Communication and the
Aging Process
(PGPS-86)

Related Titles

Baltes/Hoyer BEHAVIORAL GERONTOLOGY
Danziger INTERPERSONAL COMMUNICATION
Garnica/King LANGUAGE, CHILDREN AND SOCIETY: THE
  EFFECT OF SOCIAL FACTORS ON CHILDREN LEARNING TO
  COMMUNICATE
Goldstein/Hoyer/Monti POLICE AND THE ELDERLY
Keddie ACTION WITH THE ELDERLY

Communication and the Aging Process

Interaction throughout the Life Cycle

Lois M. Tamir
University of Michigan

Pergamon Press
New York • Oxford • Toronto • Sydney • Frankfurt • Paris

Pergamon Press Offices:

U.S.A. Pergamon Press Inc., Maxwell House, Fairview Park, Elmsford, New York 10523, U.S.A.

U.K. Pergamon Press Ltd., Headington Hill Hall, Oxford OX3 0BW, England

CANADA Pergamon of Canada, Ltd., 150 Consumers Road, Willowdale, Ontario M2J, 1P9, Canada

AUSTRALIA Pergamon Press (Aust) Pty. Ltd., P O Box 544, Potts Point, NSW 2011, Australia

FRANCE Pergamon Press SARL, 24 rue des Ecoles, 75240 Paris, Cedex 05, France

FEDERAL REPUBLIC OF GERMANY Pergamon Press GmbH, 6242 Kronberg/Taunus, Pferdstrasse 1, Federal Republic of Germany

Library of Congress Cataloging in Publication Data

Tamir, Lois M   1954-
   Communication and the aging process.

   (Pergamon policy studies)
   Bibliography: p.
   Includes indexes.
   1. Interpersonal communication. 2. Maturation (Psychology) 3. Aging. I. Title. II. Title: Live cycle.
HM132.T36 1979   301.14   79-17115
ISBN 0-08-024621-4

Printed in the United States of America

To Ron:
Our dialogues allow us to share
in the joys of communication.

Contents

Foreword

The number of Americans over the age of 60 will increase by 16 million in the next 30 years, an increase of fifty percent over the current figure of 32 million. This span of 30 years is well within the expected life careers of today's students and recent graduates. Tomorrow's older Americans will be better educated, healthier, and better organized politically. They will also enjoy greater financial security, through improved pension benefits and other forms of financial planning. As a result, they will expect a higher level of educational and recreational opportunities, health benefits, and other social services than that which is currently provided.

Older people start new careers, provide invaluable advice to government and businesses, travel, volunteer time and effort for worthwhile causes, return to school, become grandparents, make important discoveries in the sciences, and express their creative energies in the arts and humanities. On the other hand, older people also require assistance in adapting to visual and auditory losses, to difficulties of motor coordination and speech following stroke, and to the crises of widowhood, retirement, loneliness, depression, the deaths of friends, and one's own dying. In short, there is a tremendous need for well-trained and highly motivated professionals, who are knowledgeable regarding the opportunities and the problems of aging, to fill a great variety of careers in the rapidly expanding field of gerontology and services for the aging.

A major social science theory in the study of late adulthood and old age has been the life-span perspective. Aging cannot be sufficiently understood as a separate stage of life, but instead must be viewed in the context of the preceding stages of childhood, adolescence, young adulthood, and middle adulthood. It would not be correct to say that from the life-span perspective the experiences of early life fully determine the quality of later life; rather, the experiences of early life provide the background and a framework for interpreting the goals, activities, and pleasures of aging and late adulthood. The life-span perspective has been stimulated by the journal Human Development and by the West Virginia University Life-Span Developmental Psychology Conferences. For the first time, a chapter on life-span developmental psychology will appear in the Annual Review of Psychology (1980).

This maturing of the life-span perspective calls for a level of writing that rises above the merely encyclopedic; it calls for writing that is also critical and selective, providing heuristic frameworks and presenting important and stimulating questions for further research and discussion. Communication And The Aging Process, by Lois Tamir, represents a significant advance in these respects, and is an excellent introduction to the life-span perspective. A wide range of topics is covered, from attribution theory to role-playing, from baby talk to personality, from adolescent socialization to sex differences. Unlike many social science writers, this one is refreshingly frank in acknowledging that not all the answers are known yet, that studies sometimes present contradictory results, and that social science research methods can be less than perfect.

The most unique feature of this volume, however, is the organization of the material around a single theoretical perspective – communication. Why communication? Social communication is not merely the exchange of messages, it is the construction of shared meanings and intentions. Communication is an essential factor in the establishment of identity and self-respect and in the adaptation to change and coping with crises. Communication is not merely a linguistic process, but depends upon the social context, which includes the participants themselves. Distortions in communication can result from strains in social relationships; for example, identity diffusion and lack of direction following widowhood or retirement. Conversely, social relationships can be strained as a result of ambiguities and misperceptions in the communication process.

Consistent with the life-span perspective, Lois Tamir has examined the development of the communication process, beginning with infancy and early parent-child interactions, to intentions, semantics, and changes in the ability to understand another person's point of view. Indeed, the notion that this book concerns only gerontology is solidly dispelled by the chapter on "Origins of Communication," which is an area of special expertise for the author.

Communication during aging presents several unique features. Lois Tamir observes that, unfortunately, for many older persons the sensory and perceptual abilities necessary for communication begin to decline just as communication itself becomes increasingly important. Older people must communicate not only with each other, but also with the younger generation. The latter consists of family members, friends, neighbors, students, policymakers, researchers, program planners, doctors, nurses, and human-service providers. At least two aspects of the changing social context in old age may have a marked impact upon communication across the generations: First, as Lois Tamir outlines, the paradigm for communication is established in the context of parent-child relationships. As the two generations grow older together, however, there is often a reversal of roles and status with respect to dependency, economic power, and emotional strengths. Second, human-service providers sometimes grow accustomed to helping individuals who are less able to help themselves — for example, children, the emotionally disturbed, and the mentally retarded. It is a mistake to consider older persons similarly, although this often happens. The great majority are quite able to evaluate information and come to reasonable decisions on their own. Their problems derive in large part from a society structured to provide inadequate economic benefits and unfulfilling social roles for older people, and from the impact of physical disabilities and disease. But in general the elderly do know what they want, and what is best for them.

Indeed, it must be kept in mind that today's older generation has been active in raising families, managing businesses, establishing government policies, and contributing to the arts, among other things. No doubt there is an accumulated wisdom which ought to be communicated to the younger generation. Just as those who do not adapt to the rapid rate of social and technological change may be victims of "future shock," so the younger generation — through lack of communication with older adults and failure to make use of stabilities provided by experience, tradition, and coherent values — may lose contact with the past and become victims of "past shock." Clearly both generations, and society as a whole, can benefit from increased and more effective communication. Nevertheless, the task is not easy, and much more remains to be learned. As Lois Tamir observes, although young and old may share the same language, they may not share the same speech community; that is, they may have different rules for the use and interpretation of language behavior. Among the topics treated within a communication framework by the author are parent-child relations (a provocative, sensitive section of the book), intimacy and self-disclosure, attitudes held by the young regarding aging, and the role of family, friends, and neighbors as potential communication partners with the elderly.

The importance of underlying philosophical models and theoretical orientations in the interpretation of social science data is gaining increased recognition. These orientations display a variety of names — interaction, transaction, contextualism, dialectics, open systems — but have in common a focus upon the reciprocally-defining relationship between the individual and the social environment. Lois Tamir has made good use of these new, process orientations in considering the impact of changes in the social environment upon the self-concepts and the communication patterns of the elderly. In particular, the dialectical principle of development through contradiction is used effectively in setting forth the characteristics of mature, adult thought; it also describes the tension in late adulthood between greater freedom and greater uncertainty, both of which are implied in the loss of norms and roles which follows retirement.

In summary, Lois Tamir captures the critical issues of aging from both the life-span development and the communication perspectives.

She explores the lives of older persons with a sympathetic touch, but also understands the importance of wrestling with theoretical issues and attending to the details of research methodology. Frequent familiar examples and illustrative data are provided. This book will be of interest to people in the fields of psychology, education, nursing, communication, social work, occupational therapy, sociology, and physical education. It will stimulate persons now in communication to become involved in gerontology. And perhaps most importantly, it will provide students, researchers, and practitioners with a new tool — the communication framework — for understanding the human aging process.

John A. Meacham

Department of Psychology
State University of New York
at Buffalo

Preface

The field of life-span development is coming to the attention of increasing numbers of social scientists. The field, however, is in its infancy. We are struggling to develop concepts that help us understand the process of development from infancy through old age. As a student of developmental psychology, I was drawn to this struggle. Having spent several earlier years working in the field of communication and language development, I began to see connections between the two fields. This book represents a synthesis of the two areas of study: communication and life-span development, with special emphasis upon later life.

Social scientists have explored many aspects of the lives of older adults. The elderly have been studied in terms of their intellectual skills, personality, residence patterns, economic situations, and biological characteristics. These are important areas of study, for they hold great potential for improving the quality of life of the older adult. But how do older adults use their skills in everyday life? How do they deal with their social world? How do they communicate? To answer these questions, we need to pull together our knowledge from many fields. We need to know about development prior to old age, for each and every aged adult has a long and complex personal history. We need to know what the communication process is all about. We need to know how the social and psychological characteristics of the older adult fit together and mold his concept of the self and his place within the world. We need to know what other people think about the elderly, for communication is a two way process; a dialogue is jointly constructed. This book provides answers to these questions based upon our most recent knowledge in the emerging field of life-span development.

Communication is a powerful concept and analytic tool for examining the issues of development throughout the life cycle. It is the key to understanding how the infant gradually develops into a socially sensitive child. It enables the young adult to gather information from the social world, establish goals, solidify values, and develop into a mature adult;

it informs the aging adult as to his social identity. It also allows the older adult to transform his social identity by means of developing new definitions of himself and his social world. These are the basic issues addressed within this book. The intent is to examine the world of the individual throughout the stages of life, but to stress the continued potential for change as the individual transforms his environment and his self by means of continued dialogue within the social world.

Acknowledgments

This book was written with the support and encouragement of many persons. I am indebted to Toni Antonucci, Tom Hickey, Martin Hoffman, and Jacquelynne Parsons for their insightful commentaries on the manuscript. I would like to thank Bill Hoyer and Gwen Bell for their editorial assistance, and I would like to acknowledge the many others who provided the intellectual stimulation and encouragement necessary for the production of this book, including John Meacham, Ruth Riegel, and the members of the Family and Sex Roles Project of the Institute for Social Research at the University of Michigan. I would also like to thank Mary Bierlein, who did such a fine job in typing the final copy of the manuscript.

The project of synthesizing the fields of communication and life-span development, ultimately resulting in the writing of this book, was initially undertaken under the guidance of, and with the insights gained from, my mentor, Klaus Riegel. He died shortly after I had begun this project, but his influence is everlasting. His brilliance, paired with his gentle guidance, provided the sustenance necessary for breaking into a new field. I am greatly indebted to him.

Finally, I would like to thank my husband, Ron Tamir, for his careful reading of the manuscript at all stages of production, the challenging questions he was always ready to put forth, the insights he continually provided, and his encouragement and support throughout. I dedicate this book to him.

Introduction

This book represents the first step in the emerging field of life-span development to describe the process of development from a communication perspective. Communication provides the link between the individual and the outside world, and interaction between the individual and members of society is the means by which the individual develops throughout the life cycle. Communication can be stifling, or communication can be enriching, depending upon the form and the function of the social dialogue. Both the form and the function of the dialogue, however, become transformed as the individual advances through the stages of life. The individual constructs the social dialogue with others, but at the very same time the individual is shaped and molded by the form it takes. The process is dialectical. The influence is mutual. It is, in essence, the basis of the developmental process. Communication and development go hand in hand throughout the life course. This book describes how the two are connected from infancy through old age.

Chapter one, "Development Throughout the Life Cycle," provides a basic introduction to the concept of development. It discusses the issues of stages of development throughout the life cycle, the impact of life crises and societal expectations, and the methods used by researchers to measure human development. It also makes note of the differences between male and female development and explains how socialization is a part of the communication process. These basic concepts provide the conceptual background tools for the reader who then goes on to view the actual stages of development.

Chapter two, "Communicative Interaction," is also an introductory chapter. It examines the process of communication in social interaction. It is arbitrarily divided into three basic sections, each of which approaches the issue from a different perspective. "Interpersonal Cognition" discusses the cognitive processes put into action when individuals interact. "Social Interaction" discusses how social knowledge is used in the construction and interpretation of messages in interaction, and "Communication" discusses how social relationships are managed and transformed by means of the way in which the social dialogue is understood.

Chapter three, "Origins of Communication," examines how communication skills first come into being. It examines the very first social system of which the infant is a part, the mother-child relationship, and how communication and language emerge within this context. It also discusses the way in which the very young child further develops these skills in interaction with adults and children of similar age. The concept of egocentrism, the inability to see the world as others do, in childhood is introduced. It is a concept that often pervades discussions of other stages of life, and is critically analyzed in this chapter and in chapter eight.

Chapter four, "An Overview of Adolescence and Adulthood," provides the conceptual bridge between developments of early and later life. It examines the widening social world of the adolescent and the increasingly sophisticated dialogue between the adolescent and society. Adult development, too, is reviewed from a communication perspective, as the adult establishes a social position and then goes on to assess this position during middle age.

Chapter five, "The Psychological Characteristics of the Aged," and chapter six, "The Social World of the Aged," provide the reader with background information on the elderly, information that is used in the following chapters to examine communication. Chapter five reviews the biological, cognitive, and personality characteristics of the aged. Chapter six reviews the social position of the aged, including the attitudes held by others about people who are old and the role transitions that occur when the adult reaches old age. We must clearly understand both the inner and outer world of the older adult in order to understand the impact of communication upon the aged.

Chapter seven, "The Social Networks of the Aged," looks at the social networks that provide the basic context of communication during old age. It examines the impact of the family, the community, and friends upon the social position and well-being of the older adult. These social networks provide basic social supports to the aged, who are confronting a new set of social relations by virtue of their old age.

Chapter eight, "Communicative Interaction and the Aged," integrates the information discussed in previous chapters in order to provide a picture of how the older adult communicates with society and its younger generations. It examines the impact of personal, cognitive, and sensory changes upon dialogue skills. It also describes how communication between young and old generations can be fraught with ambiguities, or can enrich the quality of life. The form that the social dialogue between the young and old takes depends upon the way in which they define their social relationships, the social context that they perceive, and their willingness to take the role of the other in social interaction.

"A Final Note," chapter nine, pulls together the basic concepts which appear in chapters one through eight. Development is continual from infancy through old age. With development each individual increases in complexity. Communication in the context of an ever-changing social world contributes to the complex history of the individual.   Throughout his development, the individual defines and redefines the self, the other, and the social world in the context of social dialogue.

1 Development Throughout the Life Cycle

The individual changes qualitatively throughout the life cycle in the context of an individual-environment system. Each individual experiences the social structure and manages personal crises and change in accord with life stage, cohort, sex role, and the increasing individual complexity that comes with development. Throughout life, the individual is touched and molded by society, and in turn he restructures the social world in a reciprocal and dialectical manner. This is achieved through communication, both verbal and nonverbal, explicit and implicit, confirming and contradicting, throughout the life cycle.

MODELS OF DEVELOPMENT

A controversial issue recognized by theorists of development concerns the question of whether there are stages across the life cycle. Some assert that there can be no stage theory of development, especially in contemporary American society (e.g., Fiske, 1977), for the way in which development occurs varies from person to person. However, the majority of social scientists do acknowledge a qualitative difference in the behavior of the individual at different points across the life span.

Models of child development and young adulthood are usually inappropriate for the elderly (Ahammer & Bennett, 1976). Different factors, such as biological or environmental, operate more or less forcefully at different points in the developmental process. For example, the development of the infant is largely a function of biological growth patterns, whereas the middle-aged adult can actively seek out new situations in his environment in order to achieve personal change. Also, the relationships between environmental stimuli and their accompanying behaviors change across the life span (Baltes & Willis, 1977). While a young adult may react to a test of his skill as if it were a challenge and opportunity to perform, the aged adult becomes anxious and fearful of failure. Therefore, any conceptualization of life-span

1

development must account for qualitative change, whether or not it is labeled as a stage theory.

The most thorough analysis of stage development has been achieved by Van den Daele (1969). He critiques developmental analyses that are confined to a single, invariant sequence of stages because they minimize intra- and inter-individual variations. Specifically, it is difficult to justify a theory which states that all individuals go through stage A, stage B, and stage C in the same order, at the same age, and in the same way, regardless of circumstances. Nevertheless, the single sequence, he states, is an important starting point for developmental analysis. This is because there are qualitative changes across the life span.

Van den Daele uses a simple sequence model to illustrate how development may encompass qualitative change, yet allow for and in fact promote individual variation. Specifically, he describes a cumulative model of development where either all or some of the elements of previous stages are retained as one enters each new stage of development. One form of cumulative model, labeled a multiple progression model, implies the coexistence of earlier and later stages as well as the option of developing in alternative directions. For example, following stage A, the person has the option of progressing to stage B1 or B2; from stage B1, he has the option of progressing to C1 or C2 or C3, and so forth. This ultimately leads to intra- and interpersonal differences. People act differently from one another due to the cumulation of their prior experiences and current paths chosen. They vary their actions from one situation to the next, since a variety of options is continually open.

Overall, for different areas of behavior such as cognition, motivation, and personality, different forms of these stage models are required. The fact remains that qualitative changes do occur. A stage model, especially if it is cumulative and multiple, can account for a variety of different behaviors depending upon the options available and the corresponding paths of development followed by the individual along the sequence of stages. Social scientists do concede that there are basic social and psychological processes that occur in a defined sequence and that continue throughout the life span (Maddox & Wiley, 1976).

Two Models

Given the assumption that change occurs over the life course, one can draw on two major theoretical orientations of development, which are best described by Reese and Overton (1970) as the 'mechanistic' and 'organismic'. The mechanistic model assumes a passive individual in an active environment. The organismic model assumes an active individual in a passive environment. The prototype of the former model is the machine, and of the latter model the biological organism. Both these models are overly confining since they limit the focus of behavioral development to only one aspect of a changing system: either the environment or the individual, but each perspective has much to offer to the concept of development.

Specifically, from a mechanistic perspective we can describe the impact of environmental variables on behavior. Change in an environment supporting one set of behaviors can lead to the development of a new and different set of behaviors (Ahammer, 1973; Mischel, 1969). For example, remove the opportunity to work from the adult aged 65 and he finds new ways to utilize creative energy, make friends, and spend time (or in some cases, kill time). The statement that "life span psychology is environmental psychology" (Klausner, 1973, p. 72), therefore, requires serious consideration. Environmental variables do have a profound impact upon the individual under various conditions of development and change.

On the other hand, from an organismic perspective, developmental change occurs in a spontaneous and active way. This is best described by Werner and Kaplan's (1963) principle of increasing differentiation and hierarchic integration: the individual becomes more differentiated with development and over time develops many different capacities. These capacities become integrated with one another; each system becomes interrelated with the others. Thus every behavior, whether an outward bodily movement or internal cognitive process, gains significance solely in terms of its role in the overall functioning of the individual. For example, language develops as a means of organizing thoughts about the world, of interacting socially with others, and of accomplishing many other tasks more efficiently, in addition to its being an inborn human endowment. One of the major strengths of the organismic perspective is that it maintains the integrity of the individual — the individual's ability to direct his development and to avoid stagnation by continual, self-directed, and active change.

A Better Approach

The mechanistic and organismic perspectives in themselves are insufficient for explaining human development. They present an either/or argument for the primacy of either environmental or individual activity. Instead, the environment and the individual in their mutual interaction or negotiation must be considered. This more dynamic model of development has been referred to under a variety of labels by different theorists. These labels include dialectical, interactional, transformational, transactional and open systems theory (e.g., Baltes & Schaie, 1973; Baltes & Willis, 1977; Fozard et al., 1977; Hultsch & Hickey, 1978; Knudtson, 1976; Looft, 1973; Lowenthal, 1977; Meacham, 1977; Nesselroade, 1977; Nesselroade & Baltes, 1974; Sameroff, 1975; Sigel & Cocking, 1977; Van den Daele, 1975). Looft (1973) identifies the major focus of this perspective as that of the relations between the environment and the individual, which assume more importance than environmental or organismic variables in and of themselves. Meacham (1977), McCall (1977), and Sameroff (1975) emphasize the concept of continual transactions between, and interdependence of, elements within the individual-environment system. And Sigel and Cocking (1977) state that the process is continual and ongoing. The individual is in a constant dynamic state, although he does achieve temporary periods of stability.

A key concept in this dialectic and relational approach to development is contradiction. For example, once the individual recognizes discrepancies between what he thinks and what he sees, he will reorganize his thoughts so that they better account for reality. Sigel and Cocking (1977) describe the overall developmental process as one of interact-conflict resolution-equilibration, which results in a temporary resolution and a sense of balance, or equilibrium, until the next discrepancy occurs. Contradiction and change are inevitable correlates.

Qualitative change, to the naked eye, often appears as a sudden jump from one state to the next. In actuality, smaller changes occur in sufficient quantity to cause a qualitative shift in the entire system (Riegel, 1966; Wozniak, 1975). This concept nicely complements Van den Daele's (1969) model of development, since it accounts for movement from one stage to the next.

Finally, a more dynamic developmental model renders the issue of discontinuity versus continuity through the life cycle a useless one, for both occur. The individual needs to maintain continuity in order to preserve a coherent and consistent sense of self, yet he must also experience contradiction and discontinuity in order to develop. Stability is easy to measure and understand; change is not. It is the current challenge of developmental psychologists to measure, analyze, and explain just how and why this change takes place throughout development across the life cycle.

Development at All Levels

In a similar vein, a developmental psychology and its model of development must incorporate the knowledge of other disciplines, such as sociology, anthropology, and history. In the words of Baltes and Schaie (1973), a developmental model must "incorporate notions about individual-society interactions and cultural-biological change parameters, and permit for descriptive and explanatory discontinuities" (p. 394). More philosophically, Mannheim (1952) states that "any biological rhythm must work itself out through the medium of social events" (p. 286). In other words, we need to study the development of society as well as the development of the individual, and then see how they intersect.

On a concrete level, the need for a multidisciplinary approach has been shown by Nesselroade and Baltes (1974), who found that adolescent personality, presumably a stable characteristic, actually varies according to age, cohort, sex, and time of measurement. They conclude that these results point to the need for recognizing that personality development is not predetermined. Instead we must focus on developmental models that emphasize interactive changes in both the individual and society. Van den Daele's cumulative multiple-sequence model accounts well for this orientation.

It's Irreversible

Finally, in any coherent developmental model a major characteristic of development is the irreversibility of the process as the individual advances from one level to the next (Anderson, 1958). That is to say, one can't go back, one can't repeat the past. Hence, even if primitive modes of behavior are resorted to by the individual, the individual cannot be conceptualized as repeating a former developmental stage, since he is no longer the same individual as he was in the past. When the elderly behave in childlike ways, we must be careful not to attribute the same status to the older adult as we do to the child.

An Example

A theory of development which accounts for many of these issues is Mead's symbolic interactionism (Mead, 1934). Although it is loosely formulated, concentrates mainly on the development of self, and is not scientifically derived, its emphasis upon the interdependence between outer-social and inner-psychological conditions is enlightening (Riegel & Brumer, 1975). According to the theory of symbolic interactionism, the 'self' develops through a process of social experience and communication and continues to develop and change throughout life (Kimmel, 1974). The self is composed of the 'me' and the 'I', the social and individual components, respectively. The 'me' corresponds to the various social roles the individual plays (e.g., worker, student, friend), whereas the 'I' is the more personal core of the individual. It corresponds to the stream of consciousness and creativity of the individual, superseding any single social role. The self then intervenes between the environmental stimulus and personal response, but influences both (Seltzer & Atchley, 1971).

Whether or not one agrees with the specific dynamics of symbolic interactionism, the premise remains that the individual-environment system is one of reciprocal influence. While inner-psychological processes guide one's actions within the outer-social world, the social world guides one's inner-psychological processes and self-development. Their intersection provides contradictory experience as well as confirming support. The process is continual, reciprocal, dynamic.

A developmental model must incorporate the concepts of (a) qualitative changes in behavior through the life cycle, (b) the influence of the environment and of individual self-directedness, (c) the interdependence of the environment and the individual, (d) development through contradiction, (e) simultaneous continuity and change, and (f) the irreversibility of development over time.

THE LIFE CYCLE

No uniform theory of life-span development is recognized. Instead, it has been viewed from a number of vantage points: the social, historical, and the psychological. This section discusses the issues salient within these perspectives.

Society Informs

Patterns of life-span development vary according to where one is located within the social structure (Bengtson et al., 1977). This includes cultural, demographic, and economic factors as well as specified opportunities, norms, expectations, commitments, and resources that tie the individual to the social structure (Elder, 1977). Society informs the individual, both formally and informally, whether he is early, on time, or late in his developmental achievements (Neugarten & Datan, 1973). The woman pregnant at age 14 is early; the man who completes high school at age 40 is late. This type of information plays an important role with regard to the individual's self respect and esteem and thereby influences further development. Being off time requires explanation and justification to others who may not approve. The social mechanism of age grading, whereby members of the various age groups of society face certain requirements (such as high school attendance) and opportunities (such as retirement) in the social structure by virtue of their age, further informs the individual about what society expects from him (Atchley, 1975).

The concept of socially imposed variation corresponds to the observation that in more primitive and highly stable cultures, developmental changes are defined primarily biologically; whereas in more complex and changing societies, biological, psychological and social maturity do not develop at the same rate (Conger, cited in Labouvie-Vief & Zaks, in press). Maturity may be biological, but it develops in a cultural context.

An example of a social indicator of an individual's maturity is entry into the labor market (Neugarten & Moore, 1968). This is often an event which transforms the individual's social status in terms of new self-sufficiency and economic independence. Correspondingly, the relationship of the individual to the work world correlates with his social-participation behaviors. Wilensky (1968) found that those individuals who had smooth, well-ordered work careers (as opposed to more chaotic experiences) had more intense and satisfying associations with family, friends, the community and formal associations. We can see that various social realms of behavior and statuses are intricately inter-related.

Similarly, historical events such as improved health care influence the composition of life-course events. For example, recently there has been a steady increase in the number of postparental years (that is, those years between the last child leaving home and the onset of widowhood) due to improved physical health (Kimmel, 1974).

The Cohort

The concept of cohort, therefore, becomes a key issue in understanding how the individual develops. The cohort is a group of people who share a certain set of experiences. Most typically, this is a group born at the same time in history and experiences the same set of historical and social events. Mannheim (1952) describes the process of 'fresh contact' whereby each cohort encounters social-historical events from a unique set of perspectives. Because of their less extensive personal histories, these perspectives are different from those of their predecessors. Since successive cohorts encounter social-historical change at different life stages, they are influenced in different ways (Elder, 1977). The classic example of a cohort is those individuals who experienced the depression era. Within this historical period, those who were young at the time experienced it differently from those who were older. Relevant to today is the cohort born in the baby boom era, who again face a set of experiences unique to their age and placement in historical time.

It is also important to note that successive cohorts in turn influence the structure of society (Riley, 1976). The youth movement of the 1960s had a major impact upon the popular culture of its time. Finally, the pattern of aging exhibited by a cohort is a reflection not only of history, but also of the particular within-cohort group to which one belongs, such as sex, race, and social class (Riley, 1976). The middle-class elderly adult, for example, follows a pattern of aging different from a member of the lower class in our society.

Events, Tasks, and Tracing a Concept

In order to systematize conceptions of the life cycle, many social scientists have identified life stages in terms of major events (Atchley, 1975). For example, one event often considered pivotal is that of parenthood and its various substages of rearing and launching offspring into the world (Elder, 1977; Gutmann, 1975). Other researchers have described distinct adaptive tasks that become salient to the individual at different periods of life (Emmerich, 1973). The young adult must choose a career; the elderly adult must learn to compensate for decreasing sensory capacities. The concepts of major events and adaptive tasks are not mutually exclusive.

On a more general level, life-span theorists identify the major blocks of time of the life cycle as those of childhood, youth, adulthood, and old age (Havighurst, 1973b). None of these systematizations of life-cycle development are comprehensive in and of themselves, yet they are useful in organizing data and in marking off points of reference. The concepts of general blocks of time (e.g., childhood, old age), major events (e.g., entering the labor market) and adaptive tasks (e.g., identity formation in adolescence) are referred to in the chapters which follow.

Instead of tracing major life stages or transitions, it is often more informative (especially for specific research purposes) to trace a particular concept in its development across the life span. An example is that of attachment relations. There are qualitative shifts in attachment formation and realignment across the life cycle. To illustrate, Hartup and Lempers (1973) specify the relationship between physical proximity and the attachment between mother and child: during infancy and childhood the child and mother display approximately equivalent power in maintaining physical distance; through adolescence, mothers assign primary responsibility to the child for initiation of attachment behaviors; children gain maximal control during adulthood, whereas parents often regain partial control when they encounter old age. On the level of more general interpersonal commitments, Erikson's theory of the stages of man has been viewed as one in which the individual moves over time from dyadic (two-person) to a more all-encompassing level of commitment to others (Lowenthal, 1977). Concern about contributions to society becomes increasingly more prominent as the adult approaches later adulthood and old age.

From Childhood to Old Age: Transitions

The accumulation of experience throughout the life course makes it increasingly more difficult to predict an individual's place from age alone (Atchley, 1975). The typical two-year-old's physical appearance, cognitive skill, and family life can be described but what about the 35-year-old, the 50-year-old, the 80-year-old? In view of the continuous and cumulative change through the life course and the multiple paths of development available (as suggested by Van den Daele), one is usually unable to predict adult life outcomes solely from information relevant to childhood (Neugarten, 1969).

More identifiable are transitions from one stage in the life cycle to the next. These transitions, if not marked by any one major event, are often difficult to identify, however. The precursors of old age are in middle age, and there is considerable continuity in life style from mid to old age (Bennett & Ahammer, 1977; Carp & Nydegger, 1975). Age does not cancel out, for example, sex, race, and class membership, which provide continuity from one life stage to the next (Bengtson et al., 1977). Nevertheless, much research characterizes middle age as a time of fulfillment and old age as one of relative disadvantage (Chown, 1977).

Similarly, gradual qualitative change in thought and behavior from adolescence to adulthood are found. The adolescent exercises new and abstract skills outside the realm of practical considerations in order not to forclose the possibilities of various life-course paths (Labouvie-Vief & Zaks, in press). The transition to adulthood is characterized by commitment and responsibility. Values crystallize.

The extensive personal history and multiple paths of development experienced renders the adult more complex than the child and more differentiated from others as he proceeds through life (Neugarten, 1969). Personal and social experiences remain with the individual through development since one can never unlearn something, although it may be modified (Rose, 1962a).

Development is irreversible. Any attempt to negate a former behavior, perception, or world view will directly imply what is being negated (Mannheim, 1952). The cumulation of experiences, thoughts, and adjustments, building one upon the other (even in their negation) continually provide an increasingly individualized basis for interpreting the world and reacting to events (Neugarten, 1977). During the course of qualitative shifts across the life cycle, a person's behaviors are always linked to both present and past experiences (Williams & Loeb, 1968). Communication, as we shall see, is a prime example of this process.

Adjustment Throughout the Life Cycle

The concept of adjustment throughout the life cycle in itself is related to personal history. Evaluating the individual's adjustment behaviors as normal or abnormal is dependent upon the individual's patterns of coping throughout life (Gottesman et al., 1973).

Coping with stress (such as entering a new situation, confronting a challenge, or losing a spouse) must be judged in this manner. Research has shown that similar potentially stressful situations are perceived with differing degrees of apprehension by different individuals: those ranking high on encounters with stressful situations, but low on preoccupation with stress, have higher morale than those with little stress and high preoccupation. In addition, different age groups deal with stress differently, depending upon prior history and current situation (Lowenthal & Chiriboga, 1973). Therefore, the concepts of stress, coping, and adjustments cannot be conceived as a unitary phenomenon across the life span. They vary with age, stage, and historical background.

An account of life cycle development must acknowledge: (a) the impact of the social structure; (b) the influence of cohort membership; (c) the interrelatedness of the individual's various social statuses; (d) the multiple possibilities for categorizing life-course events; (e) the indistinct borders between various life stages; (f) the increasing individualization with age; (g) the determining power of the individual's personal history; and (h) the lack of uniformity of concepts (such as attachment, stress, and adjustment) across the life cycle.

CRISIS AND CHANGE

A prominent issue that life-course theorists debate concerns how and why crisis and change occur across the life span. Research and theory present contradicting opinions, and there is little consensus on how to define a crisis itself. There are crises without personality transitions, and there are personality transitions in the absence of perceptible crises (Brim, 1974). Expected or on-time life events, radical as they may be, do not often constitute crises (Neugarten, 1970). Women who expect menopause to occur are usually not too perturbed when it does. Nevertheless, much research does show that conflict or crisis co-occur with change, within the context of the individual-environment system.

Synchronizing Planes

A particularly useful tool for defining various forms of crises has been provided by Klaus Riegel (1975b). He describes four planes of development: the inner-biological, the individual-psychological, the cultural-sociological, and the outer-physical. Contradiction, or lack of synchronization between any two of these categories (including two of the same category), constitutes a crisis situation of major or minor magnitude. For example, a woman might find difficulties reconciling her desires for family (individual-psychological) and career (also individual-psychological). A more catastrophic natural disaster such as a hurricane (outer-physical) may interfere with an individual's plans to settle in a new home (individual-psychological) or may do physical harm (inner-biological) to the individual. For the elderly, negative attitudes held by society (cultural-sociological) interfere with the maintenance of self-esteem (individual-psychological), and even with physiological functioning (inner-biological). This conceptualization of crisis is sufficiently broad so as to account for a variety of crisis situations, but it does not specify how the individual attempts to cope or adapt.

On a more specific level, Lieberman (1975) states that two major and frequently co-occurring events that are considered crises are loss of person, place, or thing, and the encounter of a new situation in which the person must change his usual ways of behaving (such as relocating to a new neighborhood). Chown (1977) adds that crisis situations may be most disruptive when a person's freedom of choice becomes restricted as a result. This implies more limited avenues for adjustment.

A theme running throughout these various definitions of crisis involves the disruption of a smooth course of events. These changes need not be approached in a negative manner if the process of coping leads to new growth and self-enrichment. This is not to undermine, however, that many crises are unfortunate and may not lead to positive change.

Self-Preservation Or Alteration?

On a psychological level, studies on crises of transitions to new conditions (such as widowhood) have found that a common pattern is one of conservation. Specifically, people act conservatively, attempting to maintain their self-image, even under especially stressful conditions (Morris, cited in Back, 1976). On the other hand, Chown (1977), in a review of crisis research, concludes that people's opinions about themselves are likely to alter as a result of such crises (including retirement, loneliness, and widowhood), and morale is similarly affected. These opposing views need not constitute an either/or decision, however. In light of the individual variation in patterns of adjustment, the many types of crises individuals face, and the span of ages during which they face them, both these views account for many cases in themselves.

Interpretation: Pro and Con

A key to understanding why the management of crises differs from person to person and situation to situation concerns the impact of the individual's perception and interpretation of the situation (Albrecht & Gift, 1975; Lowenthal & Chiriboga, 1973; Thomae, 1970). Thomae (1970) concludes from a body of longitudinal data (primarily focused upon an aged population) collected in Bonn, Germany, and from a review of other crisis literature, that perception of change rather than objective change is related to personal behavior. The individual's major concerns, expectations, and motivations influence his perception of change. In the Bonn data, although it was clear that economic and health factors influenced the behavior of the elderly, the perceived quality of the situation was more often correlated with their behavior than was their behavior with the objective quality of the situation (Thomae, 1970, p. 5). For example, the way retirement was perceived years before retirement occurred was correlated significantly with actual adjustment to retirement.

Nevertheless, the centrality of perception, motivation, and interpretation in managing crises is not a uniform finding. Lieberman (1975), in a study of 870 voluntary and involuntary relocations to new living quarters by elderly adults, found that the central element in defining the crisis and its implications for individual adjustment was the degree of change, and not the meaning a person attached to the event (p. 152).

Self-Image and Survival

Lieberman's study also revealed another major concept relevant to the examination of crisis across the life span. Specifically, the personal characteristics that promote successful adaptation at one stage of the life cycle may be nonadaptive at other stages. Lieberman found that "those elderly who were aggressive, irritating, narcissistic, and demanding were most likely to survive crisis" (p. 155). Cross-cultural research has shown a similar pattern of survivorship (Neugarten, 1977).

Fascinating as the results are in themselves, more crucial is the underlying interpretation of these findings. It appears that those personality characteristics that promote survivorship are also those characteristics that enable the elderly adult to maintain his self-image. And it is this maintenance of one's self-image that protects the individual from extensive deterioration in old age. In contrast to younger adults, who have access to a broader network of group and social supports, the elderly adult is primarily reliant upon the self to maintain a clear self-image, and to survive (Loeb, 1975). The implications for how the elderly adult communicates with others are closely tied to this issue, and are described in later chapters.

A review of the concepts of crisis and change results in the following conclusions: (a) crisis involves lack of synchrony at various points in the course of development; (b) a crisis may potentially lead to an effort to preserve one's self-image, or to personal alteration; (c) the interpretation of the situation sometimes, but not always, influences one's behavior; and (d) maintaining one's self-image under crisis conditions may be more crucial during old age than during any other stage of life.

METHODOLOGY

Most knowledge about development is obtained by means of careful observation and analysis, formally known as empirical research.

The Traditional Methods

The simplest and most popular method utilized by social scientists is the cross-sectional research design. This design involves testing individuals of various age groups (such as 20, 40, and 60 years old) at one point in time and comparing scores and variance between and within groups. Cross-sectional results are often interpreted as representative of age differences in behavior and personality, yet they do not account for the differing historical backgrounds and cohort membership of the groups that are being compared. In addition, cross-sectional studies tend to indicate large psychological differences between younger and older groups (Bennett & Eckman, 1973). These differences often do not appear in longitudinal studies, which follow the same persons over a period of time.

This is not to imply that longitudinal research (which can range anywhere from a period of several months to a lifetime), is less problematic. Baltes (1968) summarizes the major flaws of longitudinal designs: (a) longitudinal samples are nearly always nonrepresentative of the population at large; primarily composed of volunteers, longitudinal groups contain individuals with higher IQ's and social status than a random sample; (b) often longitudinal research involves selective dropout of subjects (that is, certain subjects decide to discontinue participation in the experiment), which may result in the noncomparability of the later with earlier samples; and (c) longitudinal measurements may be influenced by effects of repeated testing over time.

Sequential Strategies

Schaie (1965), in the first attempt to overcome the drawbacks of cross-sectional and longitudinal methods, identified the primary factors influencing development as: age, cohort, and time of measurement. Age, according to Schaie, represents the maturation of the individual. This is similar to Wohlwill's (1970) 'developmental function', which represents the direct relationship between age and behavior when effects of time and cohort are controlled. On the other hand, Elder (1977) views age as an index of life stage. Cohort locates the individual within a historical context (Elder, 1977). Wohlwill (1970) states that cohort effects represent systematic alterations in the form of the developmental function. Finally, according to Schaie, time represents purely environmental effects, and according to Wohlwill (1970) represents only temporary variations in the developmental function. It is apparent that these various definitions of age, cohort, and time do not contradict one another, and illustrate that several theorists concur as to the importance of recognizing these three major components of development.

Schaie observes that the three research methods of cross-sectional data collection, longitudinal design, and time-lag comparison (which is the measurement of groups of the same age at different times, e.g., measuring 65-year-olds in 1960 and 65-year-olds in 1970), each alone confound two of the three developmental factors of age, cohort, and time. Cross-sectional studies confound age and cohort effects; longitudinal designs confound age and time effects, and time-lag designs confound cohort and time effects. He concludes, therefore, that the three methods must be carried out simultaneously, so that pure age, cohort, and time effects may be isolated through the use of simultaneous equations representing these effects.

Baltes (1968) critiques Schaie's model, however, insofar as the three components of age, cohort, and time are not true experimental variables. They are not independent of one another; they are interrelated. Baltes instead proposes the use of two factors in a bifactorial model. He states that once two of the factors are defined, information concerning the third factor will be redundant. Therefore, the researcher need only combine two methods within the research design to derive the effects of age and cohort. A common technique (given adequate time and funding to the researcher) has consequently become the sequential research design. In this design cross-sectional and longitudinal methods are combined to study individuals of the same age range. In essence, Baltes' model is actually a refined version of Schaie's original methodology.

There is a necessity for these combined designs in order to assess the environment in conjunction with the changing behavior patterns of individuals (Nesselroade & Baltes, 1974). Our model of development is one that involves continual and reciprocal transactions within an individual-environment system. The need to use more than a single research method has also been proved by subsequent research. Substantial differences in behavior and personality development of members of different cohorts and within differing historical time settings have been clearly demonstrated by these newer, sequential research designs (Labouvie-Vief & Zaks, in press; Nesselroade & Baltes, 1974). Nevertheless, the factors of cohort, age, and time in development remain interdependent and our research methods can only approximate the separate effects of each. The advance is that we recognize that each of these factors contributes significantly to the development of the person within the social environment.

Complexity and Comparison

Usually many different variables influence development at any point in time. A behavior may be a function of personality, income, parenthood, education, and a host of other variables. In order to obtain a measure of the complexity of interrelated variables and their relationship to development, Baltes and Nesselroade (1970) suggest a multivariate instead of univariate (single variable) analysis of age and cohort by means of the sequential design. The resulting data can then be analyzed by a variety of statistical techniques (e.g., multivariate analysis of variance, factor analysis, etc.).

Taking factor analysis as an example, they caution that it is unlikely to find that the relationship among the differing variables and the ways in which they cluster together will be identical or even proportional for different age and cohort groups. However, a quantitative comparison between two age groups or cohorts must be based upon a prior demonstration of structural and qualitative similarities of those behavioral and psychological variables which the researcher wants to compare quantitatively. Therefore, if this demonstration is lacking, one can only describe differences on a qualitative and not on a quantitative level. This reminder is especially appropriate in evaluating research which covers life-span development, since there are qualitative as opposed to simple quantitative differences in behavior and psychological functioning at various age stages.

Validity

Despite methodological elegance, much developmental research appears to minimize concern with external validity, which is the degree to which results can generalize to the external world. Hultsch and Hickey (1978) specifically view external validity as the adequate representation of the complexity and reciprocal interactions evident within the individual-environment system. Multivariate analysis has the potential to uncover a portion of the complex of interacting variables, yet our measurement instruments are not quite refined enough to definitively identify mechanisms of change among these variables and their interrelationships over time. Nesselroade (1977) points out the paradoxical situation of developmentally oriented researchers, whose construction and use of measuring instruments have tended to emphasize the measurement of stability over time rather than monitor change.

Another problem involving the issue of validity concerns experimental manipulation. Nesselroade and Baltes (1974) state that sequential strategies can only be descriptive unless they are supplemented by additional experimental manipulations. On the other hand, McCall (1977) observes that there is a difference between knowing if a variable is causal in an experimental situation and if it actually causes variance in naturalistic situations. Our only recourse is to combine experimental and naturalistic observations in order to understand developmental processes better.

The Sample

On the level of sampling in life-span research, especially in projects that span the later years of life, selective survival constitutes a problem in both cross-sectional and longitudinal data collection techniques. On many psychological levels (such as personality and intelligence) there are qualitative differences between those who survive and those who die within the period of observation (Elias et al., 1977). Also, refusal to participate, which is common in studies of older subjects, tends to produce study populations similar to volunteers in spite of efforts to select subjects randomly (Maddox, 1965). On the other hand, the problem of obtaining volunteers is sometimes avoided by utilizing captive samples such as institutionalized aged, who are barely representative of their age group, since they constitute only 5 percent of the elderly population. It is also important to be aware that in quasi-experimental designs, which by definition study individuals in those situations in which they are already found, limits generalizations and interpretations of causal variation (Schaie, 1977). Studies of the effects of housing arrangements among the elderly are typically done this way, and must be interpreted cautiously.

Research in Action

A study illustrative of several methodological points discussed in this section has been carried out by Woodruff and Birren (1972). Using mail questionnaires of the California Test of Personality, they were able to obtain data during years 1944 and 1969 from a cohort born in 1924 (middle-aged adults) and data during 1969 from cohorts born in 1948 (college students) and 1953 (high-school students). The utility of comparing simultaneous longitudinal and cross-sectional data becomes apparent from Woodruff and Birren's results. They found no significant differences in the longitudinal comparison of personality scores for the 1924 cohort (that is, the middle-aged adults had not changed from 1944 to 1969) and significant differences between the 1924 and both the 1948 and 1953 cohorts (the latter two did not differ). It was concluded that age changes in personality were significantly smaller than personality differences between cohorts. Since the sample is composed only of those who consented to fill out the questionnaires, generalization of results is limited, but the effects of cohort membership still appear to be a prominent factor in personality development.

The researchers had also asked the middle-aged group (that is, the 1924 cohort) to fill out the questionnaire a second time as they thought they had in 1944, when they were adolescents. They labeled this the 'retrospective condition'. Retrospective data is important because when only cross-sectional sampling is possible, a valuable research strategy may involve the use of retrospective (and prospective) instructions to subjects (Nardi, 1973). Specifically, Woodruff and Birren found that the 1924 cohort scored significantly lower when they described themselves as adolescents than they had actually scored when they were at this life stage in 1944. These adults perceived a discontinuity between their adolescent and adult personality that did not actually exist. It appears that the time of measurement had influenced the cohort's retrospective evaluations of themselves, since their retrospective accounts were more like those of contemporary adolescents than those of their own adolescence. They had evidently internalized the stereotype of the adolescent prevalent in 1969. This phenomenon is further substantiated by the fact that 67 percent of these adults had adolescent children at the time of the second personality measurement. It is crucial, therefore, in analyzing retrospective and prospective data, as well as all contemporary data, to assess the various historical, current, and personal influences impinging upon an individual's account of his past, present, and future.

An assessment of life-span research methods must take into account: (a) how well the research has identified the effects of age, cohort, and time of measurement; (b) the structural comparability among subject groups; (c) external validity and the generalizability of interpretations; and (d) how well the sample represents the population at large.

A NOTE ON SEX DIFFERENCES AND THE LIFE CYCLE

Any discussion of life-cycle development and communication must take into account the behavioral and psychological differences between the sexes. Although the issue of sex differences is not a major focus of the chapters that follow, it is necessary to outline some basic sex differences that appear throughout the life cycle and influence social behaviors.

From the Beginning

Numerous studies have documented sex differences in behavior that appear shortly after birth (Korner, 1974). Parents treat their male and female infants differently from the time of birth. Lewis and Freedle (1973) have found, for example, that mothers of three-month-old infants vocalize more to their female than to their male infants. They also observed that infant vocalization in response to maternal behavior is more likely for female infants than male, and that at three months the female infant is better able to detect whether she herself or another person is being spoken to by the mother. After following their sample longitudinally for two years, Freedle and Lewis (1977) concluded that their data reflected differential socialization by the mother of the social responsivity of the male and female child.

Lewis and Cherry (1977), in a study of two-year-old children and their mothers, go so far as to suggest a relationship between physical distance within the mother-child dyad and verbal development. They posit that the mothers who encourage physical independence in boys and allow girls to stay close by may be in part responsible for female language becoming more socially oriented, and male language more abstract. In the same vein, Nelson (1973) found that girls are faster language learners than boys. She suggested that the consistent sex differences in the rate of language acquisition may be related to the fact that boys more frequently conceptualize the world and language use differently from the mother and therefore take longer to learn it. At this point, however, we cannot identify the mother as the sole determiner of the child's verbal behavior, since she herself may be responding to the infant's own propensities, which may be influenced by such factors as maturation and neural development.

The Social Sex

Throughout the life cycle differences in social and communication behaviors by the sexes are found. In general, females are the more socially sensitive sex. For example, females are more affected by the nonverbal cues of spoken messages than are males (Argyle et al., 1972).

These sex differences also appear in social-participation patterns throughout old age. A five-year study in Bonn, Germany, for example, found that elderly females were significantly more active in and satisfied with the acquaintance role (Schmitz-Scherzer & Lehr, 1976). Other studies have shown that elderly females are more socially integrated within their neighborhoods and communities than are males (Bengtson et al., 1977; Rosow, 1967).

Intimacy and the Sexes

On a more intimate level, females are more likely to have confidants and to establish a confidant relationship with someone other than their spouse (Lowenthal & Haven, 1968). On the other hand, relationships between men often resemble parallel play, or meet task oriented goals rather than intimate interpersonal needs (Lowenthal & Robinson, 1976,

p. 434). Consequently, males are more dependent upon their wives in order to fulfill their need for intimacy. For example, the Bonn study showed significantly more activity in the spouse and less activity in the neighbor role by elderly males. It is therefore not surprising that widowers are more likely to remarry than widows (Troll, 1971). Although this is in part due to the fact that more elderly women survive in old age than men, men adapt less well to the loss of a spouse. Whereas females can turn to friends and family for emotional support, males lack this mutuality and intimacy with one another as a means of emotional support (Lowenthal, 1977; Lowenthal & Robinson, 1976).

It follows that at the level of family relationships, females are more deeply involved than are males (Anderson, 1976; Troll, 1971). Troll (1971), in a massive review of family literature, concludes that family interaction is both more intense and more frequent for females than males. Males see their family relationships as more obligatory, even if enjoyable. Females feel close to their parents even if they do not agree with their parents' values.

Social Positions

Interpersonal differences between men and women are paralleled by their different positions within the social structure. They play different social roles (e.g., homemaker versus corporate executive) and are afforded different opportunities, although this is changing more and more.

The differing social positions of men and women influence how they perceive the timing of their lives. The social definition of old age is more apparent for men than women, and is typically determined by age of retirement (Neugarten & Moore, 1968). Women view their age status in conjunction with the timing of the family life cycle, particularly with the development of their children. Males view their age status in conjunction with their progress in the work environment (Neugarten, 1968b).

Consequently, attitudes toward personal aging differ. Females in general hold more negative stereotypes about aging (McTavish, 1971). This is due in part to the ambiguous position of the older woman who no longer has a family to care for, nor a more feminine 'youthful' appearance, but also to the stereotypes dominant in society. For example, one study found that subjects evaluated the voices of older females significantly more negatively than those of older males and of younger females in terms of hypothetical personality dispositions (Ryan & Capadano, 1978). The communication process serves to get these points across to the aging adult, and influences self perception accordingly.

The inevitable conclusion is that even if an overall model of communication over the life course is drawn, sex differences appear throughout, from infancy until old age. The nature of sex differences may very well undergo change in modern society because of the rapidly rising number of alternatives for female and male life styles. Nevertheless, as it stands now in the realm of verbal development, interpersonal relations, family interaction, life histories and self-images, sex differences are the norm and not the exception.

A NOTE ON SOCIALIZATION AND THE LIFE CYCLE

Communication across the life cycle is a major means of socialization, and socialization is the key to understanding the individual-environment system. Socialization, on a societal level, enables the social system to continue over time (Bengtson & Black, 1973). On an individual level, socialization through the life span is necessary for personal adaptation (Albrecht & Gift, 1975). Through socialization the individual becomes integrated within the social system and finds meaning within it. This section explains several basic concepts of this process, how it changes through the life cycle, and is linked with communication.

Its Reciprocal Nature

Both the socialization of the child and the socialization of the adult are interactive and reciprocal processes (Albrecht & Gift, 1975; Emmerich, 1973). While the socializer interacts with the socializee, he himself may change in the process and acquire new values, attitudes, and behaviors, rather than reinstitute old ones without modification (Riley et al., 1969). Because the individual is continually open to new developmental paths, there is a pull towards change as well as toward continuity. The socializer and socializee, be they mother and child, husband and wife, worker and boss, learn from one another as they adapt to continually changing environmental conditions (Bengtson & Black, 1973).

Its Variations

Age of the individuals involved in socializing experiences affects the nature of the interaction process (Riley et al., 1969). There are qualitative differences, for example, between peer interaction as a socialization experience for the child, and socialization of the child by the parent (Hartup, in press).

There are many and varied agencies of socialization throughout the life cycle, including the family, place of employment, school, friends, neighbors, political groups, and advertisers (Bernstein, 1970; Brim, 1968). In addition, socializing agencies and institutions socialize individuals in accordance with the nature of the social setting in which the agent and individual interact. Settings vary, for example, in the degree to which individual differences are encouraged or reduced and in the social climate (or general level of feelings) communicated in diverse ways to the individual (Wheeler, 1966). Family and work environments are good examples of these contrasts.

Differing agents of socialization achieve varying degrees of prominence for the individual at different points in the life span. While the impact of a work supervisor may be temporary, the marital relationship continually influences the individual's adjustment and development (Brim, 1968).

While socializers and those who learn from them (especially when they are members of different cohorts) respond to events in the environment differently, societal events in themselves influence the socialization relationship. This relationship, in turn, differs from generation to generation (Bengtson & Cutler, 1976). Inkeles (1969) specifically identifies those aspects of the social system that continually influence socialization at all stages of the life cycle as: the ecological, economic, political, and value systems of society.

Ideal and Real

Any characterization of socialization must take into account that actual socialization often does not correspond to the ideal model (Riley et al., 1969). Successful socialization ideally leads to a "transformation of identity" (Bengtson & Black, 1973). The socialized individual internalizes new perspectives and behaviors which permeate all other social positions and roles. Ultimately, however, we must conceptualize the success of socialization along varying degrees of a continuum. The least successful socialization occurs for the role of the aged individual.

The Child and the Adult

An especially formative socialization experience involves the parental influence on the child. Unlike adult socialization, where emotional involvement is neutral and there is little power differentiation, the socialization of the child, particularly by the parent, is characterized by high levels of affect and large power differentiation (Brim, 1966). Consequently, according to Brim (1966), what children learn in the context of interacting with their parents is often viewed by the child as inherent in the world. Effects are long lasting.

Adult socialization, in contrast, does not typically require that the adult occupy the position of learner. Much adult socialization is acquired through a trial and error process, and new material is appended to and integrated within attitudes, values, and behaviors acquired earlier in life (Brim, 1966). The major task of adult socialization is not only to learn new roles, but also to develop the capacity to integrate multiple roles and to vary role behavior in accordance with the demands of the situation (Brim, 1968; Rosow, 1974).

Self-initiated socialization typically becomes a greater source of individual change for the adult than are efforts by others to motivate the individual to change (Brim, 1968). The most successful adult socialization is voluntary (Rosow, 1974). In our rapidly changing modern society, it is often necessary that adults be socialized and resocialized in order to accommodate adequately to the demands and needs of society (Inkeles, 1969). Individuals vary, however, in the degree to which they voluntarily change their various roles and skills during adulthood.

And the Old Person

During the course of adult socialization, there is a distinction between role socialization and status socialization (Wheeler, 1966). Status is a broader concept than role, and involves the life style of the individual. The state of being an elderly adult can be conceptualized more as a status than as any one specific role; and in the process of acquiring this status, it has been suggested that the individual is 'desocialized' instead of socialized by society (Bell, 1967). Rosow (1974) states simply that people are not effectively socialized to old age. For example, there are few esteemed rites of passage (such as graduation and marriage) that mark the transition to old age. Instead, the elderly adult undergoes a change of status in individualized ways (Rosow, 1974). In other words, there is no one right way to become old.

There are few norms or instructions as to what constitutes appropriate behavior for the elderly. When roles (such as spouse and worker) are lost, there are no new roles to replace them, and there is no anticipatory socialization, rehearsal, or identification with the elderly role (Rosow, 1974). Rosow lists various factors that reverse optimal conditions for successful socialization to old age; these include a devalued position, ambiguous norms, role discontinuity, low motivation for or resistance to acquiring the new status, and lack of rewards for appropriate behaviors. In contrast to the younger portion of the population, who view change in a positive light, the elderly consider lack of change in a positive manner. Those who retain a youthful outlook and appearance are most esteemed and admired. This tenuous position of the older adult will influence with whom and how he chooses to interact.

Socialization as Communication

Overall, socialization is embedded within the communication process (Woelfel, 1976). One of the major conditions for successful socialization is the quantity and quality of time spent between the individual and the socializing agent in interaction (Wheeler, 1966). The way one views oneself and one's place in society has been communicated in various verbal and nonverbal ways to the individual. Cicourel (1972) observes that "socialization experiences revolve around the use of language and linguistic codifications of personal and group experiences over time" (p. 249). Similarly, Lewis and Cherry (1977) state that language, meaning, and communication are simultaneously the "goals" and "means" of socialization (p. 237); and Ryan (1974) asserts that the "process of language acquisition itself constitutes a form of socialization" (p. 185).

Knowledge about norms and roles and about one's related self-concept are transmitted by means of communication. The process is mediated by the composition of society and its value systems. One's views about the social world and about both personal and cultural history differ, however, among the various age groups of society as they exist at any one point in time and as they communicate within and across generations. The process of being socialized into the various age groups of society is determined by qualitatively different mechanisms across the life cycle.

2 Communicative Interaction

Communication is the process that links the individual to society. It is essential to the developmental process. Communication in interaction is complex and multifaceted. It involves cognitive skill, social knowledge, and personal intention, as the individual adapts to society and structures his view of the world and himself.

INTERPERSONAL COGNITION

When people communicate, a variety of cognitive processes are necessary to ensure the success of the interaction. These include decision making, problem solving, information processing, and role taking (Lee, 1975). Each participant must determine the goal of the interaction, how to achieve this goal, and most importantly, how to influence the behavior of the other participant. Knowledge about the immediate social environment, or in other words, the social context of the exchange, is necessary information for the conversation participant. Of most crucial importance, however, is the fact that there are implicit presuppositions each participant holds about the other, which in turn influence the nature of the messages transmitted. Therefore, a cognitive approach is a good starting point for explaining how people perceive each other and the social context, as they embark upon a social interaction.

The process of perceiving the environment and others in it is transactional (Toch & MacLean, 1967). Specifically, the way a person perceives the things around him is not simply a matter of precisely knowing what's 'out there'. Instead, perception is a creative act. The individual 'sees', or rather interprets, what is perceived in terms of prior knowledge, current concerns, personal disposition, and developmental factors such as age, generation, and historical background. Hence, the perceiver enters into a transaction with the environment. Objective reality and individual activity interact in a dialetical way.

The end result is the unique perception of the social world and its social objects by the active, and interactive individual. The hungry person perceives reminders of food in the environment; the defensive person perceives the potential insults of others; and the elderly person perceives those messages which tell him he is useless.

This section first reviews the general ideas of attribution theory, a theory which provides a framework for how people perceive their social environment. Other concepts central to interpersonal cognition are elaborated. These include the drive for consistency, the impact of early cues upon perception, stereotyping, attraction, and role taking, all of which influence how interpersonal information is perceived, processed, and put into action.

Making Attributions

Attribution theory is helpful in exploring interpersonal cognition because it explains how the individual searches for and interprets social meanings in interaction (Shaver, 1975). Attribution theory assumes that the perceiver tries to identify the causes of the behavior he sees. When the perceiver makes attributional judgments about another individual, he is also developing a set of expectations concerning this stimulus, the target person (Nardi, 1973). Ultimately, the aim of social perception is to discover the underlying regularities in the behavior of others (Heider, 1958). In this way the social environment becomes a more predictable and controllable situation for the individual. Factors that influence the predictions by the individual are the stimulus person, the social context, and the characteristics of the perceiver (Bengtson et al., 1977; Kelley, 1973; Nardi, 1973).

The centrality of perceiver characteristics to the processes of person perception is critical. Straightforward attributions about the environment or the target person are relatively simple to identify. For example, one may attribute poor performance on a test to the unfairness of the tasks requested (environment) or the lack of skill of the testee (person). However, the interaction of the perceived and perceiver characteristics can result in a complex set of attributions and expectations (Nardi, 1973). There are multiple personal factors involved in perceptual attributions about others. As the perceiver identifies the actions, motives, affects, and beliefs of the target person, the perceiver characteristics such as prior experience, intelligence, empathy, affect, and self-concept all serve to influence his cognitive evaluations of the other in direct and indirect ways (Heider, 1958). These in turn influence the nature of the interaction.

Many of the assumptions that influence our perception of the environment and attributions about others have been internalized. Therefore, there is a general tendency of individuals, as they interpret their social environment, to experience these interpretations as constituting intrinsic features of the persons and situations they perceive (Heider, 1958). Once perceived as intrinsic, the features become nearly impervious to change.

On a developmental level, Abelson (1976) describes the perceptions of the social environment in terms of scripts — specific sequences of events expected by the individual. Experiences accumulate, an episode at a time, until more general categorical scripts are constructed by the individual. An attitude, correspondingly, is a group of scripts concerning a particular target object or person.

Scripts are acquired through observation, participation, or both. In childhood, the development of many scripts is derived from situations that are observed and not participated in. Hence, a middle-aged adult develops scripts about interacting with his co-workers by means of much accumulated experience. The child develops scripts, on the other hand, about interacting with elderly adults by observing how his parents and others behave in this situation. It is important to acknowledge, however, that so long as interaction with the social environment is continuous, so is the possibility of modifying the various scripts, which mediate social encounters under many and varied circumstances. Contradictory experiences in the context of an interaction serve this purpose, but how open people are to experiencing contradiction is another story in itself.

Comfort in Consistency

People are self-corrective. More precisely, they are self-corrective against disturbance. If the individual is unwilling to accept what is obvious, then his self-corrective mechanisms work "to sidetrack it, to hide it, even to the extent of shutting off parts of the process of perception" (Laing, cited in Bateson, 1972, p. 429). In most general terms, people like to be consistent.

Once the person feels he understands a social situation, smaller inconsistencies are readjusted or rationalized. The individual is more concerned with maintaining a coherent picture of a situation than recognizing discrepant information (Greene, 1976). In turn, what the individual believes to be true influences his behavior much more than what is truly 'out there' (Heider, 1958). Within a social interaction, each person reinterprets incongruent information within the spoken message and the social context in order to maintain a sense of consistency and coherence in terms of how he understands and functions in society (Fishman, 1972). Research has shown that material congruent with a person's attitudes is better remembered than material incongruent with one's own views (Flavell, et al., 1968).

A special case of this overall phenomenon is Festinger's theory of cognitive dissonance (McLeod, 1967). When the individual cannot explain or justify his actions in terms of existing and objective information, he actively seeks out information consonant with his views. This, in turn, reduces any inconsistencies and dissonance in making a particular decision and acting upon it. The elderly adult states he enjoys his place of residence because he's lived there for 30 years and takes comfort in its familiarity. He does not admit that the neighborhood has deteriorated and that in fact he is too poor to move.

First Impressions And Stereotypes

When the individual encounters another individual, he notices what is salient and concrete about him (Greene, 1976). On this basis first impressions develop, and the first impressions tailor his perceptions of the situation thereafter. They can change, but they're difficult to change, in the light of our consistency-seeking individual.

Erving Goffman (1959), a sociologist, has elaborated these ideas using terminology from the theatre in an enlightening and entertaining way. He describes the formative power of initial observations by showing that perceivers, or 'audiences', tend to accept an individual's 'performance' as evidence of his capacity to perform his present routine or any routine. For example, if the performer is initially observed losing his temper, we conclude he is a nasty person.

Goffman similarly uses this terminology to describe how stereotyping tends to occur. The audience typically accepts the self projected by the individual as representative of his colleagues, or 'team', and his social affiliations. If the elderly performer is forgetful and slow, we assume his age-mates are similarly incompetent.

Related to Goffman's observation that the individual is considered a representative of his group, is Hamilton's (1976) description of the cognitive processes involved in stereotyping groups and group members. He states that the individual first constructs human groupings and then determines the characteristics and behavior patterns representative of the groups rather than the reverse. A common categorization method utilized by the perceiver is identifying those who are 'like us' and those who are 'not like us'. For example, the adolescent may categorize everyone over 30 as 'not like us' and everyone under 30 as similar to himself. What makes these groups different is decided upon afterwards. Once groups are formed, there is a tendency to overestimate the similarities among members within the same group, and the dissimilarities among members of different groups. Hence, all old people are considered alike, and presumed to have little in common with someone aged 25, at least according to stereotyped groupings.

Attraction

Heider (1958) describes how interpersonal relations based upon mutual attraction are in themselves affected by cognitive groupings of similarities between individuals. Heider cites early experimental support for the tendency to like individuals whom one perceives to be more like one's self and one's ideal self. This concept is important, for example, when examining friendships between elderly people who dislike their own aging.

Heider also finds a tendency for the individual to increase, either cognitively or overtly, the similarities between himself and a person he likes during the course of the relationship. In addition, proximity and amount of contact appear to affect mutual relationships in fairly specific ways. When attitudes are originally similar, proximity serves to increase these similarities; with slight dissimilarity, mutual assimilation may occur, provided the friendship strengthens; and with strong dissimilarities, there is an increase in hostility.

These principles of interpersonal attraction constitute a special case of the preference for balance, a concept which originates with Heider. Not only are balanced relationships between individuals and their attitudes towards objects considered to be more pleasant, but the layman typically assumes that interpersonal relations will be in balance (Kelley, 1973). Heider has hypothesized that in order to achieve a balanced situation, the individual will either change his attitude towards the other person, or his discrepant attitude towards a mutually perceived object. However, there have been many exceptions to this idealized notion of restoration of balance and equilibrium within a relationship, even during the time that Heider originally had proposed this hypothesis. In fact, often the individual must juggle both positive and negative feelings about the other person in an ongoing relationship. Family relations, as we shall see, can be ambivalent yet cohesive.

Role Taking

When two people do not know one another well, a mismatch between what the perceived person is really like and how in fact he is perceived is likely. While the perceiver is well aware of his own personal history and internal consistencies, he feels less constrained about assuming a variety of dispositions about the other. Research has shown, for example, that when individuals are asked to perceive their own life courses, they note continuity and stability, whereas when they are asked to perceive the life courses of others, they note discontinuity (Nardi, 1973).

The major force impeding the acquisition of accurate knowledge about the other is the egocentrism of the perceiver. Egocentrism (about which we have more to say in later chapters) is the inability to take the role of the other, to view the world as he sees it. The role taker must synthesize information concerning general knowledge of people and behavior, patterns of social role expectations, and direct perceptual input concerning the other person (Flavell et al., 1968). He must also simultaneously consider the different points of view of himself and the other in relation to each other (Feffer & Suchotliff, 1966). In a situation of mutual role taking, the awareness of the other as a perceiving and evaluating individual may lead to a state of self-consciousness (Heider, 1958). But the role-taking process in itself is not necessarily deliberate or conscious (Flavell et al., 1968). Within the interpersonal encounter, through role taking, an understanding and 'decoding' of each message involves a temporarily established shared cognitive representation by participants of the physical and social relationships at hand (Rommetveit, 1972). Mutual understanding is achieved in this context.

By means of role taking, in its ideal form, the individual can simultaneously exercise his perceptual skills, guided by his unique background experience, yet learn of the social environment and modify his perceptions in accordance with what is newly communicated and understood. However, the work of role taking is clearly less strenuous when two people are alike to begin with. Members of the same cohort share similar perceptions; the 20-year-old and 80-year-old often do not. Similarly, we shall see that young children, though egocentric, share similar concerns and views of the world, and often communicate effectively as a result.

On the opposite end, when communicative interaction in its ideal form is absent, it may result in a state of pluralistic ignorance, a situation where persons either do not engage in the process of comparing attitudes and ideas, or already assume that others share the same perceptions (Shaver, 1975). This situation renders all individuals concerned ignorant of the true state of affairs. Enlightenment and personal change cannot be achieved.

By means of the multiple role-taking experiences that occur throughout life, a person not only develops his own response patterns, but also internalizes the responses of others within his own repertoire of perceptions and responses (Brim, 1966). Since cognitive change, as a function of continual social exchanges, is also occurring continually, it is difficult to pinpoint precisely when and where a particular viewpoint has been incorporated and integrated within the existing thoughts of the individual. Nevertheless, the influence of others is significant throughout the life cycle. It is clear that those processes of perception and cognition exercised by the individual are bent towards continuity and a predictable understanding of the social environment, a conservative bent in light of our susceptibility towards change in the individual-environment system.

A basic feature underlying the structure and content of interpersonal interactions is the perception of the social environment and its participants. The characteristics of both the social environment and the perceiving individual influences the nature of the evaluations of the target person and the subsequent messages which are communicated. Principles of attribution theory are especially useful in describing how the perceiver organizes the information available from the surrounding environment. The perceiver strives towards developing a predictable picture of the social environment consonant with his view of the world and personal attitudes. Hence, incongruent information is reinterpreted so that it is consonant with the perceiver's own world view. Initial information exerts a particularly formative influence upon the development of attitudes and the evaluation of others. Stereotyped attitudes are a special case of this phenomenon. Attitudes can change, however, in response to a relationship, although they also first determine with whom one wants to relate.

The most accurate interpersonal perceptions take place within the context of mutual role taking. When this occurs, the individual becomes most open to change, because to truly take the role of the other, one must acknowledge thoughts different from one's own, and recognize their value and logic. However, this task is considerably lightened when two people share a similar background, since differences are minimized, perceptions shared, and communications clear from the time they begin.

SOCIAL INTERACTION

Social relationships between members of society are intricately related to how they communicate. Social relationships dictate the content of communicated messages, yet communicated messages serve to define social relationship (Hymes, 1971).

This section discusses the more social aspects of communicative interaction. First the field of sociolinguistics, which studies how language is used in social settings is examined. Then the particulars of social interaction and the social relationships involved are discussed — specifically, how participants manage to maintain surface agreement within their interaction and how power, control, and intimacy influence the social interaction.

Before these issues are examined, the concept of a social situation must be defined. Most simply, a social situation occurs when two individuals are in each other's presence (Goffman, 1964). To the extent that each individual is becoming aware of the other, he experiences some degree of self-consciousness as he attends to the nonverbal and subsequent verbal behaviors of himself and the other (Barnlund, 1970). To the extent that it is difficult not to interact when two individuals are in each other's presence, one cannot speak of a state of no interaction within a social situation (Watzlawick et al., 1967). Even the act of silence conveys a social message of indifference in the presence of two potential communicators.

Sociolinguistics

Each message communicated in a social interaction is determined by two components: the social features of the situation and the personal intent (Ervin-Tripp, 1972). The language used by each participant makes reference, implicitly or explicitly, to these social features (personal intent aside). Language has the dual function of both representing and altering a social situation. In light of this potential for modifiability, the understanding of a social situation and even the social norms that are required, can be negotiated and reconstructed. Hence, behaviors are always tentative, continually tested throughout the interaction (Back, 1976; Bernstein, 1970; Cicourel, 1972). The individual may enter an interaction believing himself to be the superior. He may leave the interaction with the understanding that the other is now the one calling the shots. This transformation has been achieved by the way in which language has been used during the course of their social interaction.

The field of sociolinguistics studies precisely how language is used in social settings and how language makes reference to its social features. Its principles are useful to us, therefore, in our examination of these social interaction processes.

The social features of interaction that sociolinguists study include the participants, settings, topics, and interaction functions and forms (Ervin-Tripp, 1968). Insofar as participants are concerned, their sociological characteristics are important. These include factors such as age, class, status, and social position. These participant characteristics appear in all cultures and determine social relationships as well as their verbal expression (Bengtson et al., 1977; Ervin-Tripp, 1968; Fillmore, 1972; Hymes, 1974).

Most typically, specific variations of these features occur simultaneously. For example, in the work setting supervisor and employee talk only about work-related topics. Conversation is formal and messages politely conveyed. Research has shown, however, that shifts in form of speech co-occur with role, topic, and/or setting changes (Ervin-Tripp, 1968; Fishman, 1972; Schegloff & Sacks, 1973). Supervisor and employee discuss football at the company party. Talk becomes informal. They act like pals. Situational factors influence not only language forms, but also the degree to which an individual is willing to express what he truly believes (Freedle, 1975).

To the observer, the language form itself indicates social categories (Gumperz, 1972). The use of the word 'sir' clearly implies social distance between speaker and hearer. However, often the sociolinguist must attend to extralinguistic factors (that is, factors that are not solely linguistic) in order to interpret the language spoken (Ervin-Tripp, 1972; Lakoff, 1972). Correspondingly, in many social situations the spoken message may mark social distinctions in the absence of any exclusive linguistic form (Lakoff, 1972). Research has shown, for example, that the subordinate social status of the child is reflected in the types of utterances addressed to him, although these utterances do not take any one particular grammatical or lexical form.

Insofar as all socialized individuals are either consciously or unconsciously aware of social norms, ranges of acceptable behavior, and basic principles of conversation, interaction between strangers is facilitated (Cicourel, 1972; Ervin-Tripp, 1972; Fishman, 1972; Freedle, 1975). Each person assumes some form of social organization in the absence of information about the other's actual status or role. The fact that there are ranges of normative behaviors and choices for expressing social distinctions is especially informative for interpreting social meanings for participants who are either strangers or acquaintances (Hymes, 1974; Labov, 1970).

In addition, deviant or unexpected utterances often call conscious attention to the interpretation of social meanings within the interaction, redefining factors such as personal status or social situation for the participants (Ervin-Tripp, 1968, 1972). In our supervisor and employee example, if the supervisor suddenly declares that he feels like a failure, status relations are bound to shift and the more confident employee may ultimately take charge.

A shared language does not imply shared sociolinguistic rules between individuals (Ervin-Tripp, 1972). An 80-year-old and 20-year-old may both speak English, but their rules and regulations for language use may be barely comparable. A concept utilized by sociolinguists for identifying rule systems is that of the speech community. A speech community is a group of people who share rules for the conduct and interpretation of language behavior of at least one variety; a speech field is the range of communities with which the individual is able to communicate (Hymes, 1972b). The categorization of speech communities varies along a number of dimensions, depending upon how general the communication characteristics examined are. Hence, not only might ethnic groups constitute such communities, but also, for example, cohorts or generations, or the elderly of a housing project who share a set of norms and expectations for behavior.

Related to the concept of speech community is the activity of identifying members and nonmembers. Typically, adequate recognition of terms, locations, ideas, and activities within the stream of conversation differentiates members from nonmembers, or strangers (Schegloff, 1972a). Schegloff (1972) describes 'trouble' in the interaction when either the speaker's analysis of the other as a member was incorrect, or the hearer is not a fully competent member. On the other hand, mutual recognition and selection of the 'right' terms exhibit a state of "we know where we are, who we are, and what we are doing at this point in conversation" (Schegloff, 1972, p. 130). This is a comfortable state, no doubt.

Keeping in Line

On a less abstract level, the various works by Goffman (e.g., 1955, 1959, 1962, 1964) identify more precisely the pragmatics of social interaction. His analyses of human tendencies and rules of interaction provide insightful explanations for a variety of interpersonal behaviors. As we discuss his work, however, we must keep in mind that Goffman does not account sufficiently for the potential for personal change through interaction. His theories of behavior can be characterized as mechanisms for the maintenance of status quo, mechanisms which are nonetheless exercised quite frequently during the course of social interaction.

First and foremost, Goffman (1959) asserts that the maintenance of surface agreement in interaction and the desirability of avoiding open conflict concerning the definition of the situation are basic characteristics of social interaction. Additionally, the individual will often give the impression that the present interaction and partner are both special and unique. Goffman had developed the concepts of 'face' and 'line' in one of his original descriptions of social interaction in 1955. The line is the individual's pattern of verbal and nonverbal acts which express his view of himself and the situation. All participants are assumed to have taken a line. The face is the positive social value the individual has claimed for himself, and although it may constitute his most personal possession, it is ultimately 'on loan' from society. Maintenance of face is a condition, not an objective of the interaction, and the individual depends upon the social encounter to support his line. Moment-to-moment decisions as to what actions will maintain face, made either consciously or unconsciously, dictate behaviors. Typically, therefore, the individual will neither overtly nor covertly commit himself to a personal conception that interpersonal events are likely to discredit (Goffman, 1962).

Interactions become problematic when information discrepant with an individual's line is introduced, leading to a sense of shame and inferiority. For example, the individual who poses as an authority on children becomes embarrassed when he cannot control his own child. In addition to 'poise' as an individual mechanism for suppressing shame, participants attempt to save the face (and feelings) of one another, and the greater the power and prestige of the individual, the greater the attempt by others to save his face. The impetus towards saving face, called 'face work', is so strong that lack of effort on the part of one individual is compensated by the other. In Goffman's (1959) stage terminology, if the audience employs tact, the performer must act in ways to render this assistance possible (p. 234).

Should an 'incident' occur whereby there is a failure to save face, and should an offender continue to offend, methods such as tactless retaliation or withdrawal will deny the offender the status of interactant and deny the reality of the insulting incident. More typically, however, preventive procedures for redefining interpersonal assumptions counteract these disruptive events, especially when cooperative individuals participate in an interaction. Nevertheless, should an individual be deeply involved in or identified with a particular role he is trying to project, a disruptive interaction may seriously discredit his self-conception (Goffman, 1959). This becomes an increasing possibility with the onset of aging.

Power in Interaction

A fundamental component of social interaction is its power relations. Power relations are usually complementary, so that greater dominance of one implies greater passivity of the other (Ahammer, 1973). Sussman (1976), in a review of the properties of small groups, similarly notes that rewards for group members who interact may be unequal. Nevertheless individuals continue these relationships, unequal as they are, because they are perceived as better than the alternative, which is often no relationship at all. It is power relations that underlie this inequality of rewards derived from the relationship. Sussman concludes that social interaction, when it extends over a period of time, involves a continuous process of losing or gaining power during each episode. And power lost or gained, in turn, tailors the nature of each episode that follows. Even in relationships where power is equally shared, there is a continual danger of social competition over time (Watzlawick et al., 1967).

The 'principle of least interest' (Waller, cited in Bengtson & Black, 1973) represents one social mechanism of power display. Specifically, the person who is least invested within a relationship is the most influential of the two, since he has the least at stake. However, these notions of power relations are actually too simplistic. Distribution of power may differ within a single relationship for different areas of behavior and different aspects of the relationship. While the husband may dictate the financial behavior within the marital relationship, the wife may have final say on raising the children, without deferring to her marital partner.

Expressions of power may be explicit or subtle. Brown and Gilman (1960) for example, find that the egalitarian ideology of the United States is so predominant that conventional expressions of unequal power relations are suppressed. Instead, subordination is expressed unknowingly through body language. Nevertheless, the observer is usually able to identify the individual or group with lower prestige or power, as subtle as the cues may be (Goffman, 1959). In line with Goffman's (1959) emphasis on maintaining the status quo, he states that the observer is ill disposed toward the individual who refuses to keep his place, be it of high or low prestige.

Naturally, the person with greater power and control has the greater advantage in interaction. If the individual in control is a significant person to the other member, his evaluation has the power to increase or decrease the member's self-esteem and respect (Brim, 1966). Most serious, however, is the ability of the member in power to influence the self-concept of the weaker member, an ability which increases as the internal and external resources of the weak member diminish. This danger is confronted by the elderly adult, although it can occur at any stage throughout the life cycle.

The Positive and the Negative

Regardless of the power differential, social interactions can be characterized as positive, as negative, or as somewhere in between. However, the individual is drawn towards positive social cues that reinforce the individual's past and present outlook, and away from negative cues that contradict established attitudes and behaviors (Barnlund, 1970). This concept is naturally tied in with the preference for consistency, so common in social behavior. It also explains why individuals avoid contacts or topics which potentially threaten their face.

Experimentally, it has been shown that positive behaviors by one participant are related to positive behaviors by the other. For example, in research with children, high correlations have been found between positive reinforcements children give to others and how popular they are (Gottman et al., 1975). Other research has shown that when the child acts in a positive manner with an adult, the adult produces a more favorable evaluation of the child on intellectual and social dimensions (Bates, 1976). In general, within an interaction, positive reinforcements elicit positive reinforcements, and negative reinforcements elicit negative reinforcements (Ahammer, 1973). The latter situation is the more likely of the two to terminate most quickly.

A special case of negative interaction involves attempts to change behavior (Ahammer, 1973). This form of interaction is usually unpleasant, since prior knowledge of the learner is discredited, as he is subjected to new learning conditions. The result is decreasing attraction to the teacher, be he friend, neighbor, family, or professional. Teaching an individual to accept the status of 'old person' is an example of this form of social interaction, which is sometimes avoided, sometimes learned, and nearly always confronted by the aging adult.

Intimacy in Interaction

A major dimension of interpersonal interaction involves the degree of intimacy and shared knowledge between participants. There is a continuum along which interactions range from highly intimate to highly constrained. More formal and constrained relationships are dependent upon external norms to dictate behavior, whereas intimate relationships are more spontaneous and less subject to the constraints of social norms (Cicourel, 1972). We also find that the more formal the interaction, the less personal the information that is conveyed (Lakoff, 1972).

Members of a culture need to participate in both formal and informal social relationships. Formal relations allow the individual to exercise his social roles and maintain the social system in the process. Informal and intimate relations in turn provide a release for the member of society. In Goffman's (1959) terms, they allow him to relax 'backstage' until the next 'performance'.

The closer the relationship, the greater the overlap of interests and attitudes, and the greater the likelihood that the speech will take a specific and personal form (Bernstein, 1970). To the outside observer, therefore, messages cannot be understood without extensive background knowledge of the context and the history of the relationship. Most often in these relations communication is condensed (Bernstein, 1970). A few words go a long way, since intention is taken for granted and assumptions are shared. Thus, when the husband says to his wife as he returns home from work, "It happened again," she knows precisely what happened, to whom it happened, why it happened, and how he feels about it, without further cues from her apparently distraught spouse.

Research has shown that the more previous information shared by speaker and hearer (although not necessarily intimate companions) the less complete are verbal statements, the fewer words used, and the fewer repetitions made in an interpersonal exchange (Ratner & Rice, 1963). Similarly, when people write sentences to themselves, they contain fewer words than sentences addressed to others (Werner & Kaplan, 1963). Correspondingly, when there is someone with whom one shares a close relationship, sentences become more like those to self and less like those to others when partners interact.

Rules for Everyone

Several rules and regulations for interaction apply to all parties concerned, whether or not their relationship is intimate or constrained. It is important to recognize that these rules exist within the individual's many and varied interactions. Sociolinguists have been especially insightful in discovering just what these rules are.

One basic rule of interaction, for example, is that participants take turns in speaking (Sacks et al., 1974). Although only one person is permitted to speak at a single time, there are variations in turn-taking patterns in accordance with the social relationship. Some get more turns than others, depending upon factors such as status and power, as well as on the social context of the exchange.

A related feature of conversation is the 'adjacency pair' (Schegloff, 1972b; Schegloff & Sacks, 1973). An adjacency pair is a pair of utterances whereby once the first utterance is spoken, a second, adjacent utterance must follow from the listener. Hence, when the individual hears, "Hey, you know what?," he is obliged to answer with, "No, what?." In cases such as this one, should the individual originally approached choose not to respond to the initiator of conversation, strong social (or rather antisocial) inferences are made (Schegloff, 1972b). In general, the individual who supplies the appropriate reply to the initial utterance of an adjacency pair, indicates that he has understood the goal of the speaker (which was in this case to begin a conversation) and that he would like to comply. As a result, the speaker of the first utterance sees that his intentions are recognized and congenially accommodated by the other (Schegloff & Sacks, 1973).

It is these basic rules of interaction that link one social act to the next. Since all participants can play by the rules, they rely upon them to sustain interactions, which vary with social setting, social relationship, and social goals.

Social interaction is an integral human behavior exercised throughout the life cycle. Social relationships and the contexts in which they occur influence the form and the function of interaction, yet the interaction can transform the social relationship and redefine the social context by means of the messages exchanged. Sociolinguists have helped us to understand the ways in which relationships, settings, and language are intertwined, and why a mutually shared language does not insure an accurate understanding of messages spoken. Nonetheless, individuals strive to agree, to avoid conflict, and to preserve their 'face', as they negotiate power, form intimate relations, and examine and re-examine themselves and others.

Social interaction is an excellent means for encouraging individual change. However, the individual must be open to change and personal reassessment for this change to occur. On the other hand, if change is not valued by the individual, he must rely upon sturdy inner resources to counteract the explicit and implicit forces of change during the course of social interaction.

COMMUNICATION

Communication is essential to human development. It enables the individual to understand others and the social world as they change throughout the life cycle. Communication promotes stability, self-assurance, and consistency. It also promotes development and reorganization of the individual, of his relationships, and of his social environment. These processes are discussed in this section, which examines the constructive and disruptive effects of communication in interaction.

This section describes some general characteristics of interpersonal communication, then narrows in on the theory of speech acts, a theory which explains how people derive meanings from the utterances they hear. The importance of social context and dialogue content is stressed in an analysis of how messages are interpreted, how relationships are managed, and how communicators work to achieve mutual understanding.

The Communication Process

Communication creates meaning as opposed to merely messages, and in this way aids the individual in understanding personal and social experiences (Barnlund, 1970). Language is essential to the process. Language categorizes experience and channels our perception of the social and physical world. But the process is not static; it varies and changes. As long as we communicate, we are affected by communication and are subject to personal change as well as personal confirmation at all stages of life.

Some part of the self is revealed in nearly all communication (Pearce & Sharp, 1973). It can then be accepted, rejected, confirmed or discredited by the listening participant. How the participant in fact reacts makes or breaks the social relationship.

The strains built into our social system and its patterns of social relationships are managed or exacerbated within communication (Hulett, 1966b). Hence, if society is age graded, and each age group holds stereotypes of the others, discrepant attitudes and inaccurate perceptions surface during communication.

All behaviors become potential messages when people interact. Action and inaction, interest and indifference, all convey information to the other. In the words of Watzlawick et al., (1967), "One cannot not communicate" (p. 49). Communication can take place even if it is not intentional, conscious, mutual, or successful. On the other hand, when communication is intentional and mutual, the participants are able to affirm their own identity, recognize each other's identity, and view themselves as a mutual collectivity, a 'we', in relation to other social groupings (Habermas, 1970).

Two basic features of communication that facilitate mutual understanding are redundancy and feedback. There is typically an increase in redundancy and explicitness when a message overtly fails (Bates, 1975). However, nearly all messages contain redundant features in the absence of any requests for clarification. Redundancy, in fact, is already built into the system of human communication due to the various defects and ambiguities in language, and the inadequacies of human senders and receivers (Schegloff, 1972a). This redundancy feature of human exchange manifests itself at both verbal and nonverbal levels of communication (Erickson & Schultz, 1977).

Just as redundancy clarifies ambiguities within utterances, feedback clarifies messages across utterances. Research has shown that increases in feedback between communicators performing a task result in both more successful communication and greater confidence of subjects in their success. The absence of feedback results in increased distress on the part of both speaker and listener (Flavell et al., 1968). In less structured situations, however, interpersonal feedback is often ambiguous. It may indicate error on the part of the speaker in, for example, his estimate of the capacities and needs of the listener, compliance with norms and assessment of the social context (Hulett, 1966a). In these cases, more continual feedback is necessary in order to facilitate mutual adjustment.

Feedback is a crucial feature of communication because all communication is to some extent ambiguous. The more ambiguous the content of a communication, the more personality, motivation, and past experience influence the perception of the message (Fearing, 1953). When content is relatively unambiguous and congruent with the needs and attitudes of the listener, it is accepted with minimal modification. If incongruent, the receiver may reject or deny it, or else initiate overt conflict.   Goffman (1955) concludes that communication is a less 'punitive' human endeavor than the discovery of facts, since communications may be "by-passed, withdrawn from, disbelieved, conveniently misunderstood and tactfully conveyed" (p. 230).

Speech Acts

An analysis of how messages are understood is provided by the theory of speech acts. J.L. Austin originally introduced several of the major ideas of speech-act theory in 1962. These ideas were expanded and elaborated by Searle (1965, 1969, 1975), which in turn extended the field of linguistics to include theories about the human processing of communicated messages. The value of Austin's work is the attention it brings to the idea that words and utterances 'do things'. They are actions in themselves. Austin defines a 'performative' as the issuing of an utterance which performs an action. A simple example is the declaration 'I now pronounce you man and wife', which, under appropriate circumstances, performs this feat. However, few cases are as direct as this particular performative.

More typically, communicated messages are speech acts rather than pure performatives. And speech acts are a combination of locutionary and illocutionary acts. The locutionary act is simply the act of saying something, of making the sounds. The illocutionary act corresponds more to the performative function of the utterance. It is what the words do. For example, the illocutionary act warns, commands, promises, and describes. Searle (1965) adds that the illocutionary act is the minimal unit of linguistic communication.

The illocutionary act itself is composed of two components. These are the actual content (called the propositional content) of the utterance, and the illocutionary force, which is how the speaker intends the utterance to be taken by the hearer. The hearer attends most carefully to the force of the utterance and uses the context of the utterance to guide his interpretation. Hence, the statement, "Watch the door," does not mean one must continuously view the door as one would view a movie screen. Instead, it is a warning, since the door is likely to open any moment and slam directly into the hearer's face. Meaning of the illocutionary act, therefore, is a matter of both intention and convention (Searle, 1965).

An additional component of the speech act is the perlocutionary act, which is the effect of the illocutionary act upon the hearer's feelings, thoughts, or actions. Whereas illocutionary acts are conventional, perlocutionary acts need not be (Austin, 1962). We can never know for sure how the listener will react to the spoken message, as clear and intentional as it may seem.

Within speech-act theory, communication is achieved by having the hearer recognize the speaker's intention to communicate specifically what he intends (Searle, 1965). Austin refers to this process as 'securing uptake'. It is the process by which the speaker conveys the meaning and force of the utterance to the listener. Often the success of the speech act is also dependent upon adherence to basic rules of conversation (Grice, cited in Bruner, 1974/5; Lakoff, 1972). Some of these rules are that: (1) speakers must stick to the point and not repeat obvious information; (2) speakers must be truthful and should assume that the hearer will believe them; (3) answers are expected in response to questions, and compliance is expected in response to commands. On occasion these rules are violated, although such violations can be recognized and repaired by participants. At other times, violations are deliberate, in order to achieve specific intents such as humor, irony, or manipulation (Bruner, 1974/5).

A common form of speech act is the indirect speech act (Searle, 1975). The speaker says one thing but means another. In these cases the hearer must differentiate the intended act from its literal meaning. Successful interpretation is dependent upon the hearer's rationality, cognitive ability, and shared background information. Speaker, not sentence meaning, is primary. For example, "Can you lower the temperature," is usually taken not as a request for information on the hearer's ability to move the thermostat lever, but as a request to move the lever because the speaker is feeling a bit too warm. Another example of an indirect act is provided by Schegloff (1972a). When a random pedestrian is approached on the street with a request for directions to a nearby location, he may reply "I don't live here." The pedestrian does not mean to embark upon a conversation concerning his personal living arrangements. Instead, he is communicating his inability to give accurate directions to the lost solicitor.

A major criticism of speech-act theory involves the idea that except in obvious cases, there are no clear cut methods for recognizing the intention and force which underlie an utterance (Turner, 1974). Although in agreement with Austin's premise that words 'do things', Turner (1974) faults Austin's two conditions for the effectiveness of performatives: set conventions and appropriate setting. These conditions cannot be taken for granted, as Austin's analysis implies, but instead may have to be jointly determined or forcefully asserted as bases for further communication (Turner, 1974). Although this process is hinted at in the concept of 'securing uptake', it is not adequately described by either Austin or Searle, although it is a necessary condition for successful communication. Speech-act theory does, however, clearly prove that there is no one-to-one correspondence between the meanings of messages and the utterances which express them (Rommetveit, 1972). And in order to fully understand the speech act, the total situation must be considered.

The Total Situation

Although words are often used in interacting, communication is not solely a linguistic process. The selection of words is based upon features of the social environment, features that lie outside the structure of language and within the structure of society (Basso, 1972). For example, parents are referred to by their role ('mom') and children by name ('Jack') in order to differentiate the status positions and social responsibilities of each (Brown & Gilman, 1960). Similarly, nearly all encounters are structured by the ages of the participants (Neugarten, 1968a). Speier (1972) gives the example of the three-and-a-half-year-old who asserts, "Somebody give me some milk; please can I have milk," at the dinner table. This act of communication displays the mutual recognition of the child's restrictions in performing certain activities (such as getting milk from the refrigerator) and his right to have them done for him. Were a 25-year-old woman to speak the same utterance, the implications would be quite different.

Hence, the effect of communication is dependent upon the social context – participants included – as well as on the actual content of the message. In fact, Bateson (1972) asserts that without context, there can be no communication. Context is both 'out there' as well as inside the heads of communicating individuals, who in turn communicate effectively only if their personal contexts agree.

Utterance By Utterance

The total situation is one form of context which aids in interpreting messages. A more specific context is formed from the content of utterances both preceding and following each successive utterance within a dialogue. Typically, we do not speak in clear, even sentences. Speech is more spontaneous and irregular than the written word (Soskin & John, 1963), and spontaneous speech is governed by utterance-to-utterance decisions about what to say. Correspondingly, the relation between utterances defines communication, not each utterance in and of itself (Watzlawick et al., 1967).

The idea that each communication can be 'magically' modified by the accompanying communication illustrates that the meaning of the chain of dialogue is continuously transformed (Bateson, 1972). Dance (1970) likens the communication process to a helix, which is always moving forward yet reflective of its past. Each turn in dialogue also narrows down the number of possible moves by the speaker that follows (Watzlawick et al., 1967). Communication, like development, is both irreversible and unrepeatable as well as complex (Barnlund, 1970). It is a dialectical process.

Each turn in conversation refers not only to topics of concern, but to what was previously said. Hence, when people take turns in speaking, they may extend or even complete the utterance before theirs; and they always incorporate the ideas (and frequently the same words) of the previous utterance into their own (Duncan, 1972; Speier, 1972). Consider, for example, the following:

(a) "We're invited to eat there tomorrow."
(b) "Should we bring some wine?"

Utterance (b) clearly assumes what is stated in utterance (a). Specifically it assumes that there is an invitation to dinner. Also consider (c) and (d):

(c) "We're invited to eat there tomorrow."
(d) "Dinner? Tomorrow?"

In this case utterance (d) implicitly assumes what is said in (c) but is asking for further elaboration upon the topic of concern.

Often the chain of conversation is advanced in this manner, with repetition of and reference to the content of the previous message. This behavior displays that meanings are understood, that participants are willing to continue their talk, and that each recognizes the significance of what the other is saying, as they work to construct their dialogue.   And as we shall see in chapter three, the ability to participate in dialogue in this manner becomes a major achievement of the very young child.

More technically, however, theories are offered about how the individual processes a sequence of utterances on a cognitive level. A particularly insightful description of this process is contained in the 'given-new' strategy of Clark and Haviland (1974). The given-new strategy suggests that an utterance is understood by first discriminating what information has been previously given, and what information is new. Utterance (b) in our example presupposes a dinner invitation. This is the information assumed to be given. The new information concerns the problem of whether to purchase a bottle of wine. The listener determines the address in his memory for the information that is already given (the dinner invitation). The new information (buying wine) is then placed at that particular address.

Listeners, therefore, expect that each utterance they hear contains given, presupposed information, plus the assertion of new information. If the presuppositions of an utterance do not match what the listener already assumes, the given-new strategy fails. If the listener to (b) had presupposed that the invitation was to eat a quick, early breakfast, the suggestion of wine might have left him confused, since coffee would be more to his liking. If presuppositions fail, however, an alternative procedure is available. The listener will treat the true presupposition (a breakfast invitation) as new information in itself and will set up a new address in memory in which to store the correct information. When presuppositions are incorrect and given information is misunderstood, the utterance takes longer to comprehend. When speaker and listener follow different paths of thought and make different assumptions about what they are saying, communication can be difficult, tedious, and strained until mutual understanding is achieved, if at all.

The Dual Message

Communication is indeed complex. Messages have multiple meanings. They tell about society, situation, dialogue, and most importantly, about social relationships. In fact, every message transmitted from speaker to hearer conveys two basic pieces of information: information about the world, and information about the relationship between the speaker and hearer. Nearly all theorists of communication have discovered this dual aspect of communication, and each has described it with different terms. Bateson (1972) describes the metalinguistic (linguistic) and metacommunicative (social) components of communication, Hymes (1974) the referential and stylistic meanings of utterances, Halliday (1973a, 1973b) the ideational and interpersonal functions of messages, Habermas (1970) the analytic and reflexive aspects of language, and Watzlawick et al. (1967) the report and the command within communication. It is also observed that the relationship aspect of any communication classifies the content, or report of the message. How the individual perceives the interpersonal relationship shapes his perception of the message transmitted. Although these two components of communication are intricately interrelated, communicators may disagree about the relationship or about the message content as they negotiate an interaction.

However, communication about the relationship is largely unconscious (Bateson, 1972). Nevertheless, to the degree that it underlies the content of any communication, a difficulty in the relationship cannot be left unresolved (Watzlawick et al., 1967). If left unresolved, the message content may be seriously distorted. Resolution of the social relationship, therefore, is of utmost importance to the success of human interaction.

Actions and Words

Just as communication about the interpersonal relationship is largely unconscious, it is also largely nonverbal and involuntary (Bateson, 1972). Watzlawick et al. (1967) utilize computer terminology to describe the expression of both the linguistic and social components of communication. 'Digital' communication is like linguistic communication. Arbitrary signs are manipulated by means of logical syntax. 'Analogic' communication is like nonverbal communication. It is 'thing like' and imprecise. Digital language has the advantage of a complex, precise syntax, but lacks the semantics to express relationships. While analogic language possesses the semantics, it lacks an adequate syntax for resolving ambiguous definitions. Both, therefore, must operate together.

Nonverbal communication, though subtle and imprecise, has quite an impact on human exchanges. Research has shown, for example, that nonverbal cues can have greater influence upon subjects' evaluations of messages than do verbal cues (Argyle et al., 1972). This occurs despite the fact that analogic, nonverbal material is not consciously assessed by the listener.

The power of the nonverbal component of communication accounts for the fact that in face-to-face communication adjustment to listener needs are more likely since in this situation nonverbal cues can be detected immediately (Fearing, 1953). Examples of nonverbal social cues include lack of respect, subordination, informality, and anxiety (Brown & Gilman, 1960; Ervin-Tripp, 1972; Hulett, 1966b). How something is said is essential to what is said, and certainly influences the social response (Hymes, 1972b).

Managing Relationships

The relationships implied by messages and their nonverbal components are rarely defined deliberately or consciously. However, the more healthy and secure the relationship, the more the relationship aspect of the communication remains far in the background. And the more sick or unsteady the relationship, the more a struggle concerning its nature is at the forefront of the communication effort (Watzlawick et al., 1967).

Watzlawick et al. (1967) describe the punctuation of communication as the means by which the relationship is displayed on verbal and nonverbal levels. Punctuation organizes the conversation in terms of its social relations. It determines, for example, who takes initiative, who is dominant, and who is submissive. Since the punctuation organizes the act of communicating, it is necessary for the coherence of the ongoing exchange; the nature of the relationship as well is dependent upon the punctuation of the communication.

Most typically, discrepancies in punctuation occur in those cases where at least one participant possesses information different from that of the other, but does not realize it. Should this not be resolved, or should overt conflict over the punctuation occur, an interactional impasse results, leading to mutual charges of "madness" and "badness" (Watzlawick et al., 1967, pp. 93-94). This conceptualization is strikingly similar to the occurrence of an 'incident' as described by Goffman, where one participant refuses to save the humiliated 'face' of the other.

Self-concept correspondingly is managed from the relationship per-spective. Watzlawick et al. (1967) observe specifically three forms of self-concept management at the relationship level of communication: (1) The individual's self-concept may be confirmed by the other, insuring mental development and stability. With a firm sense of one's own identity, the individual can more easily and confidently incorporate what he learns from the social environment, and develop in selected directions. (2) The individual's self-concept may be rejected by the other. Although this is painful to the individual, it assumes at least some recognition of what is rejected and therefore need not destroy the reality of the individual's self-concept. (3) The most pathological condition is the disconfirmation of the individual by the other. In this case there is no attention paid to the individual's self-concept at all, since the individual himself is discredited as a viable source for defining his own self-concept. Should the individual be subjected to the com-munication of disconfirmation, it inevitably leads to personal self-doubt and loss of a sense of effectiveness, a situation likely to be encountered in the social world of the older adult.

Self Disclosure

A related dimension of communication is the degree to which the individual voluntarily offers personal information. Pearce and Sharp (1973), in a review of self-disclosure research, find that most communi-cation settings promote little sharing of personal information, while a fewer number of settings encourage a great deal of self-disclosure. Additionally, the amount of private disclosure by the individual is unrelated to behavior in more public settings of communication.

Two-person parties are more likely to share private information than are larger groups. The presence of a more neutral third party inhibits the occurrence of self-disclosure. The highest degree of self-disclosure occurs between individuals who are very close and between those who are strangers. And while there is a strong relationship between friendship and self-disclosure, the process of self-disclosure occurs gradually, as the relationship becomes more stable and enduring. With strangers, however, the disclosure may occur immediately, especially when no future contacts are expected. In most cases, an increase in disclosure by one participant results in an increase by the other.

It is important to note, however, that although self-disclosure may facilitate mutual understanding, there is little definitive evidence linking affection and self-disclosure. Not all high self-disclosers are sought out by others. Nevertheless, throughout the life cycle the individual needs to participate in close interpersonal relationships and to have a confidant. Sharing one's intimate thoughts with another enables the individual to maintain his identity and support his self-concept. And at different stages of the life cycle, confidant relationships become more essential to the individual in performing this function. Adolescence and old age are examples of these stages, and are described in later chapters.

Intersubjectivity

Many of the ideas discussed in this chapter can be summarized by a single concept: intersubjectivity. Intersubjectivity between communicators is the ideal communication experience. The philosopher Habermas (1970) best describes this ideal.

According to Habermas, pure intersubjectivity between communicators occurs when the relationship is symmetric. The play for power does not interfere. The relationship is mutual, reciprocal, equal. Intersubjectivity in communication is possible when individuals acknowledge and understand one another and know and understand their own selves. Confirmation of the self-concept of the self and the other is thereby achieved. Intersubjectivity, in the same vein, incorporates speech-act theory, since each individual recognizes the intention of the other's speech act. Mutual recognition additionally includes the certainty that the other can behave according to recognized social norms. The communication then ensues at two levels of exchange: communication about the world, and metacommunication on the level of intersubjectivity.

At the other end of the continuum, Habermas describes pseudocommunication, where by means of reciprocal misunderstandings, neither participant is aware of a communication disturbance. Instead, participants display a pseudoconsensus concerning what is occurring in conversation, what they are thinking, and what they are meaning. Neither corrects the other, because neither is aware of their faulty assumptions.

To the extent that intersubjectivity is an unrealized ideal, various approximations to this state exist. One never truly perceives the social world in a manner identical to the other, yet individuals can perceive themselves and others in highly comparable ways. When the links between social behaviors and the meanings they intend are misunderstood, a redefinition and correction of assumptions can quickly reestablish a consensual understanding, provided that participants are willing to work toward this goal. Taking the role of the other is the primary means towards this end.

Habermas notes that deformation of pure intersubjectivity is most often induced by the social structure, which is largely based upon asymmetric power relations. Similarly Hulett (1966b) observes that distortions of communication may often be attributed to sociological factors such as inbuilt strains in systems of social relationships and the persistence of dysfunctional ways in which to talk about various issues. Finally, the individual may accurately perceive the needs of the listener, yet not necessarily communicate messages in a manner responsive to the listener's needs; the speaker may have inadequate information about the hearer and not seek to obtain the correct information; or, the speaker may himself be uncertain of his own identity, his ability to predict the listener's response, or he may be unknowledgeable of social norms of behavior (Fearing, 1953; Hulett, 1966b). All these factors are disruptive to the communication process and further remove the participants from an intersubjective state. It is this state of intersubjectivity towards which communicators strive in their attempts to confirm the identity of speaker and of listener, and to form a unified and collective sense of 'we'.

The utterances we construct refer simultaneously to topics of concern and to those dimensions relevant to defining the social context. Meaning is derived by means of integrating both the social context of communication and the sequencing of utterances within the dialogue. When communicators hold common assumptions and perceive their worlds in similar ways, communication is vastly simplified and information efficiently exchanged. If not, communicators need to define their assumptions, their contexts, and themselves. The potential for growth under these circumstances is great indeed, assuming that the identities of speaker and hearer are recognized and confirmed within the communication.

Messages are communicated verbally and nonverbally, as they clarify or distort informational content and interpersonal relationships. Relationships are exhibited by communicated behaviors as well as negotiated by these same means as they aim towards either stabilization or dissolution. While mutuality, symmetry, and intersubjectivity are held as communication ideals, they are only approximated within social exchanges and may be distorted at various levels of interpersonal perception, personal motivations, and social knowledge.

Throughout the life cycle, the individual participates in endless communication exchanges, ranging from pseudocommunications to idealized intersubjective relationships. The benefits or damages which result from these experiences depend upon the developing individual, his life stage, identity, and social resources, as he moves irreversibly through the stages of life.

3 Origins of Communication

The roots of complex communicative skills are established early in life. The infant is a primitive communicator, but a communicator nonetheless. He develops the skills of taking turns, making reference, and sharing topics. In cooperation with the caretaking adult, the infant develops language skills. With social, linguistic, and cognitive growth, the child gradually takes the role of the other. He learns of a self which is separate from others and learns of ideas that are different from his own. Interaction with peers of similar age aid him throughout this process, as he discovers intentions embedded in speech and achieves mutuality of influence. This chapter describes these early processes of the development of communication. The process is traced from the time of birth, where caretaker-infant relations prevail, to the time when children interact on their own, communicating with peers and coping with an ever widening social world.

CARETAKER-CHILD INTERACTION

The infant, from the time of birth, is embedded in a social system. The newborn is predisposed to respond to the social world. The infant is especially attracted to the human voice, the sounds of speech, and the human face (Bruner, 1975; Freedle & Lewis, 1977; Lewis, 1936; Lewis & Freedle, 1973; Richards, 1974a, 1974b; Ryan, 1974; Stern, 1974; Thoman et al., 1977; Watson, 1972). The adult too is predisposed to respond to the newborn infant. The infant's babyish appearance alone engages parental attention, but additionally the infant's smile, vocalizations, imitations of the adult, novel responses, developmental progress, and general modifiability are highly attractive to the adult caretaker (Bell, 1974). The caretaker-infant unit therefore becomes the first social system in which the infant participates (Bell, 1971). And it is this situation which serves as the context for the child's socialization and development of communication.

The caretaker-infant dyad is a highly interdependent system, each member influencing the behavior of the other, their relationship superseding the individual characteristics of each. Yet each member has different aptitudes and behaviors to contribute to their social system. The relationship is asymmetric. Most obvious is the difference in communication skills. Whereas adult speech is both analogic (nonverbal) and digital (linguistic), the infant begins solely as an analogic communicator (Harris, 1975). Caretakers therefore use many means of communication besides vocal ones to interact with the infant (Ling & Ling, 1974; Stern et al., 1975). The infant serves as a powerful elicitor of communications from the caretaking adult.

The caretaker initially fits her behavior to the infant's so that interactions appear contingent (Kaye, 1977). The ability to take turns in interaction, called mutual phasing, becomes one of the infant's earliest developmental achievements, and changes the nature of the relationship. Interaction of caretaker and child involves mutual readjustment and developmental change from episode to episode, as the infant acquires numerous skills, and the caretaker changes her responses over time. Each dyad establishes communication routines unique to their own shared relationship, yet more general sequences of dyadic interaction take place in the course of early human development.

This section examines the basic features of the earliest caretaker-child interactions, including infant rhythms, facial alignment, prelinguistic conversations, and joint activities with objects. The role of the caretaker is discussed in terms of the impact of caretaker sensitivity, precursors to later developmental progress, and the changing nature of the interaction with the onset of language.

Face-to-Face

During the first months of life, biological mechanisms regulate the infant's attention (Brazelton et al., 1974). Infancy researchers describe a cycle of attention and inattention to social stimuli, particularly the mother. There are mild peaks of engrossed attention followed by slight withdrawals by the infant (Bateson, 1975; Brazelton et al., 1974). The mother must anticipate the infant's biological regularity and adjust her stimulation accordingly. If not, infant and mother have difficulties coordinating interactions, with the infant displaying increased tendency towards withdrawal from the mother (Brazelton et al., 1974; Kaye, 1977; Richards, 1974a).

During the attentive phase of interaction, the face-to-face alignment held by mother and child promotes communication (Harris, 1975; Kaye, 1977; Stern, 1971, 1974). By three months of age, mutual gaze patterns of mother and infant begin to look more like those of adult participants in social interaction (Stern, 1971, 1974). Watson (1971) characterizes this position of facial alignment between caretaker and infant as one in which the infant initially comes to know his social world. Within this setting the participating adults become increasingly prominent features of the infant's perceptual environment.

The mutual orientation of mother and child, paired with vocal behaviors, gives a conversational quality to the interaction. It has been labeled 'proto-conversation', and is the precursor to mature conversation for the infant (Bateson, 1975; Stern et al., 1975). Turn-taking behaviors are gradually learned by the infant, taking forms such as smiling games at six weeks and chainings of vocal sounds and physical gestures by mother and infant by three months of age (Bateson, 1975; Bloom et al., 1976; Lewis & Freedle, 1975; Richards, 1974a). An important lesson of social interaction has been learned by the infant who proto-converses: one turn at a time.

Researchers, particularly Stern et al. (1975), however, have reported another pattern of dyadic conversation, a coactional pattern. Behavior of mother and infant is simultaneous; they do not take turns. Coactional conversation too has been observed at three to four months of age. This mode of interchange is more similar to nonverbal systems of social behaviors such as gaze, posture, and rhythm patterns. It is an analogic mode of communication. Although the dyads observed by Stern et al. (1975) displayed both coactional and alternating (that is, turn-taking) modes of interaction, one mode usually dominated each interaction. Either the interaction was primarily a coactional or primarily an alternating form of exchange.

Both these modes of social exchange persist throughout the life cycle. Turn taking is an efficient means for exchanging information between speaker and listener. Coactional patterns of human exchange too convey information between communicators, but the information exchanged is different. Its message is primarily social in nature. Because coactional patterns are emotional and socially arousing, they have a group-bonding effect upon participants. Examples are prayer, cheers, and celebrational behaviors, which are integral components of the adult social world. They are nonverbal outlets for the expression of basic social feelings. During infancy, correspondingly, coactional behaviors paired with mutual gaze and high arousal are essential contributors to the emotion-laden mother-child attachment (Stern et al., 1975).

Both alternating and coactional patterns of early social interaction are therefore important and necessary for the cognitive and social growth of the developing infant. Turn taking permits efficient processing of dialogue information. Simultaneous arousal promotes a mutuality of social concern.

Joint Action

Whether coactional or alternating, nearly all behaviors that the infant displays are subject to maternal interpretation. The mother finds meaning in her infant's behavior whether it is meaningful, intentional, or random (Bates et al., 1975; Bruner, 1974/5, 1975; Ryan, 1974). Much of this tendency on the part of the mother is due to her need to see regularity and predictability in her infant's behavior (Kaye, 1976). However, the mother's interpretations become most important to the infant when they begin to participate in joint actions, an activity best described by the developmental psychologist Jerome Bruner (1974/5, 1975).

Joint action requires three components: mother, infant, and object. Joint action ensues when mother and child focus jointly upon the object. This is achieved by four months of age when infants begin to follow the mother's line of vision towards some object. Similarly, mothers tend to follow the infant's line of vision and to comment upon the target object, as they grasp it, tap it, shake it, and name it (Bruner, 1974/5, 1975; Kaye, 1976). In this context, mother and child share interest and information, elementary and crude as it is, about their physical and social world. This is the context in which they communicate and ultimately develop linguistic skills. Most importantly, the mutual focus and mutual sharing can be considered the earliest efforts on the part of the dyad to establish intersubjectivity, the interlacing of perspectives, and mutual social confirmation (Ryan, 1974).

Joint action enables the infant to recognize the referential nature of language (Shatz, 1977). Phrases heard serve to stabilize the similarities of behaviors over time (Lewis, 1936). Additionally, the structure of joint infant-caretaker activity is generalized to interactions with unfamiliar adults. When infants approach strangers to initiate an interaction, they typically direct the adult's attention toward an object or toy. The object then serves as a mutual focus upon which they base their social exchange (Rheingold et al., 1976; Ross & Goldman, 1977).

Maternal Power

In light of the asymmetric relationship between mother and child, and the unequal distribution of knowledge, skill, and will, the mother has an undeniably significant impact upon the interaction patterns and the development of the infant (Ainsworth et al., 1974; Brazelton et al., 1974; Kaye, 1977). Maternal sensitivity to the infant's needs and proclivities is essential. It provides the most beneficial environment for infant development. Maternal sensitivity, for example, influences the speed and facility with which the child acquires language (Cross, 1975; Nelson, 1973). Nelson (1973) has shown that young children develop either an expressive, socially-oriented, or referential, label-oriented mode of language use on their own. Mothers then either accept or reject this mode of language use. The nonsensitive, directive mother is unaware of her child's language preference and skills. She fails to build upon them. This slows the process of acquisition. The lack of fit between mother and child can also result in emotional upset by the second year of life (Nelson, 1973).

There are many individual differences among mothers in their approaches to mother-child interaction (Lewis & Freedle, 1973; Lewis & Lee-Painter, 1974; Moerk, 1974; Sameroff, 1975). Yet within the dyad there are stable interaction patterns, which have been observed during the earliest days following birth (Freedle & Lewis, 1977; Osofsky, 1976). All patterns indicate, however, that the accepting, sensitive mother facilitates the development of secure mother-child attachment and the child's cognitive mastery over the physical and social environment (Ainsworth et al., 1974; Hartup, in press; Nelson, 1973). Maternal characteristics evidenced during the first years have correlated with developments as far ahead as ages two and three (Elardo et al., 1977; Freedle & Lewis, 1977; Nelson, 1973; Stern, 1971). Additionally, when mismatch occurs between the child's mode of language use and the maternal preference (which is either referential or expressive), frustration is eased only when the child reorganizes his own system of language to correspond with that of the parent (Nelson, 1973).

These relationships are not meant to suggest that the infant or child does not influence maternal behaviors as well. However, it does appear that the more sensitive mothers are the caretakers who most allow the child to influence their behaviors, and who build upon the capacities that the child displays developmentally. Nevertheless, studies of infant individual differences indicate that some infants from birth are more easily handled than others, which may either facilitate or discourage the responsive tendencies of the mother (Thomas et al., 1968).

The Developing Dialogue

There is a basic continuity of interaction patterns throughout the first years of life, but the quality of the interaction undergoes considerable change from the first to second year. Both the structure and the content of mother and child communications become increasingly sophisticated as they begin to take the form of linguistic dialogue (Bates, 1975; Bloom et al., 1976; Escalona, 1973). Once language does develop, both the parent's language and the child's change together as the parent remains aware, often preconsciously, of the child's developing capacities (Bloom et al., 1976; Blount, 1972; Lord, 1975; Moerk, 1974).

Accordingly, the mother modifies the complexity and the content of her language to the child in response to the child's level of development. Her speech is not geared, however, towards teaching the child the grammar of language. Ultimately, the aim of the mother-child dialogue is the construction of meaningful exchanges in the context of mutual engagement. The functions her utterances perform override the need to teach specific rules of syntax (Cross, 1977; Newport et al., 1977; Snow, 1977). Correspondingly, the content of maternal language deals with the child's focus upon the immediate environment. She takes cues from the child by observing how and what he attends to within the physical and social world (Bloom et al., 1976; Cross, 1975; Ling & Ling, 1974; Moerk, 1974; Tamir, 1979a, 1979b).

A basic feature of the parent-child dialogue is the adult's acceptance of the child's nonstandard speech, rendering the child an equal

partner in the dialogue (Soderbergh, 1974). Similarly, the adult maintains a conversational flow by making proposals the child is willing to
accept and by responding to the child's utterances in a manner less
complex than spontaneous adult speech (Lord, 1975; Soderbergh, 1974).
Techniques such as imitation and expansion, or repetition of child
utterances indicate acknowledgment of the child and maintain continuity of conversation (Blount, 1972; Soderbergh, 1974). The most
effective parent-child conversations are those in which the child
initiates the topics for discussion. The parent then incorporates the
topic within her own responsive utterances and proceeds to expand upon
them (Cross, 1975; Soderbergh, 1974). Note how similar these behaviors
are to the conversation-tying procedures used by adults who interact.
Adults too expand the utterances they hear, incorporating what is
previously said, as they construct their dialogue utterance by utterance.
It is these behaviors which promote effective social exchange, and are
satisfying to all participants.

To illustrate the concept of topic elaboration, Nelson (1973) provides examples of mother-child dialogue of both a linguistically accelerated and a developmentally stifled child. Jane, who evidenced rapid
acquisition, had an exceptionally accepting mother. A portion of their
dialogue at 14 months of age went as follows:

   Jane: Baw.
   Mother: Ball, yes.
   Jane: Uh, uh, boo?
   Mother: Ball. (p. 104)

On the other hand, Paul experienced considerable difficulty once he
began to use words. A portion of their dialogue at age 17 months went
as follows:

   Paul: Go.
   Mother: What? Feel.
   Paul: Fi.
   Mother: What's that? A dog? What does the dog say? (p. 105).

A comparison of these dialogues demonstrates how well the parent
promotes or avoids the sharing of underlying concerns and presuppositions of the child. In the process the parent either succeeds or fails
to confirm the child's sense of social and cognitive competence. The
mastery of language and the development of interactive skills by the
child follow suit.

In accordance with the sensitive parent's conversational behaviors,
Bloom et al. (1976) have found that similar patterns of conversational
sensitivity develop in the young child. Specifically, the child learns to
construct utterances which incorporate the ideas of the preceding
utterance spoken by the parent in dialogue. When a topic originated in
the adult utterance, Bloom et al.'s young subjects gradually learned to
incorporate it within their contingent replies. With development the

children displayed an increase in the number messages which shared the topic of the prior utterance while adding new information to it. This process corresponds to the child's increasing ability to exercise the 'given-new' strategy of conversational understanding, as described in chapter two. The child has come to expect that each utterance in dialogue contains assumed information, and the addition of information that is new. The child becomes increasingly able to logically combine the given and new, as he jointly constructs conversational meaning.

The infant experiences his first communicative interactions within the social system of the mother-infant unit. The system continually undergoes developmental change, although early behaviors correlate with developments that occur later in time. The fundamental asymmetry of the dyad members if reflected in the different means by which each adjusts to the other. Initially, infant behaviors are dictated by biological rhythms to which the mother must adjust. Eventually, the infant gains more control over mutual phasing within their encounters and learns to focus attention upon shared objects. Throughout, maternal sensitivity to the infant's abilities and developmental changes is an important component of the interaction. The mother is the major interpreter of the prelinguistic infant and the major dialogue partner with the language developing child. With successful development, the child comes to incorporate the interactive skills displayed by the parent, ranging from the ability to focus jointly upon objects in the world, to the ability to incorporate the assumptions of parental utterances within the child's own as they continue their developing dialogue.

LANGUAGE DEVELOPMENT

Language develops in a social environment. The process of learning language is both cognitive and social. The child must learn that words are symbolic and that words convey messages.

The ability to learn language is an innate human endowment, and the internal language structures which develop are the same for all children. Yet the use of language depends upon the sociolinguistic environment (Blount, 1972). The social environment is conveyed and constructed through words. Hence, origins of social behavior and interpersonal cognition are intricately related to the development of language. Variations in the social conditions for language development, plus the differing cognitive aptitudes and propensities of language learners serve to explain the wide range of individual differences displayed by children in both speed and method of language acquisition (Bloom, 1976; Moerk, 1977; Ryan, 1974).

Learning language is not simply a process of accumulating words and grammatical rules. Rather, old means of communicating are transformed into new, as skills are acquired and abilities improve. The preverbal interactions of child and caretaker are precursors to mature language processes. They undergo successive transformations of form, content, and use (Bloom, 1976; Bruner, 1974/5; Richards, 1974a; Tamir, 1979b).

However, there are differences between the precursors and language itself. During infancy, action and communication are one and the same (Dance, 1970). The noises and gestures of the infant are not learned initially but are biological in origin. They are not intended to represent perceptions or feelings; they are the actual felt experience of the prelinguistic infant (Bloom, 1976). On the other hand, language requires the use of vocabulary and grammar, the digital components of social dialogue (Halliday, 1973b). Nevertheless, the conventions of communication prerequisite to participation in dialogue are acquired before any language appears. These include the ability to alternate turns, to participate in reciprocal exchanges, to influence others, and to establish joint reference (Bruner, 1974/5; Freedle & Lewis, 1977; Kaye, 1976; Ryan, 1974). Hence, dialogue precedes monologue, and caretaker-infant communication provides the structure and support for the elaboration of language skills in dialogue, skills that express the social world and the relationships within it (Harris, 1975; Jaffe & Feldstein, 1970; Kaye, 1977).

Language development involves the acquisition of several related skills. Most important are the acquisition of words, the construction of sentences, and the ability to respond appropriately within a dialogue exchange. No single explanation of language development can account for this complex phenomenon. It is not purely referential, purely syntactic, or purely social in origin or practice. In order to summarize several of the major theoretical views which address the problem of language acquisition, this section reviews how researchers have used the theory of speech acts to explain language development, the importance of joint action for the development of linguistic structures and reference, and an analysis of the development of linguistic and conversational skills within verbal dialogue.

Early Speech Acts

The initial communications by the preverbal infant perform basic functions but have little structure (Bruner, 1974/5; Halliday, 1973b; Harris, 1975; Lewis, 1936). The infant's first cries, whether or not the cries are intentional, serve the function of expressing needs and securing satisfaction (Ainsworth et al., 1974; Bell, 1974; Bruner, 1974/5). Development, in turn, can be viewed as a process of functional continuity in conjunction with continual structural reorganization (Piaget, cited in Ryan, 1974).

From the perspective of speech-act theory, Bates et al. (1975) have skillfully examined the relationships among function, intention, and form in the development of communication and language. They posit three stages of the development of communication, the first of which is the perlocutionary stage. During this stage, the infant's behaviors have a systematic effect upon the listener, but there is no intentional or conscious control over the resulting response, called the 'perlocutionary effect'. The infant makes various gestures and sounds to which the adult responds. Yet the infant is unaware of his power to communicate these messages and in turn to control the responses received. The infant cries and is given a bottle, a perlocutionary effect.

The second stage is the illocutionary stage, observed at about ten months of age. During this stage the infant displays a capacity for intention, called the 'illocutionary force' of the message. But intention is expressed in nonverbal ways; hence the child's communications lack a 'propositional content'. The infant may deliberately attempt to use the listener as an agent towards some goal, such as reaching for a cookie, or intentionally direct an adult's attention towards some object. The researchers suggest that this stage corresponds to an early stage of cognitive development, where the child develops the ability to analyze means-ends relationships and uses materials in the physical world in order to achieve set goals. Actions that previously were means towards some goal now become signals which are ritualized and communicative. The gesture of reaching has become symbolic. Extending an arm means, "Get me that cookie." When the child begins to use one-word utterances, these too are purely illocutionary. They indicate clear and specific intentions, yet they lack specific propositional content. The child cannot express linguistically the propositions he may mean. The force is there; the words are not. At this stage the illocutionary force of the utterance can be expressed by means of the child's intonation (Dore, 1975; Halliday, 1973b). A wild screech has a different force than a contented grunt of social delight.

The final stage is the locutionary stage, where the child verbally constructs propositions to achieve an intended effect. This corresponds to a more advanced stage of cognitive development. The child has developed the capacity for internal representation of the external world and the referential use of words within it. He is now on his way to participation in mature interpersonal dialogue.

The observations and analyses of Bates et al. insightfully link the concepts of speech-act theory with the development of communication. However, they analyze the development of intention in communication rather than the linguistic structures used to represent them (Dore, 1976). Nevertheless, their contribution is significant. Theorists of life-span development are now able to view basic functions of communication as continuous throughout the life cycle. Intention in communication arises quite early in life and is continually exercised thereafter. Intention is expressed in more sophisticated ways as the young individual develops, yet it powerfully conveys meanings to others as it achieves both expected and unexpected social effects.

Topics in Action

Intention develops within the context of joint action of caretaker, infant, and object. More than intention develops within this context, however. The structure of the interaction within this form of setting ultimately becomes transformed into the structure of language in dialogue.

Our sentences in everyday talk are composed of topic and comment. Take for example the sentence which states, "The weather is lovely today." The mutually perceived topic, the weather, is commented upon as being lovely. "How lovely!" conveys a similar message if speaker and hearer are looking outdoors. Hence, the topic-comment structure of the utterance assumes the feature of joint attention plus an implicit or explicit comment upon the jointly attended topic (Bruner, 1974/5, 1975).

Correspondingly, the topic-comment structure of communicated messages originates within the early sequences of joint activities in which the infant takes part. Bruner reviews the research and theory that illustrates this assumption about the development of language.

The child initially uses gesture, sound, and later, language, as a means for commenting upon action jointly undertaken. Research has found that the first vocal comment occurs at about nine months of age. Within the setting of joint activity, the child vocalizes either when he is about to perform his piece of the action or as the action comes to an end. During the course of joint activities and with the aid of adult interpretations and expansions, the child eventually acquires the concepts of agent, action, and object. Mastery of these parts of speech is necessary in order to construct linguistic utterances. With development and social activity, these utterances become increasingly grammatical as well as semantically clearer.

Additionally, the child, in the maintenance of joint attention, begins to approach a state of intersubjectivity. Recognition that others have intentions originates within this context (Bruner, 1974/5). However, to reach such a state, considerable development and distancing from the other is required. Werner and Kaplan (1965) note that early joint activities (which they label the 'primordial sharing experience') are characterized by little differentiation between self, other, and object of focus. With development, there is progressive distancing between these components so that the sharing experience with the other is transformed into communication to the other, and ultimately a recognition of intention of the other, as well as of the self. Hence, within these early exchanges the social functions of language develop, as do those rules of linguistic utterances which make reference to things in the world.

Meanings in Action

The development of reference, more commonly known as semantic development, begins before the child utters his very first words (Freedle & Lewis, 1977; Lewis & Lee-Painter, 1977). The earliest use of reference by the child is the act of indicating, of getting the other to view the same object as the self. The easiest way to achieve indication is by having the mother follow the infant's line of vision. This is usually supplemented, however, by the gesture and sound of the active, preverbal infant (Bruner, 1974/5). Werner and Kaplan (1963) state that the first act of reference is a social and not an individual act. It is achieved by means of mutual exchange and handling of objects. It is no surprise, therefore, that when the child begins to label verbally the objects he perceives, he learns the names specifically of things he acts upon (Nelson, 1973).

At about six to nine months of age, midway between the use of gesture and the competent use of words, the infant uses systematic vocal sounds as the first structured system of reference (Halliday, 1973b). These are the infant's own, personally constructed words. Since semantic development begins quite early, there is a basic continuity in development in terms of meaning, but not in terms of the forms used to express it. Prior to the child's use of words, he recognizes that the words of others are labels that refer to things. Correspondingly, the child's own nonstandard labels, which precede the conventional use of words, indicate that the child has learned something about the referential nature of speech (Ryan, 1975).

Overall, there is a gradual development from a presymbolic use of words, where meanings may be quite subjective and the word not truly differentiated from the thing it represents, to mature reference, whereby the word serves the dual purpose of referring to and representing the thing it labels (Ryan, 1974; Werner & Kaplan, 1963). Ryan (1974) also asserts that since the child's initial words may not have clearly defined meanings for the child or the listener, the adult's interpretation provides crucial information for the child. Interpretations enable the child to gradually learn what meaning he has conveyed. This knowledge can then be used to further a consensual understanding of the meanings of words and the uses of language.

A major impetus for the child to acquire and use conventional words is the fact that they provide the most effective form of communication. Reference is clear, meanings are understood. Further, the child has increased his capacity to discriminate objects within the physical world as well as relations within the social environment (Lewis, 1936). This development corresponds to the child's growing inclination from ages two to five to describe his experience and observations in words (Moerk, 1974).

Overall, reference is a continual function exercised in communication and language, but its structure and its form change rapidly from birth, from vague to precise, from analog to digit, from personal to conventional, in the context of social dialogue.

Dialogue in Action

Once the child enters into verbal dialogue, a supportive environment continues to be important. However, environmental factors do not influence the development of particular linguistic structures in clear and direct ways (Newport et al., 1977). The linguistic structures used by the adult become effective in teaching the child rules of language only after the child has the cognitive skills enabling him to use these structures (Snow, 1977).

The child typically concentrates on the utterances addressed directly to him, especially when they refer to aspects of the current situation he is attending (Farwell, 1975). Additionally, the child tends to listen selectively to those words at the beginning of each utterance (Newport et al., 1977). Hence, there are several features of maternal speech which directly correlate with the acquisition of specific language structures by the child. For example, mothers who ask many questions which begin with an auxiliary verb (e.g., Are you going?) have children who learn to use auxiliary verbs more rapidly. However, at the present time such clear and consistent correlations are rare in the research findings that deal with the development of linguistic structures (Newport et al., 1977). The language to the child is therefore not necessarily a teaching language. Instead, it is an attempt to share topics of interest and create meanings in the world of the child, a process achieved by means of the give and take of a mutually constructed dialogue.

Just as the child learns many linguistic structures indirectly, the child's comprehension of linguistic structures in dialogue is often indirect as well. Shatz (1977) has shown that the tendency of the child between 19 and 34 months is to respond to utterances with action, even when utterances do not request an action but rather ask for information. Shatz concludes that cognitive – more than grammatical – strategies are utilized by children of this age range in interpreting verbal messages. The child who listens to the utterance of the adult simply considers which actions might be plausible given the context of the utterance. This procedure is usually an effective one for the child since adults often intend their utterances to elicit active behaviors from the child.

Rules for participation in linguistic dialogue are acquired gradually by the child, as competent a converser as he may appear. The child might give the appropriate response, yet his strategy is different from that of the adult. While the adult attends to the subtleties of language, the child attends to the things he can do. With increasing experience and social interaction, the child comes to understand better the intentions of others. This occurs in a mutual context where topics are shared and meanings elaborated.

The development of communicative and linguistic skills undergoes continual reorganization from infancy through early childhood. Precursors to mature language use are traced to social interactions during the first year of life where the taking of turns, the sharing of topics, and recognition of intention evolve. Throughout the process of language development, perceptual, cognitive and social factors influence the child's receptivity to new information and its assimilation. An actively interpreting adult facilitates the development of semantics and grammar as well as the skills of dialogue, although the lessons are often indirect. However, the child is an efficient processor of that information in the social and physical environment relevant to his needs and capacities, as he develops strategies for processing language and for participating in conversational settings during the first years of life.

A NOTE ON BABY TALK

Investigators of child language have recently begun to analyze the language spoken to the child as carefully as the language spoken by the child. Simplification of the speech addressed to the child is a universal phenomenon, although the forms these simplifications take may vary from culture to culture (Blount, 1972). Sociolinguists have noted that all speech communities have at least one form of language use, technically termed speech register, which is confined to dialogue with individuals who are unlikely to understand standard adult speech. This speech register is referred to as 'baby talk' and has been most thoroughly reviewed by Charles Ferguson (1977).

The major characteristic of baby talk, compared to standard adult language forms, is its reduced scope and simplified structure. While some features of this speech register are similar across all cultures, others vary from one community or from one family unit to the next. Baby-talk forms themselves diverge in greater or lesser amounts from standard adult language. The features of baby talk manifest themselves at all levels of language analysis. They appear at the levels of word selection, intonation, gesture, tone, phonology, and grammar.

Additionally, a single individual simplifies his speech in different ways, depending upon the social situation. We find a variant of the baby-talk register in the increased redundancy and explicitness of speech addressed to listeners we believe to be foreigners or those suspected as being hard of hearing (Bates, 1975). Similarly, the nurturant features of baby talk have been expressed by those playing caretaking roles with hospital patients, the elderly, and others requiring physical care, as well as with infants (Ferguson, 1977).

Both parents and nonparents are expert speakers of baby talk. Features of baby talk used by all include: a high percentage of questions and imperatives, more concrete (as opposed to abstract) words, a decrease in the rate of speech, longer pauses at utterance boundaries, reduced vocabulary range, nonbroken sentences, single word sentences, shorter utterances, exaggerated intonation, suffixes (as in diminutives) and the avoidance of the first and second persons (Blount, 1972; Broen, 1972; Farwell, 1975; Ferguson, 1977; Shatz & Gelman, 1973; Snow, 1972). Several of these features are so common to the baby-talk register that Broen (1972) found 21.9 percent of the utterances produced by different mothers to their children within a playroom setting to be exactly the same. Typically, however, speech simplifications produce a form of language that is still more sophisticated than that of the child. The speech modifications themselves appear to be more a function of efforts to simplify on a psychological rather than an exclusively linguistic or syntactic level (Shatz & Gelman, 1977).

Not only adults can talk baby talk. Young children rapidly acquire the ability to use a simplified speech register when talking to those younger than themselves, as has been observed in the interactions of eight and four-year-olds as well as four and two-year-olds (Farwell, 1975; Shatz & Gelman, 1977). Nevertheless, four-year-olds are not quite as adept as adults in their use of the baby talk register (Gelman & Shatz, 1977; Sachs & Devin, 1976; Shatz & Gelman, 1973, 1977).

In the baby-talk speech register, language is modified in accordance with the assumed cognitive level of the listener. The babyishness of the language used changes with the age and developmental stage of the listener (Blount, 1972; Broen, 1972; Cross, 1975; Shatz & Gelman, 1973, 1977; Snow, 1977). The child will usually provide cues for the speaker that indicate whether or not he is understood or even attended (Cross, 1975; Shatz & Gelman, 1973). The child's responses, more than the child's linguistic production, guide the speaker's use of a simplified speech register (Farwell, 1975). Research has shown, for example, that although adults may tape-record a form of simplified speech to a hypothetical two-year-old, more extensive speech modifications are produced when the child is actually present and producing many cues of attention and comprehension (Snow, 1972). Speech modifications are therefore a product of joint interaction as well as of the underlying presuppositions held by the speaker about the listener (Snow, 1977).

Simplified speech is based upon an effort to communicate, rather than, for example, an effort to teach language (Gelman & Shatz, 1977; Newport et al., 1977). Many of the separate features of baby talk serve different, specific functions. For example, questions and repetitions are utilized as probes for feedback or as elicitors of attention (Farwell, 1975). Coaxing, on the other hand, is a more general function served by the baby talk register (Broen, 1972; Ferguson, 1977).

At the level of the social relations within the interaction, baby talk serves the function of socializing the listener (Farwell, 1975; Ferguson, 1977). It is this function that makes the baby-talk register relevant to life-span development. The speech register spoken indicates to the listener both the speaker's evaluation of the hearer's responsibility within the conversation and the social role he is expected to play (Blount, 1972). Typically, the user of baby talk assumes that the listener is incapable of recognizing subtle or intricate meanings. This, in turn, strongly suggests that there are limited expectations concerning the cognitive skills of the recipient of these messages (Bates, 1975). The listener in these cases can be a two year old, a foreigner, an elderly adult or some other subordinate. Hence, baby talk, especially when spoken within a nonnurturant context, can convey a message of childhood status to the listener (Ferguson, 1977). A very young child accepts this message. A competent adult may not.

A major component of communicative competence includes the ability to adjust one's speech to listener capacities and needs. A speech register utilized for this purpose is that of baby talk. Young children are its most frequent recipients, but simplified speech also occurs in situations where listeners are suspected of having difficulties comprehending information and subtleties common in adult language. Social implications become apparent within these contexts, representative of the relative statuses of speaker and listener in the social encounter.

EGOCENTRISM

The concept of egocentrism is elusive and abstract, yet fundamental to the study of human development. Egocentrism is the absence of the capability to recognize or predict the point of view of another. The egocentric communicator is unable to assess the thoughts and concerns of the listener. Messages in turn are not tailored to listener needs. They may give the appearance of talk for the self rather than talk aimed at getting a message across.

Early in life, egocentrism is total; taking the role of the other is absent. Egocentrism decreases gradually with increase in knowledge, cognitive skill, and linguistic sophistication (Flavell et al., 1968). The gradual shedding of the blinds of egocentrism is achieved through the process of decentering. Attention that is formerly centered on self becomes centered upon the other. The infant learns to differentiate himself from those he perceives. The child learns to differentiate his own perspective from those with whom he interacts (Looft, 1972). Communication improves and mutuality is enhanced.

This section examines how developmental psychologists view the concept of egocentrism, and discusses how the developing child breaks through the confines of egocentric thought. It also looks at why egocentrism may not be an adequate description of childhood, since we are dealing with a social child in a developing social world.

Birth of a Concept

The developmental psychologist Jean Piaget introduced the concept of egocentrism in the 1920s. He observed young children, aged five and six, as they talked spontaneously with one another. From these observations, Piaget concluded that the children were egocentric.

He characterized much of their conversation as a collective monologue in which neither participant addressed the thoughts or views of the other. Each child followed his own line of thought and current concerns as he spoke each utterance, one turn at a time. The children were not, however, asocial. They were simply unable to comprehend a perspective other than their own, as motivated as they were to partake in a dialogue. Nevertheless, Piaget does assert that the child has not completely decentered until he reaches the adolescent stage, at about the age of 13 years (Bates, 1975).

Measuring Egocentrism

Egocentrism is an abstract concept. Ingenuity is required, therefore, to measure how much exists. Clever as our techniques are, they can only be indirect. A landmark series of investigations of egocentrism were conducted by the researchers Kraus and Glucksberg (1970).

Kraus and Glucksberg began their experiments by separating a speaker and listener by an opaque screen. The speaker and listener were each given several blocks, each block decorated with a nameless graphic design. The speaker was asked to tell the listener how to place the blocks in a specified order. Prior to age five, their speakers were unable to communicate the instructions at all. They described the designs on each of the blocks in personal and private ways, as "mummy's hat" or "daddy's shirt," for example. The researchers found significant increases in accurate performance from kindergarten through fifth grade. Kraus and Glucksberg (1970) concluded that performance improved through increased descriptiveness of speaker cues, better utilization of cues by the listener, and modification of messages by the speaker when confronted with negative feedback. It's amusing to note the extreme egocentrism of several of the very youngest subjects. With the screen before them and the listener out of sight, they would still point to each block and state confidently, "It goes like this."

Research that examines childrens' persuasive capabilities provides other evidence of how egocentrism declines with age. For example, with age there is an increase in the number and sophistication of persuasive strategies used by children. In order to persuade effectively, one needs to predict accurately the perspective taken by the other. Additionally, children become increasingly more capable of tailoring their persuasive tactics to the specific situation, be it persuasion of friend, parent, or stranger (Clark & Delia, 1976).

How to Decenter

Hence, the child develops role-taking skills and decenters from his own point of view increasingly with development. This is accomplished through participation in social interaction, especially with peers (Flavell et al., 1968; Lee, 1975; Looft, 1972; Van Lieshout et al., 1976). The decline in egocentric speech is in large part due to the negative reinforcements the child receives from peers. Other children challenge the child within their conversation. They doubt what he says or contradict his perspective. This causes the child to re-examine his own point of view and to consider the points of others. Contradiction within communication therefore aids the child in developing social skills and taking the role of the other. In turn, the child learns to interact confidently with others. It is indeed a major accomplishment to reconcile highly different, discrepant points of view.

From this perspective, Piaget suggested that more popular children are better able to account for the listener's point of view, and research has found a significant relationship between egocentrism in communication and amount of interaction among preschool children (Deutsch, 1974). The less egocentric the child, the more interaction in which he participates.   Similarly, a popular status among peers during early school years is positively related to the child's role-taking skills (Gottman, 1977; Gottman et al., 1975; Hartup, 1975, in press).

With Whom to Decenter

Piaget concluded that interaction with peers is a better means towards decentration than interaction with an adult. Adults do not necessarily confront the child's messages for clarification; instead they use their intuition to understand the child's requests. Although conversations between very young children may include such features as failure to address listener needs, predict listener responses, and confront inadequate messages, mutual understanding can nevertheless be simply achieved. This occurs when children share the same view of the world and the means of referring to it (Bates, 1975). In these cases they achieve mutuality without truly making major efforts to understand one another. Overall, the quality of interaction is different when children converse with adults and when they converse with their peers, whether understanding is mutual or whether they must work to achieve it.

An extensive study addressing the issue of egocentricism in dialogue with children and adults was conducted by Schachter et al. (1974). They examined a longitudinal and cross-sectional sample of children from two to five years of age. Within a natural, free play setting, the children over time decreased the number of utterances they directed towards adults and increased the number they directed towards children, especially after age three. When speaking with adults, the children used less mature speech than when speaking with other children. Prior to age three the children's speech, in general, was immature and focused upon personal motives. It was labeled 'primary socially interdependent speech' and was tailored to caretaking needs for information.

At about age three, speech addressed to other children included more collaborative and ego-enhancing statements. This was indicative of the increasing capacity of the child to separate self from other. The researchers labeled this form of speech 'secondary sociable speech'. Lastly, at about ages four and five, the children increased their ability to use explanation, justification, rationalization and persuasive tactics. This was labeled 'tertiary socialized speech', the most mature form of speech observed.

The researchers used these results to substantiate Piaget's claims that the child does not clearly differentiate self from other until age three. Self-other differentiation is then accompanied by increasing mutuality and reciprocity between speaker and listener in interaction. Egocentric speech slowly transforms into socialized speech by about age seven, and it does so in a context of peer interaction where the child confronts contradiction and challenge as he learns social skills and adapts to others.

Egocentrism Or Sociocentrism?

Not all psychologists are unquestioning believers in Piagetian egocentrism. Many researchers have focused upon the sociocentric nature of the child (Garvey & Hogan, 1973; Rheingold et al., 1976; Vygotsky, 1962; Werner & Kaplan, 1963). Instead of viewing the child as wrapped up in his very own world, they see the child as a social being who thrives on sharing his world with others. A major proponent of the sociocentric view is the Russian psychologist Lev Vygotsky.

Vygotsky (1962) discusses private speech – his term for egocentric speech – in relation to social behavior. He asserts that private and social speech are initially one and the same. With development they diverge. Private speech becomes internal and used for inner thoughts, and social speech becomes the means by which the child communicates with others. Initially the child's utterances have communicative intent but do not differentiate between communication to the self and to the other.

Correspondingly, Kohlberg et al. (1968) have shown that private speech and social speech by children aged four through seven frequently occur together within a social setting. If private speech were presocial, there would have instead been a striking lack of social communication. Similarly, Kohlberg et al. found more egocentric speech among peers than in the presence of a nonresponsive adult. Hence, egocentric speech is more likely to be used when the child is in the presence of hearers similar to himself, constituting a more social situation for the young child.

Between ages four and seven, however, private speech becomes increasingly covert. Eventually it is used only as one's link to inner thoughts. Private speech becomes inner speech and is put into action particularly when the speaker is confronted with intellectual challenge. Social speech remains the means of participating in interaction.

The Vygotsky perspective and its argument for the socially oriented child does not, however, fairly interpret Piaget's concept of egocentrism. Piaget did not describe egocentrism as a truly asocial attitude, but as the inability to realize social intentions effectively in social contexts. The child may want to communicate socially, but simply is not equipped to do so given his level of development. Both Piaget and Vygotsky do agree, however, in the increasing differentiation of self and other that occurs with development. When the child learns he is separate from others, he learns that messages to others must differ from those to the self. Piaget's egocentric child begins to take the role of the other; Vygotsky's sociocentric child begins to stress his social form of speech when attempting to communicate. The result is the same: a sociable child.

The controversy continues, nevertheless. Research methods are continually developed to see if the egocentrism concept truly accounts for the child's behavior. In fact, the amount of egocentric behavior displayed by the child varies with the social circumstances in which he interacts. For example, the type of activity or situation exerts a major influence upon the child's efforts to communicate and his ability to take the role of the other (Rubin et al., 1971; Sachs & Devin, 1976). Shatz (1978) states that the child is able to account for listener needs provided that there are familiar activities and that the demands of the situation are in line with his presuppositions. Under conditions where the child is confronted with an unfamiliar situation along with the task of taking the role of the other, the cognitive overload hinders adequate role-taking performance. The child is overwhelmed by the process of adjusting to the strange situation. Similarly, Maratsos (1973) found that in a simple task preschoolers were able to modify their communications of toy selection to the needs of the nearby listener. In this experiment the listener required particular information because he had no sight. The preschool children clearly displayed the ability to account for the listener's needs.

Experiments that are situation-specific and difficult to understand in themselves may not accurately reflect the true capacities of a potentially socially sensitive young child. From this perspective, the Kraus and Gluckberg (1970) experiments with graphic figures on blocks have been criticized. Longhurst and Turnure (1971) have shown, for example, that the reason preschoolers are unable to perform the communication task may actually result from their difficulties in perceptually discriminating the graphic figures. Their inability to communicate instructions to the listener effectively is, therefore, in part a perceptual problem and not caused by egocentrism alone.

Finally, many experiments dealing with egocentrism tend to focus upon the child's isolated utterances and not on their social consequences (Mueller, 1972). In contrast, the research examining the speech modifications of children talking to those younger than themselves have shown clearly that the child recognizes the listener's needs and capacities in dialogue (Sachs & Devin, 1976; Shatz & Gelman, 1973). Sachs and Devin (1976) also note that listener characteristics, such as age, provide important information to the speaker, which influences the type of speech he uses. They found that children as young as three to five modify their speech to both babies and dolls that represent babies. This illustrates the child's recognition of listener needs and capacities even when feedback is not direct. We must be careful not to undermine the child's capacities, which under the appropriate setting and circumstances may be quite sophisticated and sensitive to others.

The concept of egocentrism has been used to describe the young child's inability to differentiate his own perspective from that of the other. With development, the child gradually comes to recognize the needs and capacities of the listener with whom he communicates, and he modifies his messages accordingly. This process is facilitated by interaction with peers who confront the child with dissonant information, resulting in the child's reevaluation of the situation. However, egocentrism has been contrasted with a view that advocates the child's intrinsic sociocentrism. From this perspective, methodologies that have stressed the child's egocentrism are criticized as being abstract, narrow, and situationally unfamiliar to the child. They underestimate the child's capabilities to take the role of the other, which do manifest in more familiar and naturalistic settings.

COMMUNICATION BETWEEN CHILDREN

The child's socialization and growing social skills are strongly related to interactions with peers. Peer interactions are not repeat performances of interactions between child and parent. The nature of these social encounters is qualitatively different. Adults often impose a structure upon the form their dialogue takes with the child. Peer interactions are characterized by more equal distribution of power. Communication between children is jointly pursued as each child tests out the situation and constructs social meaning with his peer (Bates, 1975; Bloom et al., 1976; Hartup, in press; Lee, 1975; Lewis et al., 1975; Mueller & Brenner, 1977).

Patterns of interaction and attitudes towards peer relations change through early childhood with increasing cognitive, social and linguistic development (Bronson, 1975; Hartup, 1975). By preschool age, both peer preferences and stable dominance relations have developed, and these interactive behaviors are increasingly managed through language (Gellert, 1961; Hartup, 1975; Strayer & Strayer, 1976). Other research has recently begun to examine antecedents of peer relations during the first two years of life. This section, therefore, briefly surveys the changing nature of communicative encounters by same age peers from infancy through preschool age.

Infant Peers

Peer interaction during infancy is a puzzling area of study. Research performed in the last several years has yielded inconsistent results (e.g., Bronson, 1975; Kagan et al., 1975; Mueller & Brenner, 1977). Nevertheless, most researchers do agree that by the second year of life, the peer is a perceptually distinctive and special object for the child (Bronson, 1975; Konner, 1975; Lewis et al., 1975). Much of the variation in results is apparently due to the individual differences among infants. These include individual readiness to interact with an infant peer, past experience with infant peers, and current familiarity with the age peers with whom the infant is confronted (Bronson, 1975; Lewis et al., 1975). For example, longer periods of acquaintance are directly related to longer socially directed interactions during the second year of life (Mueller & Brenner, 1977).

There is a continual increase in peer interaction between ages one and two (Mueller & Brenner, 1977). Mueller and Lucas (1975) have outlined three stages in the development of peer behaviors, based upon their observations of one-year-old infant pairs. Initially, contacts are centered on objects, and actions are nonsimultaneous. Bronson (1975) notes that even if the infant desires more than a mere reaction from the other infant, he lacks the means and understanding of intention necessary for more give and take. During stage two, the rudiments of mutual regulation emerge. Turn taking and imitation occur and precede the actual direction of the behavior of one infant by the other. Once the infant becomes capable of directing his peer, their social exchanges become more complex. This gradually transforms into stage three behavior, where complementary relationships are achieved. Each member of the pair is able to focus both on each action and its complement. The actions of each are different, yet they are coordinated with one another.

Mutual engagement exists prior to age two on a nonverbal level, followed by a rapid growth of peer interactions and mutuality of influence following the second birthday (Moerk, 1977; Mueller et al., 1977). Gradually, short, one-unit verbal exchanges are chained and eventually become more extended language exchanges and routines (Lee, 1975). As the roles of listener and hearer are interchanged, there is an increase both in behaviors which elicit verbal responses and in attention (Mueller et al., 1977). However, because of their limited role-taking skills, information conveyed through the language exchanged may be fuzzy and indistinct. Its power lies instead in the fact that it solidifies the children's social cohesion. Social cohesion makes peer interaction all that more attractive to the very young child.

Preschool Peers

By preschool age, the child can readily communicate with peers using language. The question then becomes how much of this language is egocentric. Many researchers of child conversation have stressed the social nature of the child's exchanges, warning us not to assume blindly that the child is totally egocentric.

Researchers have found that preschoolers aged three to five participate in extended and focused periods of speech that is mutual and responsive. Most of their utterances have social intent, and their speech both achieves and maintains social contact (Garvey, 1974; Garvey & Hogan, 1973; Mueller, 1972). Children of this age group also have displayed the ability to adapt their speech to listener feedback. They are capable of modifying unclear utterances, provided that listeners ask appropriate questions. In fact, young listeners often do request that the speaker make clear what he means (Spilton & Lee, 1977).

A common form of interaction between preschool children is social play. Rules and roles are constructed by participants and conversation routines and skills are developed. However, with increasing ability to sustain interactions in and of themselves, play becomes a less important means for promoting social relationships. As exchanges grow longer and increasingly sophisticated, the play routine becomes less essential (Garvey, 1974; Garvey & Hogan, 1973).

Results such as these clearly convey the image of a socially responsive child, one who is sensitive to listener needs and participates in mutual exchanges. However, these very same researchers have also found that not all utterances produced communicate successfully. For example, Garvey and Hogan (1973) coded 59 percent of their preschoolers' utterances in a playroom setting as communicative. Mueller (1972), in a similar setting, found 62 percent communicative utterances. That leaves an average of 40 percent as noncommunicative. It appears that the children observed by the researchers would alternate between periods of mutual focus and periods of independent, nonsocial speech activities. Additionally, the children were less able than mature, adult speakers to overcome conversational impasses when they occurred within their dialogue (Garvey & Hogan, 1973).

Therefore, these researchers do not necessarily refute the idea that the child is egocentric, but are choosing to emphasize the nonegocentric capacities of the child. Piaget (1955) also found an egocentrism coefficient of .45, which is strikingly similar to the percentages above, especially given the contrasting views and procedures of these different investigators. The child cannot be viewed as either egocentric or socially adept, but both these features of the developing, communicating child must be recognized, as he participates in increasing exchanges within his changing social world.

There are qualitative differences between caretaker-child and peer interactions and their development over time. By the end of the first year, infants become capable of primitive interactions with age peers. Mutual engagement precedes the development of verbal exchanges, which begin to increase in frequency and length at about the age of two. During preschool years children display the ability to maintain long verbal exchanges. However, these periods alternate with independent and nonsocial activities and speech, which are more indicative of the child's egocentrism and limited role-taking capacities.

4 An Overview of Adolescence and Adulthood

The bulk of one's life is spent in the world of adulthood. In this world the individual perfects his intellectual and social skills. It is not a static world; there is continuous movement of people and history, as individuals aspire towards specified goals, yet often shift gears midway.

Adolescence is a stage of life where communicative skills mature, and the adolescent becomes aware of the options available in his social world. Adulthood is characterized by increasing commitments, social goals, and inner assessment. The maturity of adulthood enriches the communication process. For successful development throughout adulthood provides knowledge of self and social utility, characteristics that will also influence the nature of old age. This chapter examines the sequence of changes from adolescence through the adulthood years, as the individual becomes increasingly familiar with his social environment, and as he comes to know and accept the contradictions of his social and personal world.

ADOLESCENCE

Adolescence is a pivotal stage of life in modern society. The adolescent is confronted with the task of discovering his social identity and developing specific goals (Erikson, 1950). The social and historical circumstances in which the adolescent develops, in turn, profoundly influence the path of development chosen. This is not to deny that the transient and volatile cohorts of adolescents do not also exert a major influence upon their own historical times (Mannheim, 1952; Nesselroade & Baltes, 1974).

This section examines the growing dialogue between the adolescent and society. It looks at the adolescent's cognitive skills and capacity for role taking in interaction and describes the shifting alliance from parent to peer in socialization, as well as the impact of social events.

69

Competence and Consciousness

A major cognitive achievement during the adolescent period is the development of formal operations. This is the ability to reason abstractly without needing to deal with concrete objects (Piaget, 1972). This ability is incorporated within the adolescent's interactions. He is able to reflect upon his own thoughts along with the thoughts of others and to adopt the other's point of view within the process (Looft, 1972; Piaget, 1972). When the adolescent perceives the implications of the perspectives of others, dialogue participants experience a rich and enriching exchange of ideas. The stage of adolescence, therefore, is the first stage of life where ideal intersubjectivity can be achieved. Mutual understanding and mature role taking within communication are now possible.

The enriched social dialogue is also accompanied by a widening social world. The adolescent's hypothetical reasoning skills increase his perception of ideas and problems that surpass the immediate realm of experience. Perception of wider issues and the ideals held by adults often provokes intense interest by the newly enlightened adolescent. As a result, the adolescent develops ideals for improving society, which are often expressed as abstract ideologies and sometimes are put into action (Piaget, 1972).

The adolescent has outgrown the confines of childhood egocentrism. However, his role taking skills in communication are not yet finely polished. The adolescent's newly exercised ability to take the role of the other does not preclude his tendency to attribute his own preoccupations to others. The discovery that others have deep concerns has been translated into concerns that are salient to the self. The adolescent's recognition of the inner concerns of the other may exceed its ordinary limits. This results in exaggerated self-consciousness on the part of this socially sensitive individual (Looft, 1972).

The Hazards of Decentration

A related problem resulting from the adolescent's intellectual growth is the discovery that there are no objective criteria of right and wrong; contradicting points of view cannot always be resolved. The adolescent experiences a heightened sense of unease. If everything is relative, then there can be no true answers. Chandler (1975) labels this uneasy state as the 'epistemological loneliness' of youth. As the adolescent seeks objective truths, he lacks sense of certainty. The adolescent has totally decentered; he recognizes multiple views. The problem is that he must choose one while he sees that the others exist.

Chandler describes the strategies that are used to cope with this uncomfortable state. Among them are: pronounced affiliation with same age peers; a search for intimacy; the stereotyping of out-groups (such as those 'over 30'); accepting a tightly defined philosophy of religious or secular beliefs; or confining one's thoughts to an abstract level in order to avoid a confrontation with day-to-day contradictions. Chandler states that the task of adolescence is the process of 'recentering' to overcome this extreme state of decentration. Through recentering, the individual becomes committed to his own personal view while recognizing and maintaining a sense of tolerance toward other interpretations. Mature thought entails an acceptance of the contradiction that is a part of life. Mature thought, defined as such, gradually develops during the adulthood years.

Shifting Alliances

As the adolescent expands his social awareness, he becomes increasingly separate from his family. Autonomy from the family group is transferred to an allegiance to friends, and the peer group serves a major socializing role. It often reinterprets parental behavior and standards for its members (Siman, 1977).

Peer interactions usually take place within the context of leisure activities. Here the adolescent develops skills that are rewarded by peers during their social exchanges. The range of activities in which adolescents participate differs from other age groups in society (Gordon et al., 1976). Communication between the old and young is impeded, and the influence of peers becomes even more homogeneous.

However, the impact of peers varies in strength from person to person. For example, adolescent males are more susceptible to the influence of peers than are females (Siman, 1977). Similarly, research has demonstrated greater personality stability of females during this stage of life (Nesselroade & Baltes, 1974). The logical conclusion is to relate stability and friendship: the less stable the adolescent personality, the more dependence there is upon peers.

Personality and History

The adolescent increasingly participates in relations outside the home. He also becomes increasingly concerned with broader social issues. The adolescent personality, in turn, is especially sensitive to cultural change. Nesselroade and Baltes (1974) correspondingly have studied adolescents aged 12 to 17, by examining short term longitudinal samples with the sequential method of life span research described in chapter one. They found that personality characteristics in adolescence varied with time of testing, independent of the age of subjects or cohorts of which they were members. These results clearly showed that the historical influences from 1970 to 1972 exerted a greater influence upon personal change than did the characteristics of each separate age cohort. Nesselroade and Baltes concluded that their results were due to the common experience shared during this historical setting; for all the cohorts moved in the same direction within the period observed. For example, regardless of age the adolescents decreased their stress on achievement; while during this same period of time they increased in personal independence.

The researchers also found that there is increasing personality stability with age. Unlike specific personality changes which occur with social change, this stability finding strongly suggests a more general developmental process. Hence, with age personality becomes more well defined, but the form it takes is determined by its placement in historical time.

These overall findings dispute the idea of consistent and uniform stages of adolescent development. Instead they substantiate the basic idea that we look to the social and cultural conditions in which the development of the individual, especially during adolescence, takes place.

Adolescence is a stage of life where personal change and development is rapid. Formal operations are acquired and total decentering achieved. But these developments may result in dissatisfaction with society, a heightened state of self-consciousness, and an exaggerated sense of objectivity. The adolescent shifts interpersonal dependencies from family to friendship groups. Throughout, he is highly susceptible to the influences of those historical conditions that provide the context of his interactions within the social world.

ADULTHOOD

Adults occupy a unique position in modern Western society. They constitute the most powerful age group within the social structure. Both young and old as well as adults are aware of this position of power (Neugarten, 1968b; Neugarten & Hagestad, 1976; Turner, 1975).

Adults, especially in their middle years, are particularly sensitive to their social position. They set norms for social behaviors and make major decisions that affect society. It is the adults who maintain the social structure (Giele, 1977; Gutmann, 1975; Muth, 1976; Neugarten, 1968b). Even within the family unit, the middle generation is central. They structure interactions within the family and condition the grand-parent-grandchild relationship (Robertson, 1975; Troll, 1971). Within this context of power and prestige, they are responsible to attend to the needs of all.

Powerful as this position may be, adult development, too, is influenced by the historical conditions of the society within which the adult interacts. For example, the study by Woodruff and Birren (1972), which is described in chapter one, illustrates that an adult's perception of his own personal history changes with current events and stereotypes of development. At present, the adult population is influenced particularly by middle-class values. For example, there is a premium placed upon work and career development. Historical events which currently tailor the life course of the adult include an increasing tendency for people to seek second careers after the disappearance of earlier jobs or the onset of early retirement, and the increasing number of females who are entering the labor market (Havighurst, 1973a).

Along with social and cultural change within the external environment, there exists a capacity for personal change throughout the adult years. Daniel Levinson (1977, 1978), a major theorist of the development of the adult male, reconstructed the biographies of men aged 35 to 45 years and examined the lives of men in other cultures and societies. He developed the concept of the 'life structure' of the adult. A life structure includes the social and cultural world, participation in this world, and those characteristics unique to the self. He concluded that the life structure through adulthood alternates between periods of stability and transition. Transitional states are sometimes provoked by compelling events which trigger personal change. Under other circumstances transitions can occur with minimal self-reflection (Brim, 1974; Levinson, 1978).

Often change in adulthood must emanate from the individual's own initiative. The adult then seeks supportive social relationships to facilitate this change (Brim, 1968). On the other hand, some changes occur for nearly all adults. One such change is a sex-role crossover during the middle-age years. Males let loose their feminine traits and females become self-assertive. Males become more dependent and sensitive; their drive for mastery diminishes. Females become more independent; achievement becomes a goal (Fiske, 1977; Giele, 1977; Lowenthal, 1977; Neugarten & Gutmann, 1968).

This section reviews the sequence of developments occurring throughout adulthood. The field of adult development, however, is just beginning to emerge. Our knowledge and accumulated research on the topic is not extensive. The major issues that have been raised in the study of adulthood are addressed in this section. It makes note of the influence of marriage and the perception of life events, and outlines the stages of adult development from early childhood through middle age, as it explores the adult's capacity to change within a changing world.

Marriage and Change

An important influence upon adult development is the marital relationship, which provides a major socialization experience throughout life. Married individuals change more than those who remain unmarried. Personalities are more similar between older couples than newlyweds, and values are more uniform between spouses than between parent and child (Brim, 1968; Troll, 1971). The marriage relationship, however, does not remain static. Husband and wife and their mutual perceptions undergo their own process of development and change. Marital disenchantment may arise for different reasons at various stages of the relationship. Changes in husband-wife interaction and the relationship implied occur in a context of personal, social and historical events (Gutmann, 1975; Levinson, 1977; Pineo, 1968; Troll, 1971). In this sense the marital relationship is no different from other communication settings. Historical, social, and personal perceptions influence the nature of the shared relationship.

Within the marital relationship and in other adulthood contexts, the occurrence of major transitional events do not always lead to crisis conditions. A prime example of such a transition is the experience of having the last child leave home. There is little evidence of abruptness or excessive strain when emptying one's nest of children. Most studies, in fact, report increased satisfaction during the postparental stage of marriage (Back, 1976; Brim, 1968; Deutscher, 1968; Elder, 1977; Kimmel, 1974; Lowenthal & Chiriboga, 1973; Neugarten, 1970; Sussman, 1960; Troll, 1971). This phenomenon illustrates how changes that are anticipated and on time are often confronted with minimal stress.

Change is an ever-present reality of the adulthood years, whether marital or personal, stressful or pleasant, for on-time and off-time events. The initial step of adult development is taken by the adolescent, who discovers the various alternative paths of development that he may follow.

Adulthood and Commitment

The adolescent is allowed the luxury of choosing among multiple options. The adult, in contrast, must fulfill obligations to others and to society. Responsibility replaces frivolty as one enters the stage of adulthood. During early adulthood, covering the years from about 17 to 45, social and personal commitments take effect. The individual becomes increasingly stable and independent. He gradually transforms from a naive beginner to an expert capable of guiding others. Levinson (1977, 1978) best describes this process using his concept of the adult life structure.

The move from the preadult to adult world occurs in the late teens and early 20s, when the individual begins to specialize professionally in accordance with personal aptitudes and social guidelines (Levinson, 1977, 1978; Piaget, 1972). However, following initial encounters with the reality and paradoxes of the adult world, this emerging adult often feels compelled to reevaluate his view of society and its norms. A transient sense of cynicism and disenchantment may result (Loeb, 1973).

Levinson (1977, 1978) finds that from ages 22 through 28 the male individual begins to create his first stable life structure. He develops a sense of personal worth and finds a place in adult society. Goals are sustained with the encouragement particularly of spouse and mentor. Ages 28 through 33 serve the purpose of improving the first life structure. Defects of the first life structure come to the attention of the young adult. This period is characterized for some by marriage problems, divorce, and occupational change.

Levinson likens ages 32 through 40 to a ladder structure. The individual both settles down and works towards specified goals. He measures his progress by the rungs of the ladder and the evaluations offered by others. During this period, at about ages 36 through 37, a phase that Levinson labels BOOM develops, which stands for Becoming One's Own Man. Progress is rewarded, but is coupled with burdensome commitments and social pressures. The individual may attempt to break out from this predictable sequence of life events. Most persons, however, weigh the alternatives and return to business as usual. Overall, throughout the 30s, a creative and comfortable style of living is promoted by a personal adaptability within a reasonably stable context (Levinson, 1977).

The life courses of the males whom Levinson studied are fairly consistent and ordered. The life structures and events experienced by these males are neatly bracketed within specified ages. Levinson's data on the lives of the men appears strikingly systematic. We, however, must take note that self-reflection and personal change can occur at any time throughout adulthood. It is a function of personal, social and historical forces of change.

Nevertheless, the young adult is confronted with a special series of tasks. He must make a place for himself in society and learn from each situation experienced. The young adult is in the process of being socialized to the adult world. Power has not yet reached its peak; he is often the subordinate in communicative encounters. Throughout, confirmations of the self are sought, from spouse, from superiors, and from peers. Part of the struggle on the way to the top is establishing a coherent and intact sense of self, a sense that is supported by the social encounters experienced.

Middle Age Appraisal

At about the fifth decade of life, when the adult reaches the middle years, he confronts a personal transition. At the extreme the middle-aged adult experiences a 'midlife crisis'. Many changes occur simultaneously within this approximate time frame. The biological system begins to run down, the career has often reached a peak, male achievement motives begin to decline, and the woman becomes increasingly independent (Brim, 1974; Levinson, 1977, 1978). Both males and females begin to accept the inevitability of death now that life is halfway through. One's concept of time is reordered. A focus on time passed becomes a focus on time left (Brim, 1974; Neugarten, 1970).

Most characteristic of the midlife period for males and females is the reassessment of self. The individual shifts from an outer to inner orientation (Gordon et al., 1976; Looft, 1972; Neugarten, 1968a). This inner orientation is often referred to as 'interiority'. Neugarten (1970), in a study of 40- to 70-year-olds, intensively interviewed males and females and examined a number of psychological measures. She discovered an increase in interiority in these mentally and physically healthy adults by the time they reached their mid 40s. This occurred in the absence of any of the losses that accompany the aging process. The competent, well functioning adult begins to look inwards. Levinson notes that prior to this stage, the male might blame the wife for their problems. Now he looks more intently at himself as a viable source of their conflict.

During this middle adulthood stage, one's life career is reassessed. Having reached the peak of his career, the individual must either lower those expectations that have not been realized, or having achieved his goals, may now find them to be meaningless or unworthy of previous sacrifice (Brim, 1974; Levinson, 1977, 1978). Fiske (1977), in a seven year longitudinal study of middle- and lower-class adults, found that 10 to 15 years prior to retirement her subjects became anxious concerning their future. The increasing concern with time left in life, paired with the prospect of retirement causes the mature adult serious inner evaluation. The career of the adult, particularly the male, has already reached its peak. He must now look increasingly towards the self for sources of satisfaction.

This seemingly difficult period of life can have undeniably favorable results, however. Levinson notes that the adult can now nurture those personal characteristics previously hidden from view. Hence, we observe the sex-role crossover common in midlife. Males give expression to their tender side. Females express initiative towards mastery.

Although individual reassessment can be difficult and sometimes painful, if the adult does not undergo this review, a later crisis or loss of self-connectedness may result. Levinson states that near the end of the midlife transition, either new paths are pursued or a more enlightened commitment to one's current mode is once again established.

The adult becomes increasingly aware of the contradiction inherent in life, the contradiction that was so difficult to resolve for the developing adolescent. But the adult has learned to accept contradiction and accepts the contradictory parts of the self. Riegel (1973) accordingly has cogently argued that mature cognition involves the reappraisal of formal, noncontradictory thought and a consequent acceptance of those contradictions inherent within human activity.

The increasing inner orientation of the adult in the middle years has implications for the way in which the individual communicates. The process of reacquainting oneself with one's personal history, goals, and feelings, lessens the reliance upon others for self-definition and confirmation. Assurance within the social encounter is enhanced as a result. The power position of the adult solidifies with age and personal experience, often giving him the upper hand within social interaction.

The growing acknowledgment of contradiction similarly enriches the communication process. The inevitability of contradiction between speaker and listener is tolerated. Shades of grey are accepted; one need not demand black or white. Throughout, if personal self-assessment has not yet been resolved, a lack of self-definition and direction impedes successful communication. If the adult lacks assurance in self, his messages can be seriously misrepresented and intention clouded with doubt.

Middle Age Assurance

In contrast to the struggle of personal assessment that occurs during the middle-adult years, research has revealed a sense of heightened self-confidence and intellectual development during middle adulthood (Birren, 1970; Labouvie-Vief, 1977; Neugarten, 1968b). In a study by Birren, successful middle-aged male and female professionals expressed an increased awareness of their ability to develop effective strategies, their success in managing time, and skill in distributing responsibilities to others. Increasingly aware of their capabilities as well as the limits of their skill and energy, they also become increasingly aware of how much they needed to rely on others. By assigning responsibilities to their younger colleagues and entrusting them to perform these tasks, these professional adults avoided contending with an overload of information. They were able to develop their ability to abstract. In turn, they dealt with more significant and crucial conceptual issues. They displayed their competence and derived personal satisfaction as a result. Neugarten's (1968b) research similarly found that respondents perceived extensive improvement in their judgmental skills during middle age.

The middle-aged adult's growing propensity to focus upon key issues and judgments influences the nature of the messages exchanged within communication. While the younger adult is absorbing multiple sources and bits of information, the older adult has consolidated his knowledge into several basic, essential ideas. The reference and underlying propositions that characterize the messages exchanged by younger and older adults by necessity differ at a conceptual level because of their differing strategies and views. The younger adult is developing values and methods of operating in the world. The middle-aged adult has consolidated those values and concepts implicit within his thought and language. However, to the extent they deal with similar issues and topics of concern, they can learn from one another in a highly beneficial way: the younger adult acquires new knowledge; the middle aged adult forms richer ideas.

Birren's description of the middle-aged adult's emphasis on broad strategies of interaction corresponds to Levinson's assertion that the individual aged 40 through 65 is increasingly concerned with long-range goals, especially involving the growth of others with whom he interacts. Decreases in biological endurance and the avoidance of cognitive overload are compensated by an increased desire to contribute to the social world. Similarly, Neugarten (1970) asserts that the increasing interiority of the middle-adult years includes a sense of "conscious self-utilization" instead of the "self-consciousness of youth" (p. 77). This concept provides the synthesis for those contradictions implicit in the midlife appraisal. The pain of inner evaluation and assessment of the self promotes a sense of self-awareness and the social utility of the developing adult.

However, Birren's study in particular involves an extremely select sample of successful professionals. His results may not necessarily apply to those with less spectacular careers. Fiske (1977), in contrast, found in her lower- and middle-class longitudinal sample that once many of her subjects had reached the peak of their careers, they tended to become bored with their work and to withdraw from on-the-job social relationships. She also noted that these discomforting states were not confined to the less prestigious occupations.

The psychologist Erik Erikson (1977) asserts that the dominant theme of middle adulthood is the resolution of the opposing tendencies towards generativity and self-absorption. This theme neatly characterizes the issues discussed in this section. Generativity corresponds to a heightened awareness of personal development, intellectual competence, and social contribution. Self-absorption corresponds to stagnation of personal growth. The adult who is stagnated is overly absorbed in personal concerns and self-assessment and unable to perceive a satisfactory resolution. Stagnation and a self-absorbed state preclude a contribution to others, yet contributions to the social world are the means for insuring continued development.

Adults are a more powerful age group than the young or the old, yet this group is not impervious to social and historical influences. Adulthood is characterized by change and development instigated by social events along with personal insight. In the early stages of adulthood the individual establishes himself in society. He absorbs the information communicated by others as he works towards achieving specified goals. By middle age the adult carefully assesses his achievements and aspirations. There is an increasing emphasis upon one's internal world. In the process the adult achieves inner balance. As contradiction in the world and in the self is accepted and understood, communication is enriched. Under optimal conditions in middle age, self-confidence and competence flourish. Under less favorable circumstances the individual runs the risk of self-absorption and withdrawal.

The ability to change and develop does not end in middle age. The issues prominent in middle age continue through later adulthood. The individual strives to maintain a sense of self and to benefit from social encounters. A reliance upon self becomes increasingly crucial as the adult approaches old age, a stage of life that is discussed in chapters five through eight.

5 Psychological Characteristics of the Aged

A unique set of factors contribute to the psychology of the older adult. The elderly have accumulated a lifetime of experience with the world and with themselves. Many biological changes have amassed through the years. Information about life too has amassed, and the older adult reorganizes his thoughts to account for all he has learned. Finally, the personal disposition of the adult may alter during old age, depending upon the inner resources he has built throughout the years.

WHO ARE THE AGED?

The middle-aged adult eventually grows old. The point at which the individual becomes an old man or old woman is difficult to isolate. Aging is a steady and gradual process. Cognitive, perceptual, and motoric systems gradually slow down (Birren & Renner, 1977). In general, however, the individual is seen as "older" at about the age of 60 (Rosow, 1974). This section provides a general introduction to this older adult.

Different Yet Same

The elderly are more different from each other than any other age group. They constitute the most heterogeneous segment of the population (Oyer, 1976). On biological, psychological, and sociological levels, aging involves a process of continuing differentiation (Beattie, 1976). The model of development described in chapter one confirms this idea. Developmental histories become more complex with the passage of time, and each person becomes more different from the next. Patterns of aging similarly vary with placement in society. These patterns are often dependent upon the prior life styles and activities of the individual (Bengtson et al., 1977; Gordon, 1975; Lowenthal & Robinson, 1976). There is no single and uniform way in which the adult grows old.

Nevertheless, there are some general characteristics of the aged population. The majority of elderly adults live within the community, especially in metropolitan areas (Carp, 1976; Teaff et al., 1978). Those who are isolated tend to be of low social and economic status, in poor health, and unmarried (Lowenthal & Robinson, 1976). Only five percent of the elderly at a single point in time can be found in institutions (Kimmel, 1974; Shanas & Maddox, 1976). As a whole, the aged are less educated than the rest of the population (Birren & Woodruff, 1973).

Elderly females outnumber elderly males due to the higher survival rate of women. Seventy-three percent males and 37 percent females over 65 are married, and 53 percent females over 65 are widowed (1976 Bureau of Census, cited in Bengtson et al., 1977).

Economically, the aged are on the average worse off than the rest of the population, with widowed females constituting the most deprived group among the aged (Bengtson et al., 1977; Strumpel, 1973). Approximately 17 to 25 percent of the elderly are at the poverty level. However, many elderly adults are not considered to be at poverty levels but do experience a considerable drop in their standard of living. They, too, confront a state of relative poverty (Maudlin, 1976; Palmore, 1977; Schulz, 1976). There is large variation in the financial situations of the elderly, and there are more inequalities among the aged than among other age groups. Inequalities of earlier years tend to intensify with age, and there is a strong relationship between education and degree of poverty. Those who are less educated are those who are more economically deprived (Strumpel, 1973). Additionally, as a cohort, the elderly do not readily seek assistance from public agencies, due to their high valuation of personal endurance and self-respect (Trager, 1976).

Age Groups in Aging

The life stage of old age covers a great many years. A 60-year-old healthy adult is quite different from an ailing octogenarian. Hence, we find that the elderly can be divided into separate age groups: the young-old, middle-old, and old-old.

The young-old (approximately 55 to 65 years) are in relatively good health, of higher educational status, economically secure, free from parental responsibilities, caring for their own parents, and often employed. The middle-old (approximately 65 to 75 years) are typically postretirement with continued physical well-being, reduced income, increased leisure time and opportunities for community service, recreation, and educational experiences. The old-old (approximately 75 years and beyond) constitute the major problem population, characterized by ill health, poverty, and increased incidence of psychopathology. The lower educational attainment of the old-old is one of the major factors lowering their relative status from the status of younger groups of aged adults (Havighurst, 1973a; Neugarten, 1977; Pfeiffer, 1977; Streib,

1976; Strumpel, 1973). Unfortunately, much research on the elderly does not take into account these relative groupings. This, in turn, blurs the distinctions among the very different adult cohorts that comprise the aged population.

Consciousness and Continuity

The aged in America do not embody a unified subcultural group (Neugarten & Moore, 1968; Streib, 1965, 1976). The development of an aged subculture is hindered by strong family identification, the possibility of continued employment, resistance towards personal aging, weak age group identification, and the multiple differences between older adults (Lowenthal & Boler, 1965; Rose, 1962b). Elderly adults interact with one another at their own discretion, but do not express strong feelings of group consciousness based upon age alone (Rosow, 1974; Streib, 1976). Instead, social-group identification is based more upon social categories such as sex, occupation, class and ethnic group (Riley, 1976; Streib, 1976). Only a minority of elderly (such as the Grey Panthers) are activists for the aged, although they may be the more visible members of the total aged population (Rosow, 1974).

In general, there is an unwillingness to accept one's old age (de Beauvoir, 1973; Kastenbaum, 1966; Rosow, 1974). However, there are class differences. Working-class adults both age faster and accept old age earlier than do middle-class adults. Middle-class adults are more threatened by the aging process (Rosow, 1967). Perception of the self as old develops with the aid of internal cues (such as failure of endurance), social cues (such as excessive solicitousness), and direct classification as old by others (Lowenthal & Chiriboga, 1973). All these factors act jointly to consolidate an older self-image.

Most important to the development of this older self-image is an inevitable loss of roles (Rosow, 1967, 1974). The role of worker is lost with retirement, the role of spouse is lost with widowhood, and the role of provider is lost with ever shrinking economic supports. Earlier attachment relationships gradually diminish as spouse, family, and friends die. They may be replaced by new relationships, but often they are no longer mutual. Many are caregiving in nature, such as between adult child and parent or between physician and patient. And all these changes contribute to a sense of diminished social position (Bennett & Ahammer, 1977; Inkeles, 1969; Kalish & Knudtson, 1976).

Consequently, many elderly adults identify with their former statuses, whose losses have not been replaced (Rosow, 1974). But in the real world these former identities are difficult to verify. The older adult may state he's a teacher, but others assume he's no longer productive. Within the context of our rapidly changing social environment, a sense of personal continuity becomes that much more difficult to maintain (Clayton, 1975). Yet, within this context the elderly person feels further compelled to emphasize his identification with his former position and image to maintain continuity. The older adult is thereby caught in a cyclic state of affairs. Considerable inner strength and support are required to break loose from this cycle.

Disengaged or Active?

Most older adults find that their social world is no longer expanding. There is decreased membership in organized groups and increased participation in leisure activities that are homebound rather than widespread (Cath, 1975; Gordon et al., 1976; Neugarten, 1977; Rosow, 1967, 1974).

In 1961, Cumming and Henry proposed the 'disengagement theory' of aging. They suggested that with the onset of old age there is a gradual and mutually satisfying disengagement between society and the individual. This theory was suggested as an alternative to the 'activity theory', which stated that the aging individual who remains active will be most satisfied. Both theories have been challenged by an upsurge of research instigated by these opposing theoretical views.

The resulting research indicated that disengagement is neither cross-cultural nor intrinsic, but constitutes one among several alternative styles of aging. It is chosen only in a small percentage of cases (Gordon, 1975; Gutmann, 1976, 1977; Maddox, 1964; Maddox & Wiley, 1976; Schmitz-Scherzer & Lehr, 1976; Tobin & Neugarten, 1961). There may also be disengagement only for short periods during old age. Longitudinal data has shown both patterns of consistent and inconsistent social activities and resulting satisfaction over a period of time (Havighurst et al., 1968; Lehr & Rudinger, 1969; Lowenthal & Boler, 1965; Maddox, 1965; Schmitz-Scherzer & Lehr, 1976). Personality factors as well influence the degree to which the individual withdraws or remains active and derives satisfaction from the option chosen (Lowenthal & Boler, 1965; Maddox, 1968b).

Neither disengagement nor activity characterize an elderly population replete with individual differences. In addition, psychological and interpersonal disengagement does not mean total inactivity (Cumming, 1975; Maddox, 1965). The older adult can be physically active yet decrease his social contacts.

Adjustment

Many factors jointly influence adjustment to old age. Therefore, it is difficult to distinguish the effects of aging alone from other influences upon adjustment. These include a changing status, stressful circumstances, personality characteristics, and cultural and historical change (Bennett & Ahammer, 1977; Butler, 1968; Neugarten et al., 1968; Riley, 1976; Rosow, 1976b). Both inner resources and external supports contribute to adjustment.

The older adult is often perceived as increasingly more vulnerable with age, yet most elderly adults do manage to adapt successfully to the process of aging. The majority remain integrated within rather than isolated from society (Hess, 1974; Maddox & Wiley, 1976; Palmore, 1977). They continue to function within the community in spite of physical impairment. Many manage to maintain their class identity and style despite decreasing financial resources (Shanas & Maddox, 1976; Streib, 1976). Additionally, political and social attitudes, values, and beliefs among the elderly shift with the rest of the population, but these shifts take place more slowly than shifts among younger adults (Palmore, 1977; Rosow, 1974). The elderly clearly are not ignorant of trends within society. They follow the signs of the times, although it may take them longer.

A reasonably supportive social environment, particularly the presence of one or two concerned and helpful individuals, enables the elderly adult to adapt to a rapidly changing social world and to an increasingly older self-image (Botwinick, 1973; Neugarten, 1977). Losses in many areas of life occur with the aging process. But inner resources and social supports facilitate successful adaptation.

Comparing the Aged

Discussions of the research that deals with the cognitive and social skills of the elderly often compare results for the aged with those found for children and adolescents (e.g., Barker & Barker, 1961; Looft, 1972). In such cases it is important to recognize that the reasons underlying the behaviors of old and young are often very different (Bayley, 1963; Looft, 1972).

Nevertheless, comparisons are useful. They are capable of revealing similarities and differences in the impact of the social world upon the individual's means of coping. This is the case in comparisons of adolescent and elderly cohorts. These two age groups more often than not are perceived by others in ways which differ from their personal self-perceptions (Baltes & Schaie, 1973). Sharing the position of less social power than the middle-aged adult, adolescents and elderly persons experience a distinctive sense of alienation (Bengtson & Black, 1973). Correspondingly, both groups are often reliant upon peers for socialization, to boost morale, and to counteract the ambivalence of family relationships (Inkeles, 1969; Lowenthal & Robinson, 1976). In addition, research shows that adolescents and the old prefer affiliation over achievement, in contrast to the professional aims of young and middle-aged adults (Ahammer & Baltes, 1972).

However, the developmental and social circumstances providing the context for these similarities serve to highlight how these groups are also very different. Adolescents see their lives before them. The elderly see their past. Adolescents rarely view old age in a positive light. The elderly do not display the pervasive group consciousness that characterizes youth. From the differing historical conditions in which their development occurred, the elderly and the young by necessity have different views of the world. Comparisons of age groups, however enlightening, must be evaluated with caution. Eighty years of experience and maturity are not reducible to the widening world of youth.

Living in Institutions

The remaining chapters deal with the elderly who live within communities, since they comprise the overwhelming majority of the aged population.   Therefore, only a brief note describing the minority of elderly adults who reside in institutions is included in this section. The group of individuals who populate institutions that cater to the aged includes the very old, the never married, the widowed, the childless, and those who are psychologically worse off as well as closer to death (Lieberman, 1969; Shanas & Maddox, 1976). Institutionalization is nearly always a last resort (Hess, 1974).

When elderly adults enter or relocate to different institutions, there is an increased death rate the first year of relocation, especially within the first three months (Aldrich & Mendkoff, 1968; Blenkner, 1967; Lieberman, 1969). The death rate is highest, however, for the chronically and acutely ill. Survival is most likely among the elderly who are angry and demanding (Aldrich & Mendkoff, 1968; Blenkner, 1967; Lieberman, 1969, 1975).

Although preparation and a voluntary acceptance of change may decrease vulnerability, even optimal conditions have not eliminated the increased death rate following relocation (Blenkner, 1967; Lieberman, 1969). Nevertheless, under some conditions, relocation has resulted in positive change for the institutionalized adult, although Lieberman (1969) states that those factors that contribute to more positive results are as yet largely unknown.

It is clear, however, that the social environment of the institution is radically different from the day-to-day social world of well-functioning adults. Institutionalized aged are consistently treated in a subordinate manner. Communication within this context is frustrating to the elderly adult who is aware of the social relations conveyed. It is no surprise that those who are demanding and angry survive. They channel their energy towards equalizing relations and maintaining a sense of self and dignity as they communicate with others.

The aged are the most highly differentiated segment of the population, yet they confront a similar series of stresses and role shifts with increasing age. Many elderly adults are hesitant to accept an older self-image and display little sense of group consciousness. They instead identify with their former statuses to maintain a sense of self-continuity in a rapidly changing world. The social activities of older adults may narrow over time, but few disengage from society. Multiple psychological and social factors influence the aging process. Hence, it is difficult to isolate the effects of aging alone upon adjustment. The majority of the elderly do, however, adjust and remain integrated within society.   They may experience similar social influences as the young and alienated adolescents; but comparisons of age groups must be pursued with caution, for the old and young are more different than alike in their perspectives.

BIOLOGY

The elderly experience more biological changes than any other age group. These changes take place at all levels of biological organization. Genes, cells, tissues, and organ systems are affected. The aged organism represents a cumulation of biological errors that have developed throughout the life span. Consequently, the elderly are more often afflicted by disease and disability (Jarvik & Cohen, 1973; Kimmel, 1974; Shock, 1977). Due to the multiple biological changes that accompany the aging process, no single biological theory can account for all aspects of physical aging (Shock, 1977).

Biological functioning becomes more important as the individual ages, for biological systems and their rapid alteration influence other systems of behavior (Birren & Renner, 1977). However, the individual's psychological state also influences biological functioning. For example, psychological and social stresses can cause a change in nutrition and a decline in health; or the changing deep-sleep patterns of the elderly may be due to depression rather than physical changes (Labouvie-Vief & Zaks, in press; Looft, 1972; Marsh & Thompson, 1977). Both psychological make-up and biological functions influence the individual's behavior. Severe stress upon either system brings stress upon the other.

Biological changes are capable of altering the psychological and social worlds of the older adult, yet the elderly adult need not be at the total mercy of biological decrement. Compensation is possible and is often achieved.

The Nervous System

A consistent feature of growing old is the process of slowing down. The older adult takes longer to react. There is, however, a wider range of variation in speed among older adults (Jarvik & Cohen, 1973). This general slowing of behavior is in part due to the aging of the nervous system, but the precise cause remains unclear (Jarvik & Cohen, 1973).

Alterations of the involuntary nervous system result in inefficient biological regulation (Frolkis, 1977; Jarvik & Cohen, 1973; Labouvie-Vief & Zaks, in press). Frolkis (1977) suggests that this leads to irregular changes in the physiological components of various behaviors and emotions. There may be inappropriate reactions to ordinary stimulation. In addition, a decrease in biological efficiency leads to decreased ability to readjust quickly during stressful situations (Jarvik & Cohen, 1973; Labouvie-Vief & Zaks, in press; Shock, 1977).

The Senses

The elderly experience decline in the capacities of all five human senses (Lawton & Nahemow, 1973; Palmore, 1977). The decreasing capacity of the senses to register cues from the external world reduces the intensity and amount of perceptual stimulation for the older adult (Botwinick, 1973), which explains in part the changes in reaction speed (Jarvik & Cohen, 1973).

Not only does visual acuity decrease as the individual ages; the elderly may also be receiving different visual signals. Their visual processes differ from those of younger adults. For example, they attend more to movement than to color (DeLong, cited in Lawton & Nahemow, 1973). The environment for optimal visual functioning for the elderly is also unique. Older persons require increased levels of illumination for clear vision, yet they also become increasingly more susceptible to glare (Fozard et al., 1977). The visual problems of the elderly often cannot be completely overcome. It is difficult to determine the best prescriptions to counteract their many visual problems (Fozard et al., 1977).

The hearing loss associated with age has been termed presbycusis. It involves reduced sensitivity to pitch, especially at higher frequencies, which means that consonant, not vowel, sounds are harder to detect. There is also reduced speech discrimination by the adult with presbycusis (Botwinick, 1973; Corso, 1977; Willeford, 1971). Up to 25 percent of elderly individuals are hearing impaired by age 75, and approximately 13 percent or more of those over 65 show advanced signs of presbycusis (Corso, 1977; Willeford, 1971). Members of the oldest age group nearly all exhibit some form of hearing impairment (Jarvik & Cohen, 1973).

There is also evidence suggesting a cohort effect for hearing impairment. The present cohort of older adults may be exhibiting hearing loss at a greater rate than younger members of the population. This is because of the recent availability of antibiotic treatments (Bettinghaus & Bettinghaus, 1976). Cross-cultural work has also shown that more primitive and less industrialized noise-free societies exhibit significantly less hearing impairment among its elderly members (Willeford, 1971).

The symptoms of presbycusis, especially the decreased speech discrimination, are due to brain alterations at the auditory-processing centers, and are largely untreatable (Botwinick, 1973; Corso, 1977; Willeford, 1971). Elderly adults have described their perception of speech communications as sounding "fuzzy," as if the "words seem to run together" even when the speech is sufficiently loud (Willeford, 1971, p. 312).

An Optimistic Model

Many biological functions are related to psychological responses and behaviors. For example, slower brain waves co-occur with intellectual deterioration, and the oxygen deprivation of brain cells results in deficient intellectual performance (Botwinick, 1973; Marsh & Thompson, 1977). However, the biological changes that occur during old age need not be accompanied by psychological impairment (Ahammer & Bennett, 1976; Labouvie-Vief & Zaks, in press). For example, elderly adults may take longer to respond, but their responses are often accurate (Jarvik & Cohen, 1973). Behaviors are not solely dictated by the individual's biological make-up. The impact of biological changes may be tapered by the individual's interpretation, determination to excel, and the presence of other caring persons who support a self-image of competence.

Biological factors significantly influence the psychological and social functioning of the older adult, yet the majority of elderly appear to adapt to these biological changes. They continue to function in the social environment, compensating for the organic insults to their biological and sensory systems. A supportive environment and a determined adult facilitate the process.

COGNITION

Cognition has proved an easy target for the measurement of changes during old age. Batteries of intelligence tests, problem-solving, and memory tasks have been given to older adults in order to detect a decline with age. It appears, however, that the method of measurement strongly influences the shape of the results.

Types of Intelligence

Intellectual development throughout adulthood proceeds along two tracks, that of fluid and that of crystallized intelligence. Fluid intelligence is primarily nonverbal, involving perceptual and manipulative skills. Research has shown that fluid intelligence decreases prior to ages 50 or 60. In many cases the decline actually begins following early adulthood. However, decline is especially rapid among the aged. This in part is due to the general slowing of behavior which occurs in old age. In general, decrement in fluid intelligence is considered biological in origin, but fluid performance can be improved by factors such as increased physical exercise and a supportive and stimulating social environment (Botwinick, 1973, 1977; Labouvie-Vief, 1977).

Crystallized intelligence is more cultural in origin. It represents the verbal and intellectual skills acquired throughout the life cycle. This form of intelligence increases through life and shows little or no decrease in old age (Botwinick, 1977; Labouvie-Vief, 1977). Riegel and Riegel (1972) have shown that while more intelligent adults acquire crystallized skills earlier in life, less intelligent adults gradually catch up, so that the intellectual distance between the two groups tends to diminish with age.

Terminal Drop

A hidden factor influencing measures of intelligence within elderly subject samples is the distance from death of each of the persons tested. A phenomenon labeled 'terminal drop' has surfaced in the results of many independent investigations of adult intelligence (e.g., Riegel & Riegel, 1972). Approximately five years prior to death, elderly adults, on the average, display dramatic decreases in intelligence scores. Survivors and nonsurvivors, over repeated testing, exhibit differences in both initial scores and changes in scores over time (Botwinick, 1977). Studies that fail to separate out those persons who die shortly thereafter seriously confound their results and conclusions. Group averages decrease as a function of the number of subjects who are close to death, and those studies (most of which are cross-sectional) that do not take terminal-drop cases into account inappropriately support a model of intellectual decrement in later life (Labouvie-Vief, 1977; Riegel & Riegel, 1972).

The concept of terminal drop establishes a connection between biology and intelligence during the years immediately preceding death. This connection does not, however, apply to healthy and well-functioning adults (Jarvik & Cohen, 1973). Intellectual deterioration is related to biological factors when disease processes are highly advanced. This idea is expressed in the 'discontinuity hypothesis' first described by the gerontologist James Birren. This hypothesis states that intelligence and biological functions are largely independent of one another through adulthood and old age. However, when extreme levels of pathology and biological alterations are reached, biological functions begin to have a significant impact upon intellectual performance (Eisdorfer & Wilkie, 1977; Labouvie-Vief, 1977).

Methods and Misinformation

Method of measurement is a major determinant of intelligence tests results. Longitudinal and sequential designs are superior to cross-sectional techniques. For example, cross-sectional studies show highly different patterns of fluid and crystallized intelligence. Longitudinal results do not display the extremely rapid decline in fluid intelligence found with cross-sectional methods (Labouvie-Vief, 1977). Cross-sectional studies do not account for those nonintellectual differences between age cohorts that may be accounting for the lower scores of older adults. For example, older adults have had fewer educational opportunities than the young and are less familiar with new innovations in our rapidly modernizing society. Longitudinal studies, in contrast, indicate little change for a single cohort as it ages over time. Older adults within these studies display little intellectual decline (Birren & Woodruff, 1973; Labouvie-Vief, 1977).

Similarly, cross-sectional comparisons of age groups show that the elderly become more rigid. Longitudinal studies do not support this development in old age. Rigidity is more related to culture and personal experience than to some intrinsic aging process (Botwinick, 1973; Chown, 1961).

Solving Problems

When older adults are given cognitive problems to solve, they nearly always perform more poorly than younger adults. We must keep in mind, however, that much problem-solving research is cross-sectional.

Older adults tend to approach cognitive problems in highly concrete ways. They look for general themes and relations, not abstractions, to solve a problem (Baltes & Schaie, 1973; Botwinick, 1973). For example, when asked which two categories go together among apples, grapes, and knives, the older adult will typically respond: the apples and the knives. The knives, they assert, are used to cut the apples. In contrast, the answer coded as correct would be pairing the apples and grapes, for they belong in the abstract category of fruits.

Aged adults appear to have particular difficulties with tasks that are complex, especially those requiring them to think about several dimensions simultaneously (Craik, 1977; Chown, 1961). They appear to lack the ability to analyze and synthesize different bits of information effectively (Arenberg, 1973).

Even when studies of problem solving have shown no age differences in accurate performance, the strategies and behaviors of elderly adults are different from those of the young. Older adults tend to make more inquiries during the cognitive task. Often their questions are redundant, although each time they receive an answer they treat the information as new (Arenberg, 1973). Botwinick (1973) observes that the elderly behave as if they have difficulty giving meaning to the information they gain from each question asked. Once they understand the information received, they appear to have difficulties remembering it.

Memory

Most research indicates decrement in the memory capacities of elderly subjects. Both immediate memory (spanning about one second) and short-term memory (spanning several minutes) appear to decline, especially with increases in the number of stimuli to be remembered (Arenberg, 1973; Botwinick, 1973; Jarvik & Cohen, 1973; Riegel, 1966). Impairment of immediate memory may be caused by difficulties in perceiving the stimuli adequately or by interference from brain activity patterns. Similarly, short-term memory decreases have been attributed to interference effects (Jarvik & Cohen, 1973).

Deficits in memory retention covering more than several minutes are caused by problems in storage and retrieval of information. Storage difficulties are due to a greater susceptibility to interference among elderly adults (Arenberg, 1973; Botwinick, 1973). However, more recent investigations locate memory deficits at retrieval sites (Arenberg, 1973; Craik, 1977). Older subjects tend not to develop effective links to information they have stored. They fail to organize the information they learn so that it is readily accessible for recall. It appears that the elderly adult stores more information than he retrieves (Arenberg & Robertson-Tchabo, 1977; Riegel, 1966). Additionally, evidence indicates less accurate recall and recognition from the distant past by elderly adults (Craik, 1977).

However, the collection of research studies investigating memory functions of the elderly is not uniformly negative. The performance of many aged adults is comparable to that of the young (Arenberg & Robertson-Tchabo, 1977; Jarvik & Cohen, 1973). This contradiction of findings apparently corresponds to the large degree of variation among members of the elderly population in all domains of behavior.

Rethinking Our Results

Many factors besides intelligence influence the cognitive performance of elderly adults: education, pacing, cautiousness, meaningfulness, arousal, training, and reinforcement. It is important to account for these factors when analyzing results.

More highly educated elderly adults perform in a superior manner on tasks requiring the exercise of abstract thought (Botwinick, 1973). Because elderly adults are the least educated age group of adults in general, the ability to solve an abstract problem may be telling us more about the adult's education than about his intrinsic intelligence.

Speed requirements often impair the older person's performance on cognitive tasks (Arenberg, 1973; Chown, 1961). Slower pacing significantly reduces differences in performance by the old and young. The elderly are able to display their cognitive capabilities when relieved of time constraints (Arenberg & Robertson-Tchabo, 1977; Palmore, 1977).

Elderly adults are more cautious research participants than are members of younger age groups. The older adult prefers not to respond if he has any doubt about his accuracy (Elias & Elias, 1977; Jarvik & Cohen, 1973). Consequently, improved performance has resulted by requiring older adults to guess even when they are uncertain (Botwinick, 1973; Labouvie-Vief, 1977). The elderly adult, in general, values accuracy over speed, resulting in delayed response time. This in part is a function of the subject's desire for a higher degree of sensory information prior to committing himself to an answer, and in part a function of lower self-confidence (Arenberg, 1973; Birren, 1970; Botwinick, 1973).

Older adults are especially affected by the meaningfulness of a task. The use of more meaningful experimental materials reduces differences between age groups (Arenberg, 1973; Elias & Elias, 1977). This partially accounts for the poor performance by elderly individuals on fluid intellectual tasks, which are meaningless and abstract to the elderly adult (Labouvie-Vief & Zaks, in press). One study, for example, showed that highly meaningful material minimized age differences not only in overt performance, but also in physiological functions (measured by galvanic skin response) as they performed a memory task (Marsh & Thompson, 1977). Additionally, performance improves when older subjects are given increased structure and direction, thereby attributing more meaning to the experimental situation (Botwinick, 1973; Jarvik & Cohen, 1973).

Elderly adults are highly susceptible to the effects of motivation and its physiological components when participating in cognitive studies (Bennett & Ahammer, 1977; Elias & Elias, 1977). Often the experimental setting itself, anticipation of failure, and rapid pacing increase their physical and emotional arousal so that performance is impaired (Elias & Elias, 1977; Labouvie-Vief, 1977). A study by Eisdorfer, for example, showed that reduction of physiological arousal by decreasing the free fatty acids in older subjects' blood plasma served to improve their learning performance over a group receiving placebo treatment and a group of younger adults (Arenberg, 1973; Jarvik & Cohen, 1973). Elderly adults are also more susceptible to the negative effects of fatigue in the performance of cognitive tasks (Labouvie-Vief, 1977).

Finally, studies have shown that prior training and reinforcement result in improved performance on cognitive and intellectual measures (Jarvik & Cohen, 1973; Labouvie-Vief, 1977). Experience with the materials at hand and reinforcement for accurate responses clearly aid the older adult in performing to capacity. In the absence of these conditions, the competence of the older adult may be seriously underestimated.

Ability in Aging

Both the form and content of cognition in later adulthood differs from the cognitive processes of earlier developmental stages. The older adult is more concerned with judgments, attitudes, and values that have developed over a lifetime than with the fluid, manipulative skills common to intelligence testing (Flavell, 1970). Similarly, most of the older adult's daily activities involve cognitive operations less complex and more concrete than those necessary for abstract problem solving (Riegel, 1973). The growing accumulation and complexity of knowledge acquired throughout the life span leads to consolidation and simplification in terms of what is significant to the individual. In this way the developing adult is not overwhelmed by his abundance of knowledge (Ahammer & Bennett, 1976). This hypothesis is in agreement with Birren's findings concerning the changing cognitive strategies and consolidation of ideas that begin to take place during middle adulthood.

Hence, the cognitive competence of the older adult must be viewed in a context that differs from that of earlier stages of life. Poorer performance on standard measures may actually be indicating cognitive differences, not cognitive deficits. With development through adulthood, the individual becomes increasingly capable of dealing with and accepting the multiplicity of contradictions that confront him throughout the life cycle (Chandler, 1975; Labouvie-Vief, 1977; Riegel, 1973). Experience provides the basis of adult cognitive development (Flavell, 1970), and in most cases the lessons learned from experience are adaptive and progressive.

Should decrements occur, especially in conjunction with biological alterations, most elderly adults appear to adapt and compensate by means of accumulated knowledge, experience, and training (Frenkel-Brunswick, 1963; Rabbitt, 1977). Decline is not necessarily inevitable or irreversible. Labouvie-Vief (1977) correspondingly notes that most decrement appears to take place during the postretirement phase of adulthood, which is characterized by a less supportive context for the exercise of cognitive skills. Similarly, social isolation and low degrees of environmental complexity are strongly related to intellectual decline during the later years.

Change the nonsupportive context, and the elderly adult is likely to display considerable improvement. By altering meaning, motivation, and requirements for speedy action, the older adult is capable of competent behavior, especially within a social context that supports his skill. Adult cognition is more a function of personality, experience, and social factors than of inevitable biological decrement, at least until the point of severe physical pathology.

Intelligence through adulthood is composed of fluid and crystallized components, corresponding to more abstract perceptual-manipulative skills and acculturation, respectively. Biological factors directly influence adult intellectual performance only when they reach a stage of advanced biological decline. Research has shown decrement with age in problem solving and memory skills, yet conclusions must be drawn with caution. Cross-sectional research inflates the differences between age cohorts, and the experimental situations in which measurements are taken often impede optimal performance. Factors such as pacing, caution, arousal, experience, and education often influence the level of performance. Whether the older adult performs as well as a younger adult or not, the process and content of his cognitive strategies are different from those who are younger. The older adult has consolidated his lifetime of accumulated knowledge. As long as the environment remains supportive and stimulating to the individual, cognitive capacities need not decline, but the wisdom of old age can flourish.

PERSONALITY AND MORALE

Personality throughout adulthood remains consistent, yet open to change. It is shaped by a sense of personal continuity and by the historical and social events experienced throughout the life cycle. The adult interprets social events in accord with his personal dispositions, but social events, in turn, can significantly alter personal modes of behavior.

It is not surprising, therefore, that the collection of studies that measure personality changes in adulthood and old age yield results that are more inconsistent than they are consistent. Persons become increasingly unique with age, and some are more susceptible to the influence of events than are others. In general, the transition to old age is not marked by extensive personality change, and many characteristics remain stable (Botwinick, 1973; Neugarten, 1977; Riegel & Riegel, 1960). It may even be that personality becomes more consistent with aging (Kimmel, 1974; Neugarten et al., 1968). As personality becomes more consistent, either inner strength or neurotic problems aid or impede adjustment.

This section discusses those personality changes in old age that are documented by research, and the effect of personality upon the life satisfaction derived from social activity. The personality of the older adult influences the success of adjustment to aging, and a stable self-concept is a crucial component throughout the aging process.

Confusing Characteristics

Psychologists have shown that personality characteristics can and do change in old age. Caution must be exercised, however, in determining the origin of these changes. Often they are not caused by aging alone, but by the unique social forces that confront the adult who is aging.

Studies have shown that the aged are more cautious than other age groups. This cautious disposition is accompanied by an increased pessimism and less sense of control over the external world (Botwinick, 1973; Chown, 1977; Kogan & Wallach, 1962; Riley et al., 1969). There is a lower achievement orientation and increased detachment from motives towards mastery (Botwinick, 1973; Chown, 1977; Neugarten & Gutmann, 1968; Riley et al., 1969). All these characteristics are logical end-products of an environment that fails to encourage its elderly to develop and use personal skills and that sees old age as a stage of decline.

The elderly have been characterized as more rigid, conservative, dogmatic, traditional, and serious, than those younger than themselves (Botwinick, 1973; Kimmel, 1974; Oyer, 1976; Riegel & Brumer, 1975). These dispositions are most likely results of the consolidation of values that occurs during later adulthood.

The elderly display a continuation of the sex-role crossover begun in middle age. Males become more passive and sensitive; females become more dominant (Gutmann, 1975; Kimmel, 1974; Neugarten, 1977; Riegel & Brumer, 1975). Other changes during old age include an increasing preoccupation with one's inner world, reduced ego energy, decreased control over impulse life, decreased delay of gratification, and increased valuation of time (Botwinick, 1973; Kastenbaum, 1966; Kimmel, 1974; Neugarten & Gutmann, 1968; Wallach & Green, 1961). Physiological changes often lead to a state of lessened self-confidence (Kimmel, 1974). For example, some elderly adults are ashamed to participate in social events because of their deteriorating physical appearance and decreasing personal stamina. Their body image and self-esteem have been injured as a result (Simos, 1973).

Most of these documented personality changes do not occur uniformly. Some aged adults show none of these characteristics, others quite the opposite dispositions. Additionally, the way a trait is measured influences the researcher's results. A study by Botwinick (1969) found that given the option not to take any risk, elderly subjects would select a no-risk option significantly more often than young adults. However, when required to take at least some risk in making difficult decisions, elderly subjects were no different from young adults in the amount of risk they would take. Elderly adults, then, are not invariably more cautious than the young.

Evidence concerning the rigidity and conformity of aged persons is also contradictory. While many studies suggest that elderly adults rigidly adhere to opinions, others indicate greater persuasibility and increased acquiescence (Bennett & Eckman, 1973; Kogan, 1961). A finding by Riegel and Riegel (1960) helps to clarify these inconsistencies. The researchers found that elderly adults would express their opinions in general and stereotyped ways, but when asked how they would personally react to specific situations, the subjects became more flexible, not rigid in their responses.

The way the researcher asks his questions about the personality of the individual has a major impact upon the way the individual is conceived. Given our general lack of knowledge about the aging process, this phenomenon may be more true for the aged than for younger age groups.

An Inner Search

There does exist a consistent finding in personality studies of older adults. Older adults become more involved in their inner world. The process of interiority, begun in middle age, reaches its peak in later life (Havighurst et al., 1968; Kimmel, 1974; Looft, 1972; Neugarten, 1977). There is no longer a need to expand one's social horizons. Instead the older adult attempts to expand his inner consciousness. The lessened concern with social expression can be accompanied by a decreased tendency to express anger overtly (Chown, 1977).

The older adult may no longer actively seek gratification of needs. Instead, he attempts to attain satisfactions in indirect and vicarious ways. However, the lack of active motivations and curiosity about the world may in fact be a by-product of the lack of a stimulating environment (Kuhlen, 1964).

Whether active or passive, the older adult is intensely involved in his inner world. He recalls and reviews the events of his life now that death is not too far off. Butler (1968) attributes this process to the need for the elderly adult to come to terms with himself and with the life he has led. This life review is successful when there is a flexible outlook and few regrets. Erikson (1950) describes this stage of life as one where the adult achieves personal integrity as he places his life in a positive perspective, or one where the adult reaches the depths of despair because of a life unhappily lived.

Social Satisfaction

In spite of an intense inner focus during the later years, most elderly adults are more satisfied with life if they remain actively involved (Botwinick, 1973; Elias & Elias, 1977; Havighurst et al., 1968; Tobin & Neugarten, 1961). However, there is a wide range of variation from person to person in activity and satisfaction derived. This variation is largely a function of the personality of the older adult and his previous style of social activity (Bennett & Eckman, 1973; Kimmel, 1974; Lehr & Rudinger, 1969; Lowenthal, 1968; Maddox & Wiley, 1976; Schmitz-Scherzer & Lehr, 1976). Throughout, however, the adult's social encounters influence the nature of personality during aging.

There are active aged adults who are satisfied and those who are not. There are also nonactive aged adults who are satisfied and those who are not (Havighurst et al., 1968; Maddox, 1965; Neugarten et al., 1968). Many elderly adults gradually withdraw from their social activities with success. Among the most highly satisfied disengaged adults are those who are self-directed and maintain an interest in the world. Passive adults too are content to withdraw during old age. Elderly adults who are threatened by aging and who continue to yearn to achieve find solace in withdrawal from the social world, but may substitute new activities for roles and opportunities that are lost in old age (Botwinick, 1973; Havighurst, 1973a). Those individuals who had previously maintained outgoing and sociable styles of life suffer most if excluded from social activities during the later years (Lowenthal & Robinson, 1976).

The effects of social withdrawal depend upon whether the withdrawal is voluntarily chosen. If disengagement is forced upon the elderly adult, decreased morale and dissatisfaction inevitably result. Voluntary withdrawal, on the other hand, is accompanied by high morale and contentment (Botwinick, 1973; Chown, 1977; Lowenthal & Boler, 1965). Voluntary withdrawal does not imply a total end to social relations: it can mean increased intimacy with a few select confidants plus the luxury of having time for one's personal thoughts and life review (Lowenthal & Boler, 1965). Whether the adult actively pursues social interactions with others or is content to share intimate moments with only one or two, it is crucial that the decision is made by the aged adult, so that a sense of competence and self-esteem continue throughout life.

Character and Coping

The nature of the individual's personality determines how well he adapts to old age. Those who are least well-adjusted throughout life adjust most poorly to aging (Gottesman et al., 1973; Neugarten, 1977). There is no single pattern of normal adjustment, but some methods of coping are better than others.

Inner resources are crucial in coping with the problems that accompany old age (Labouvie-Vief & Zaks, in press; Shanan, 1976). Those who perceive themselves as in control of their lives are better able to cope with the stresses of aging. Those who perceive little self-competence undergo a cycle of self-defeat. As their personal resources diminish, they withdraw from the complex demands of life. This often leads to a decreasing use of mature cognitive skills and psychological defenses. The older adult becomes all the more vulnerable (Kuypers & Bengtson, 1973; Lawton & Nahemow, 1973; Pfeiffer, 1977).

A stable self-concept maintained in old age can counteract this process (Lowenthal & Chiriboga, 1973; Mischel, 1969). It is this factor that differentiates adaptation by the elderly from adaptation by younger adults. Young adults are more dependent upon their social networks and significant others to cope with the crises of living. Elderly adults are more reliant upon their inner resources. The elderly adult uses the self as a guide for coping actions. Good adjustment and a firm self-concept are strongly related in later life (Lieberman, 1975; Loeb, 1975; Lowenthal & Robinson, 1976; Thomae, 1970). Even if the older adult protects himself and maintains his self-image through angry, demanding, and aggressive interactions, he remains intact and survives better and longer than those more compliant, passive, and vulnerable (Lieberman, 1975; Lowenthal, 1977).

Happiness

The older adult must confront many losses and stresses during later life. This does not mean that he is invariably depressed. Most elderly persons, in fact, report that they are happy or satisfied with life, often to a degree not significantly different from responses by younger groups of adults (Britton & Britton, 1972; Palmore, 1977; Rosow, 1967). Life satisfaction does not necessarily decrease because of the aging process, but many reasonably satisfied older adults do report that they are not as happy as they were 20 years earlier in their lives (Rosow, 1967). Hence, elderly adults cannot be viewed as uniformly happy or sad. Some cope well and some do not, depending upon their views of themselves, their social world, and their imprint upon it.

Personal change does not occur simply by virtue of aging. Personality may, in fact, become more consistent in old age. Some personality changes take place more because of the changing social status of the older adult rather than because of an intrinsic aging process. There is, nevertheless, increased inner preoccupation during old age, as the older adult surveys his life and places it in perspective.

The satisfaction derived from continued activity or social withdrawal during later life is dependent upon the personal disposition of the individual. Those who voluntarily choose to withdraw from an active social life often maintain a high morale due to increased mutuality in the context of a more intimate set of social relations and increased opportunity for personal reappraisal. Most important in adjustment to aging is the maintenance of a firm self-concept. Reliance upon group supports is more characteristic of younger age groups.

The social world of the older adult is different from that of the young. The ways the elderly relate to their world are different as a result. This social world is examined more closely in chapter six.

6 The Social World of the Aged

The older adult experiences a social world that is different from earlier years. Others no longer react to him as a young and vigorous adult, and he in turn must relate to others in a new manner. Attitudes about old people are different from views about people in general, thus placing the aged in a unique position within the social structure, a position not especially attractive to adults of any age. The older adult is free from the roles and norms of early adulthood, yet this freedom embodies a sense of ambiguity and vulnerability. This chapter examines these features of the social world of old age, features which provide the context for communication in later life.

ATTITUDES TOWARD THE AGED

Everyone holds an attitude, whether explicit or implicit, about the aging process and about people who are old. These attitudes can vary. They can be positive or negative, depending upon the person and the context under scrutiny. People may tend to feel differently about family members and the old in general (Bekker & Taylor, 1966); they may idolize a grandparent, yet downgrade the status of senior citizens.

Overwhelmingly, however, the bulk of research on attitudes towards the elderly tells us that the general public does not view old age in a favorable light. Western culture views the older adult as a problem, not an asset (Bettinghaus & Bettinghaus, 1976). For example, in a study of a community in which aged adults resided, the younger adults felt that the elderly should be active in community affairs simply to occupy their time, not because of any special skills (Britton & Britton, 1972). De Beauvoir (1973) characterizes this situation as one in which the elderly person is viewed as an existing being ('exis') rather than a doing being ('praxis'), and thereby appears as different from the active, functioning adult.

Our society holds independence and personal utility in high esteem. To the extent that the aged lack these qualities, they are viewed as insufficient (McTavish, 1971; Troll, 1971). The elderly adult arouses negative emotions in younger adults, who fear the dependencies the aged project and the prospects of their own eventual aging (Auerbach & Levenson, 1977). The adult, when interacting with an aged person, may convey an attitude of respect, yet all the while be acutely aware of the declining status of the aged (de Beauvoir, 1973).

This section reviews the stereotypes held by the young about the old and how cultural and historical conditions support or modify these views. Individual differences in attitudes held and methods of measurement are also discussed because they influence how one responds to questions on personal attitudes. This is followed by a review of attitudes toward aging held by older adults, and how they differ from those of society at large and from one another.

Society's Stereotypes

As the person perceived increases in age, the perceiver increases the number of stereotypes he holds about that person (Bennett & Eckman, 1973; McTavish, 1971). Older adults tend not to be viewed as separate individuals. Instead, they are perceived as representatives of their age group (Rosow, 1974). This corresponds to the description in chapter two of the process of stereotyping. Perceivers first construct human groupings and then determine their characteristics. The young perceiver readily places the older adult in a separate group, a group that represents a set of people very different from the self.

McTavish (1971), in an extensive review of attitudes toward the aged, found that from a fifth to a third of adults in the United States are willing to agree with negative statements about the elderly. Tuckman and Lorge (1953), in their pioneering research in this area, found that even educated and psychologically sophisticated young adults (that is, graduate students) express numerous misconceptions and stereotypes about the aged when their responses are based on intuitions rather than on experimental evidence.

Research has uncovered a multitude of stereotypes that are held about the elderly. These include perceptions of the aged as ill, tired, nonsexual, cognitively deficient, grouchy, withdrawn, self-pitying, inactive, isolated, lonely, unhappy, unproductive, defensive, ineffective, economically insecure, rigid, having failing physical and mental powers, conservative, respectful of tradition, and proud of their children (Eisdorfer & Altrocchi, 1961; Fitzgerald, 1978; McTavish, 1971; Rubin & Brown, 1975; Tuckman & Lorge, 1953). In fact, one study found that even when college students could differentiate between the aged and the mentally ill, some of their attitudes towards these different groups were expressed in similar directions (Eisdorfer & Altrocchi, 1961).

Negative attitudes are perpetuated by the popular culture. Jokes, fiction magazines, television, and other media events poke fun at or directly denigrate the elderly (Aronoff, 1974; McTavish, 1971). More favorable attitudes toward the elderly are held in many more primitive societies, yet even here the cultural ideals and actual behavior are sometimes at odds (Gutmann, 1977; McTavish, 1971). Further, the effects of societal modernization on the attitudes of the individual are different from the effects of modernization on society as a whole. In a study of several developing nations, researchers found that current exposure to modernizing experiences do not consistently influence the individual's attitudes toward the aged for the worse. Societal modernization as a whole, however, is negatively related to overall attitudes toward the aged (Bengtson et al., 1975). The aged become increasingly useless with the advances of modern technology, and it is likely that with further modernization, subsequent generations will feel less favorably towards their elderly members.

On a more positive note, Seltzer and Atchley (1971) conducted a study of books read by children from 1870 through 1960. They hypothesized that these books had helped to develop the attitudes of middle- and upper-class children. Contrary to expectations, they found that the general picture of older people was not consistently negative. Although there were several decreases in positive attitudes toward the elderly, they were few and of small magnitude. Some differences occurred only for specific time periods or were limited in scope, rather than indicative of general negative changes over time.

In fact, it appears that in current times we are rethinking our views about the elderly, especially in light of the increasing numbers of older adults who live in society. Mass-media coverage of aging and the aged is becoming more conscious of its negative stereotypes, and is attempting to present a more clearheaded view of old age. Business, too, is catering to a growing elderly population, and is becoming increasingly aware of the public which it serves. Nevertheless, we are far from reversing our negative attitudes: a fear of aging is deeply ingrained in the culture of modern Western society.

Class, Character, and Cohort

Not all adults hold precisely the same attitudes toward the elderly. Factors that contribute to individual differences in attitudes include social class, educational level, personality, and age. Members of the poorer and less educated classes believe in more of the stereotyping of aging (Auerbach & Levenson, 1977; McTavish, 1971), yet aging is also a difficult process for members of the lower and more deprived classes. Middle-class adults, on the other hand, tend to deny old age more readily than working-class adults (Rosow, 1974).

Personality influences the individual's attitude toward the aged. When the adult feels positively toward the aged, these feelings are further reinforced by exposure to information on aging (Hickey et al., 1976). Other personal characteristics influencing attitudes towards old age include nurturance, on the positive side, and authoritarianism, alienation, and negative attitudes towards the mentally ill on the negative (Bennett & Eckman, 1973; Kilty & Feld, 1976; Kogan, 1961).

Finally, attitudes towards the elderly develop early in life. By third grade, children clearly perceive the aged as different from middle-aged adults (Hickey et al., 1968). From third grade through college, children and adolescents view old age as generally unpleasant, but their descriptions of aging become more elaborate as they grow older (Hickey & Kalish, 1968). Clearly, attitudes maintained so consistently throughout the early stages of life are difficult to counteract in adulthood.

Social factors are capable of modifying attitudes held by adults. For example, one study found less social distance and stereotyping of the aged among young adults within a sample of people aged 18 to 74. This finding strongly suggests that different age cohorts hold different attitudes towards the elderly. The younger adults within this study maintained less allegiance to the traditional work ethic of middle-aged adults. They required less productivity and independence from the elderly in order to prove their worth (Hickey et al., 1976). In turn, they would not judge older adults as a useless and burdensome group.

Attitudes toward the elderly are acquired at an early age, yet may be modified through increasing social experience and by the acquisition, confirmation, or rejection of stereotyped presuppositions. Cohort membership influences the development and maintenance of general attitudes, since each age group achieves contact with the social structure in a fresh and novel way, influenced by its socializers, yet comprising a social force in itself.

Surveys and Social Perception

Attitudes towards the elderly remain predominantly negative, although the future holds more favorable prospects. The way people's attitudes is measured tailors survey results and conclusions. Results from questions that require agree-or-disagree responses differ from the results acquired through more open ended questions. The latter allow for the person to volunteer information on both positive and negative feelings about aging, old age, as well as aged acquaintances. Throughout, however, the perceiver attempts to maintain a consistent view.

Perceptions of and attitudes about older adults remain highly subjective. They result from personal dispositions and the nature of the person viewed. For example, when adults were interviewed about the elderly living in their community, the researchers observed all-or-none type descriptions of older adults. If the person discussed was doing well in one area of behavior, such as getting on well with the family, he would be viewed as doing well in all areas of life (Britton & Britton, 1972). This type of perception points to the saliency of first impressions. If the elderly adult is perceived as declining in any area of functioning, he is likely to be viewed as similarly incompetent in other domains.

The Aged View Aging

Both culture and personal situation determine how the older adult views aging. While the older adult has developed attitudes towards aging from early through later life, he must reinterpret aging stereotypes in conjunction with current concerns and perceptions. By now it is apparent that the older adult has a poor foundation to work from. Society at large tells him that he is useless and slowly declining. Yet, when aged adults hold similar attitudes, it is only self-defeating: it reinforces the negative attitudes of the population at large (Bennett & Eckman, 1973; Cath, 1975).

Research measuring the attitudes of the elderly has yielded inconsistent results. Many studies indicate an increased favorability of attitudes and a decrease in stereotypes held, while others show no difference between the attitudes of young and old (Bennett & Eckman, 1973; Hickey et al., 1978; Kilty & Feld, 1976; McTavish, 1971). Both young and old perceive elderly people differently from people in general (Kogan & Shelton, 1972). Even if the degree of negativity by young and old is equally as strong, the specific negative attitude items selected by old and young respondents differ (Bennett & Eckman, 1973).

The attitudes held by older adults are fraught with contradiction (Kogan, 1961). The older adult may have fears about aging yet be comfortable with the self. He is also aware of the many patterns of aging within his age group. Some of his peers fit the stereotypes well, while others thrive in old age. The older adult is therefore least likely to hold clear and consistent attitudes. As we discussed in chapter five, the older adult has reached a stage of development where contradiction becomes accepted as an intrinsic feature of life.

On the other hand, attitudes held by some older adults may be a product of misinformation. Hess (1974) has suggested that many aged adults are subject to pluralistic ignorance, a concept described in chapter two in the discussion of social cognition. Specifically, when older adults fail to communicate effectively with others, they are unable to engage in the process of comparing their differing views of the world. They may in fact assume that others view aging the same way they do. As a result the adult is never quite able to check out the reality of the stereotypes he holds about the aging process and about his own behavior.

In accordance with the mixed attitudes the elderly hold towards aging and the aged, a similar inconsistency of results characterizes research that examines the self-image of the aged person (Bennett & Eckman, 1973). Although past research has shown an even split between results evidencing either positive or negative self-images, more recent research has tended to stress the positive aspects of self-perception. One study, for example, showed that aged adults view themselves as highly affiliative and responsible (Fitzgerald, 1978). This shift towards the positive is possibly due to an increasingly positive approach on the part of researchers, current change in general attitudes, or a cohort difference in perception and adjustment to aging by present aged adults. It is important to note, however, that many, especially middle-class, aged do not view themselves as being old (Hess, 1974; Hickey et al., 1978). This certainly influences whether one views one's self-image in a favorable light.

The analysis of the attitudes held by the aged must therefore distinguish between attitudes toward the self and towards others of similar age. The elderly person's self-perception may be different from that of the aged in general, depending upon his personal nature and place in the social world. For example more privileged and educated samples of elderly persons display less negative self-images, yet they view other elderly adults in a significantly more negative manner (Bennett & Eckman, 1973; Kogan & Wallach, 1962). However, class differences in self-images are not as striking after age 75 when the stress and hardships of the aging process have already taken their toll (Rosow, 1967).

Life style similarly has a major impact upon self-perception in aging. For example, older adults who view themselves as more sociable than the typical aged person are also individuals who maintain a more extensive network of social roles in old age (Fitzgerald, 1978). On the other hand, the elderly who are unequipped to live on their own effectively tend to believe in a wider range of stereotypes of the aged (McTavish, 1971). Hence, the position the older adult holds in society and the competence he displays can make or break his acceptance of the stereotyped image of old age.

Society holds a predominantly negative attitude toward aging and the aged, reflecting such cultural values and expectations as product-ivity and independence, which are conveyed to all age groups in society. Class, personality, and age group cohort influence the nature of attitudes held. Additionally, research methods of measurement help to shape the form and content of people's perceptions of the old. The elderly themselves are not untouched by the cultural setting, yet appear to display less negative views about their own self-image, especially if they are members of the more privileged social classes. In general, society's stereotypes about the aged remain unfavorable and few individuals from any life stage wish to identify with the stereotyped image of life lived by the old.

NORMS AND ROLES

The social roles the individual plays and the norms of behavior he observes anchor the individual within the social structure. The social world then becomes a predictable place in which to live, and social identity guides the individual in his interactions with others. Many norms, however, are based upon the assumed capacities of participants in a social relationship. Often norms are negotiated rather than rigidly adhered to (Atchley, 1975; Turner, 1974). This process of negotiation is especially relevant when discussing the ambiguous norms and roles that comprise the changing social world of the older adult.

This section addresses the issue of this changing social world. It explores how adults react to the loss of roles in old age and how personal style provides a bridge between early and later life. It examines the increased freedom from norms that the older adult is allowed and the way in which he confronts this new, ambiguous social world. Finally, it takes note of those people and situations that can and often do structure the social expectations of the adult during later life.

Role Reduction

In general, during middle adulthood the role obligations are numerous and overly demanding. The middle-aged adult must simultaneously juggle a diverse collection of roles, such as father, husband, friend, neighbor, intellectual, boss, employee, athlete, consumer, and expert in various fields. The greater the number of roles that the individual is capable of playing, the more likely that he is well adjusted in the social world (Goode, 1960; Sarbin, 1954). In contrast, during older adulthood, the individual must abandon many roles that are often not then replaced (Phillips, 1957; Riley et al., 1969). The older adult is left on his own to create new roles and fill the vacuum to the best of his ability. The options are not extensive.

The radical loss of social roles and the accompanying lack of norms for behavior is not especially well received by most aging adults. Many respond to the uncompensated role loss with an increased adherence to their previous norms and former social identities. They refuse to call themselves old (Rosow, 1974). As the loss of roles accumulate during the later years, eventually the older adult feels forced to identify himself as old (Phillips, 1957).

Through adulthood the acquisition of each new role is enhanced by commitment, preparation, rewards, and approval from others (Elder, 1977; Goode, 1960). The role changes occurring with aging, however, minimize commitment and preparation, and rewards are severely reduced. Few approve of the status decline experienced with old age. If the older adult behaves in a way that society might expect, he is delegated to a deviant status within the social structure: now he is a member of the unproductive segment of society (Riley et al., 1969).

Riley et al. (1969) find, in contrast, that when the elderly are given the opportunity to participate in roles that are socially approved, they express similar feelings of self-satisfaction as do young adults. Riley et al. correspondingly suggest three alternatives that are open to the older adult who is faced with an unwelcome loss of roles: a) he may replace an old role with one that is new and in line with his values – often the most difficult alternative for the adult to achieve; b) he may reorder his values and orientations towards roles so that feelings and actions no longer conflict – for example, he may state that he now wants retirement for he suddenly realizes what a rat race exists in the world of work; c) he may choose to simply accept the deviant status of old age. Selection among these alternatives by the elderly adult depends upon a combination of available opportunities, personal preference, and individual capabilities.

Style and Stability

In spite of the obvious loss of many standardized roles, such as spouse and worker, Rosow (1976b) has shown that older adults maintain more informal roles. Informal roles are roles that are not bounded by social responsibilities. They are exercised by the adult in both formal and informal contexts. Generally they correspond to the individual's personal style of interaction. Thus, one may be a nurturer, another an intellectual. It is informal roles therefore that allow for continuity of role relations from early through later life. They enable the adult to maintain a stable self-concept throughout the life cycle, which is crucial to successful survival during the later years.

Constraints and Contradiction

The loss of roles and the norms that go with them leads to a greater sense of freedom. It also leads to an increasingly ambiguous state of affairs (Markson, 1975; Rosow, 1974, 1976b). The norms of behavior society requires of the elderly are few and vaguely defined. They include such general expectations as maintaining ties with one's child, living in a separate home, and deferring to the middle aged. Several norms inform the adult about what he is not allowed to do. For example, it is generally disapproved when an older adult attempts to behave in a manner much younger than his years (Atchley, 1975; Rosow, 1974).

Clear norms and their internalization by the elderly are impeded by a lack of consensus about just what these norms are (Wheeler, 1966). There also are few people who act as role models of appropriate behaviors (Rosow, 1974). However, as long as the older individual does not behave too strangely, and as long as he doesn't lean too heavily upon those who provide for his needs, for the first time in adulthood he is allowed to say and do what he pleases. Only such factors as poor health or poverty can keep the old person from behaving precisely as he wishes (Rosow, 1974). In other words, old people are allowed to be eccentric.

The absence of norms and the structure of roles can lead to a sense of confusion. Yet, recall as discussed in chapter five how the older adult has come to accept the contradictions inherent in human activity; the elderly, more than younger adults, can accept and adapt to the consequences of their inconsistent status (Streib, 1976). The increased acceptance and recognition of contradiction in old age facilitates the individual's adaptation to a highly ambiguous social context.

Reference Groups

By identifying with others, one can learn to play their roles. The individual's reference group displays these roles and illustrates their norms (Rosow, 1967). For the elderly adult, family, friendship networks, and status groups (such as ethnic affiliations) function as reference groups. They provide role models and reinterpret norms for the older adult (Atchley, 1975; Rosow, 1967). However, in a study by Rosow (1967) a third of the elderly adults that were interviewed were unable to name an adult role model whom they wished to emulate. Fifty-three percent, on the other hand, specified personal associates they used as role models, 44 percent of whom were relatives or friends, nine percent of whom were neighbors. He concluded that for reference groups the older adult looks first towards the family, and then to neighbors and friends.

Admired role models, in general, are individuals who are young. They remind the aging adult of his former position and capabilities. Similarly, the older adult tends to look up to other adults of similar age who maintain a youthful appearance and outlook (Rosow, 1974). For many elderly, this form of identification can result in considerable internal dissonance: the older adult may be incapable of living up to his ideal.

An additional and major source of norms is the residential community (Atchley, 1975; Elder, 1977). An increased number of elderly adults living within the community increases the number of neighbors who are named as role models for the aged (Rosow, 1967). Similarly, increased concentrations of elderly adults within a community increase the number of age-linked norms that guide behaviors and social interaction (Carp, 1976). Chapter seven delves further into these issues of community life. At present the basic idea remains that the greater the sense of community established and the stronger the network of social relations, the more guidelines of behavior that can be offered to the older adult.

The roles and norms that regulate behaviors and social expectations diminish in quantity and explicitness during the later years. Loss of roles is usually unwelcome, causing the elderly adult to search for new roles, restructure his orientation towards the roles he is left, or accept a new, marginal social status. Those informal roles that convey personal style, however, help to maintain a sense of self-continuity during the process of aging. The vagueness of norms and ambiguity of role relations is more easily accepted by older than younger adults, due to an enhanced ability by the old to deal with contradiction. Many elderly are unable to specify role models to be used for guidance, although most often family and friends become their reference groups. The composition of the community in which the individual resides is also influential in the development and maintenance of roles and norms during old age.

The older adult, more than any time in life, must work to construct his social world and actively seek out guidelines for the ways in which to behave. The inner strength of the older adult will aid him in the process and help him construct the roles he can play until the end of life.

THE ENVIRONMENT

The social and physical environment of the developing individual have a major impact upon behavior and social interaction. The environment is structured by the individual's unique perception of it, yet at the same time the environment structures one's view of the world and of the self.

Press and Stress

The concept of environmental 'press' has been used to identify how forces within the environment, together with individual needs, determine how the individual behaves on a given occasion. Lawton and Nahemow (1973), who describe this concept in relation to the process of aging, show that competence, affect, adaptation, and environment press are highly interrelated. In conjunction with the changing nature of the elderly adult's social and intellectual behaviors, there is a change in the nature of the environmental press (DeLong, 1974). With aging there is an increasing influence of environmental stress (Gottesman et al., 1973).

Representative of this view is the 'environmental docility hypothesis', which posits that as the capabilities of the individual decline, it appears that the environment accounts more for behavior, the individual less (Lawton & Simon, cited in Lawton & Nahemow, 1973). This position corresponds to several changes during the aging process such as diminished health, income, and status, and increased loss of roles, which serve to increase dependency upon support from the environment (Lawton & Nahemow, 1973; Rosow, 1968). Additionally, the physical features of the environment (such as convenience of location and accessibility of needed services) can have a significant impact upon morale, regardless of the social supports available to the adult (Lawton & Nahemow, 1969).

An environment of poor quality in turn can decrease the competence and self-assurance of the aging individual (Butler, 1968). A lack of stimulation, low environmental complexity, and social isolation may result in decreased motivation and intellectual decline (Kuhlen, 1964; Labouvie-Vief, 1977). The possibility of this occurrence becomes most threatening in later life. For the older adult has less social and physical resources than during his earlier years.

Preference and Perception

The individual most often prefers a consistent and predictable setting, and during the later years of life a stable environment becomes especially important (DeLong, 1974). This in part is due to the biological changes that occur in old age: the older adult moves about more slowly and his senses are less acute (Lawton & Nahemow, 1973). Within optimal, supportive environments, aging appears to be most successful, eliminating the threat of deterioration and promoting growth or stability at minimum (Bennett & Ahammer, 1977; McTavish, 1971). Additionally, the more adapted the individual is to the environment, the more efficiently he processes and utilizes information within the setting (Fozard et al., 1977). Optimal environments vary in accordance with individual needs, however. For example, for one group of elderly adults the presence of age peers may be most crucial; another group may require access to supportive services, such as health care facilities.

An important environmental distinction involves the relative advantages of urban or rural settings. While some investigators minimize the distinction — noting, for example, that cohesive communities exist within both settings — others favor either the urban or the rural environment. Advantages of urban areas include greater contact with one's child and easier access to services. Rural areas usually are characterized by greater contact with friends, longer residence, and less impersonality, but there is also greater deprivation in terms of income, health, and services (Britton & Britton, 1972; Lawton, 1977). The preference of urban or rural ultimately resides within the person.

It is important to stress that the individual at any age is not totally passive. The environment is defined, in essence, by the individual's perception of it. The aging adult need not be at the mercy of the environment, but may seek out complexity and stimulation provided he takes the initiative. What appears to the young as a defective environment may be seen by the old as enriched. He may take comfort in its familiarity and the way it supports his level of functioning. Communication with others past and present helps to define one's personal setting. Environment and individual interact in a dialectical way as they jointly contribute to the structure of the world and of the person within it.

The environment is a major component of the individual's social and physical world. The aging adult's level of competence renders him more or less susceptible to environmental stresses. A poor environment in turn can decrease the individual's level of competence. In contrast, supportive and self-selected settings facilitate optimal adaptation to aging. Under these circumstances external information can be processed most efficiently. It is important to recognize, however, that both the individual and environment contribute to the process of change. Environmental stimulation, or lack of it, is defined by the way in which the person interprets the external world.

RETIREMENT AND WIDOWHOOD

Two losses common to old age are the loss of job and loss of spouse. Adjustment to these losses requires inner strength and the availability of a supportive social environment. Work and the marital relationship contribute to the individual's self-concept throughout the life cycle. They provide the social support system that maintains the individual's personal identity and channels his social relations. Both the internal and external worlds of the aged adult undergo considerable change during the loss of these central roles. This section briefly reviews these role transitions of later life.

Retirement

Only 12 percent of adults over 65 years are employed; and about a fifth of those retired would actually prefer to work (Palmore, 1977). Most studies indicate adjustment to and favorability of retirement during old age (Atchley, 1974; Riley et al., 1969). Adjustment is most likely when retirement occurs voluntarily. To the degree that it is expected, the effects are less dramatic (Kimmel, 1974; Neugarten, 1970; Strumpel, 1973): events that are anticipated and on time in their occurrence are not nearly as stressful as unanticipated crises. Most adults who have planned retirement are significantly more satisfied than those who were forced to retire unexpectedly (Neugarten, 1970).

The major determinant of satisfaction during retirement is adequate health and sufficient income to maintain a comfortable life style (Atchley, 1974; Gottesman et al., 1973). Those aged adults who continue to work are typically in a more favorable economic position (Schulz, 1977). Other factors contributing to adjustment to retirement include: positive attitudes toward retirement, achievement of one's ambitions prior to retirement, and the availability of social support systems such as retirement planning programs and family relations (Atchley, 1975; Kimmel, 1975; Riley et al., 1969).

The elderly adult encounters problems during the phase of retirement if he maintains a lifetime feeling of guilt about indulging in leisure. Most adults do not derive as much satisfaction from leisure activities as they do from work (Havighurst, 1973a). Often work in itself had justified participation in leisure activities (Miller, 1968). In contrast, retirement requires that the individual dedicate himself to leisure and leave the basic work in the world to the younger adult (Riley et al., 1969). Nevertheless, some elderly adults truly enjoy their leisure activities, particularly when these activities are related to life-long interests (Havighurst, 1973a; Reichard et al., 1962). There is a wide range of individual variation in the satisfaction and utilization of the immense amount of free and unstructured time of the retiree.

The marriage relationship can ease or disrupt adjustment to retirement (Oyer, 1976). Couples vary in attitudes towards retirement activities. However, consensus between husband and wife concerning domestic roles and responsibilities following retirement contributes to high morale (Bengtson et al., 1977; Lowenthal & Robinson, 1976; Rosow, 1974). Husband and wife must jointly construct a new social system within the home. They must distribute power equitably based upon their views about themselves and their relationship, for society offers few norms of behavior to guide their negotiation of changing roles (Rosow, 1974).

Whether or not retirement is voluntary or satisfying, entrance into the role of retiree simplifies one's life routines and often lessens opportunities for social interaction (Kimmel, 1974; Looft, 1972; Muth, 1976). A social identity based upon one's previous working role is no longer tenable; this is why the increasing interiority and maintenance of self-concept (as illustrated in chapter five) are so essential to adjustment during later life. They provide the aging individual with a sense of personal continuity as the social environment and his place within it are suddenly transformed.

Widowhood

The loss of a spouse is a devastating event at any age. Its occurrence is handled differently by older men and women. Males are far more likely to remarry than are females (Bengtson et al., 1977; Troll, 1971). Of course, the older men have greater chances for finding a mate: many more older women are available. Widows, on the other hand, are more likely to turn to kin. They will usually live near their children or move in if they cannot live self-sufficiently (Troll, 1971; Troll & Smith, 1976). Widows are the poorest among the aged.

Additionally, intimate friendships between older women can often satisfy social needs now that the husband is gone. In contrast, males have often failed to nurture close relations with other men throughout their lives. For males, a close and intimate relation is best achieved through marriage, for this is the only setting in which the male takes comfort in closeness (Lowenthal, 1977; Lowenthal & Robinson, 1976).

Loss of a spouse disrupts the person's psychological state and social status. Personal problems are common. In fact, in some cases symptoms appear that are similar to those following institutionalization. These include increased incidence of physical disorders and death, depression, withdrawal, apathy, and decreased activity levels (Kimmel, 1974; Lieberman, 1969). The loss of one's spouse may disturb the survivor's previous self-image, which had been based upon the partnership of the two individuals (Cavan, 1962). However, once the period of severe disturbance is over, survivors with good health and sufficient income can continue to live full lives (Troll, 1971).

On the level of social relations, widows are frequently stigmatized. Friends are embarrassed and acquaintances uncertain about how to interact with a widow (Lieberman, 1975). Relations with others that were based upon one's status as a couple are terminated or transformed (Lopata, 1975). It is those who have suffered similar losses who remain at hand. Consequently, widows tend to find more extensive social supports in communities where many other widows are residing (Lieberman, 1975; Riley et al., 1969).

Adaptation to the loss of a spouse varies from person to person. It depends upon the former relationship of husband and wife, relations with others, personal strength, and objective constraints such as income and health (Lopata, 1975).

The expectability of events, however, also influences the degree of stress the survivor experiences. Widowhood is a more common event during later life. Spouses become acutely aware that one of the pair, usually the male, is likely to die first. While both younger and older widows experience increased physical ailments following the death of a spouse, widows below 65 years of age express more psychiatric symptoms than women who are older (Neugarten, 1970). As hard as it is to be left alone, the older widow fares much better, since she knew it was bound to occur.

Retirement and widowhood are two major crises confronted by the older adult. They alter the roles and social identity of the aging individual and require a supportive social environment to cushion the blow. To the extent that these events are anticipated, they are more readily accepted and coped with. While retirement is often a matter of individual preference, the loss of a spouse is not, resulting in considerable distress on the part of the survivor. Maintenance of self-concept, consensus, and mutuality with others become crucial factors in adjustment to these radically altered roles.

Overall, the social world of the older adult has gradually transformed from one that has maximized a sense of competence during middle adulthood to one that must maximize coping skills to insure survival in old age. Social attitudes have conveyed the message that the older adult is on the decline. Roles and norms which support one's self-image are eliminated one by one. The older adult is left all the more vulnerable to stress within the environment, yet he need not succumb to these negative forces in later life. There are social supports which can enhance the quality of one's old age. Chapter seven reviews the supports of family, neighbors, and friends, which can alter the nature of the social world of the aging adult.

7 The Social Networks of the Aged

The older adult confronts a social world that is nonsupportive. He must contend with a social attitude which downgrades the aged and with an ambiguous social environment that supplies limited roles and guidelines. For this reason the social networks of the aged come into prominence, providing the adult with a social position, a purpose, and sense of security. Their absence or their nonsupport makes adjustment to aging quite difficult.

This chapter describes the social supports provided by family, neighbor and friend, and how the older adult communicates in the context of these relationships. All three supports actually serve to supplement one another. The family often takes precedence, due to affection and life-long bonds. The neighborhood defines the immediate social environment for interaction. And friendships allow for those special relations where people share their deep concerns about themselves and about the world they jointly perceive. The mass media is also used by those with social support and those without, as a one-way form of communication, unlike the jointly constructed dialogue by adult with family, neighbor and friend.

FAMILY

No social group compares with the family in its influence upon the individual. It is an organized group that naturally evolves within all human societies, and it is a primary source for the individual in developing his view of the world. Views of the world are conveyed and reinforced by communication within the family, communication that is quite different in quality from that among less cohesive group members (Bochner, 1976). Relations between family members are enduring and intense. They mold one's initial sense of self and place within the world. These relations persist throughout the life cycle of the developing individual, transcending the barriers of physical distances and separation over time (Back, 1976; Bengtson & Black, 1973; Troll & Smith, 1976).

The family is highly influential in directing its members' participation in many institutions of society (Goode, 1960; Gove et al., 1973). The structure of the family group, including number of persons and resources of money, time, and energy influence the person's behavior both inside the family and out in society (Gove et al., 1973; Sussman, 1976). Both inside and out, family relationships influence one's strategies of thinking, as each family member interprets the world in a similar way. A consensus among the family members maintains a sense of stability and hedges against anxiety (Bochner, 1976). There is a deep emotional as well as social dependence upon the family.

Yet the family fosters more discord and conflict than other social systems (Bochner, 1976). Power struggles and clashes of will can dominate much communication. The punctuation of communication, which represents how such relations are organized by each member (as described in chapter two) is often renegotiated as dominance relations change over time. Although certain themes of conflict are common to many families, each family maintains its own standards and ideals about what a healthy and happy family is truly like (Bochner, 1976).

This section discusses those issues that deal with the relationships between elderly adults and the members of their families. It identifies the modified extended family as the basic family structure in modern society and discusses the role this family plays in relation to its elderly members.

Mutuality in the Modified Family

The presence of several generations living under a single roof is rare in our society. There are also, however, few nuclear units of husband, wife, and child that are cut off from wider kinship ties. There is instead what is called the modified extended family (Sussman, 1976; Sussman & Burchinal, 1968; Troll, 1971; Troll & Smith, 1976). The modified extended family consists of a network of several related nuclear units, usually living within visiting distance. These units are connected by means of mutual aid and social activities. They interact by choice and often share affectionate relations. They do not control each other, but they offer their support. In modern urban society, so notorious for its impersonality, the modified extended family becomes that much more important (Sussman & Burchinal, 1968). This modified kinship network supports its elder members.

Most elderly adults have living relatives with whom they are in contact (Troll, 1971). With the general losses that accompany the aging process, these relations – particularly with one's child – grow in their importance (Rosow, 1967). The elderly often look to their families for norms and standards of behavior. On a practical level, it is often members of the extended family who help to arrange the elderly member's relations with formal organizations, special services, and bureaucracies (Sussman, 1976). On a psychological level, the elderly person's involvement with the family lessens his sense of feeling old as it supports an image of self-continuity and positive self-esteem (Bell, 1967; Back, 1976).

This latter feature of family support is a crucial element of communication, for the tacit confirmation of the older adult's continued sense of competence provides him with the fortitude to counteract society's image of aging. Observations of more primitive societies have shown that extended families contribute to the continued well-being of their oldest generation. Families in these cultures allow their elderly members to recall and relive their past through their current interactions with family members (Gutmann, 1976). This in turn enables the elderly adult to put his life in perspective, to perceive a continuous family life and continuous sense of self. To the extent that the modified extended family performs this function in modern society, the oldest generation is assured of self-esteem.

Within the modified extended family, the relation between parent and child is often the most intense for the elderly member. Relations with brothers and sisters, however, also can be close, particularly when the elderly person is single, has no children, becomes widowed, or still has a living mother (Troll, 1971). The older adult may strengthen ties with brothers and sisters in later life; unlike parent-child relationships, power is usually equally shared (Lowenthal & Robinson, 1976; Troll, 1971). The relationship therefore is less ambiguous, the interaction more comfortable.

Similarly, the relationship between husband and wife can be most satisfying during later life. Once the children have left the home, husband and wife are more free to dedicate their time and energy to one another (Troll, 1971). Few relationships of later life can convey the sense of self-confirmation derived from the mutuality and self-understanding when husband and wife communicate.

Family Development

The family is not a static group of related individuals. The interconnections among its members gradually change over time, as each member develops in unique ways and social trends come and go. The family, therefore, develops as its members gradually change, and in the process each member alters his perceptions of the others, sometimes imperceptibly, other times in radical ways.

For example, when a parent retires, family relations change. The parent quite possibly will now play down his children's successes at work because they may threaten the elder's position and the prominence of family ties (Bengtson & Black, 1973). On the other hand, the elderly member confronted with numerous losses may identify with the lives of his children and grandchildren in order to partake of their successes (Thomae, 1970). In either case, for better or for worse, the patterns of interaction are altered. As the identity of each of its members change, so do their relationships.

As the family develops and its members branch out in their lives, striking similarities between the generations remain. There may be a generation gap in modern day society. But this gap substantially narrows when viewed within the family (Bengtson & Cutler, 1976). Behaviors, predispositions, attitudes, values, personality traits and occupational choices are transmitted from grandparents to parents and their children (Bengtson & Black, 1973; Troll, 1971). Parent and child may differ along any of these dimensions, yet the family bonds and intensive training for life that began from the earliest years, are nearly impossible for the adult to abandon once and for all.

The Message of Mutual Aid

Mutual aid is a major form of exchange between members of the modified extended family. It includes exchange of material goods, such as food, money, and clothes, as well as exchange of services, such as watching the children and running the errands. One need not live too nearby or visit a relative often in order to be a candidate for receipt or request of mutual aid. In most cases, parents of any age aid the child as long as possible, but factors such as health and money can reverse the process (Troll, 1971). Hence, middle class adults continue to offer help to their middle-aged children. In the less advantaged working class, the children may often need to offer help to their middle-aged parents (Havighurst, 1973a).

Fascinating discrepancies arise when children and parents are asked to report on the aid they give and receive. These less than accurate reports by the members correspond to the way they perceive their relationship. Parents tend to report that they give less help than children report they receive (Bengtson & Cutler, 1976). While older parents are overly modest about the amounts they give, in many cases they view themselves as receiving quite a bit more than they do. Their children, however, tend to report quite the opposite pattern. They see themselves as generous givers and modest receivers of aid (Turner, 1975). As the parent ages, he is viewed by self and child as more dependent. As a result he is seen as receiving more aid than ever before, particularly if the roles have reversed and the parent had been the primary giver when the children were young. Both parent and child, in this context, view their relationship in a new light, yet they attempt to maintain a consistent image of self, other, and the shared relationship.

Throughout, however, the older adult dislikes asking others for help (Bengtson & Cutler, 1976). When he does, he loses leverage in the power relationship. Family relations are often defined and transformed through communication of power, which can be expressed by means of the exchange of goods and services. If the relationship is harmonious, both parties benefit from the give and take, but if a struggle for power and influence is about to erupt, it often takes form in concrete acts of services given and withheld.

Communication by Contact

The majority of elderly and their adult children prefer to live in separate homes (Bettinghaus & Bettinghaus, 1976; Britton & Britton, 1972; Hess, 1974; Troll, 1971). Factors which increase the likelihood of an aged parent moving in include decreased material resources, poor health, widowhood and the availability of many adult children (Sussman, 1976; Troll, 1971).

Elderly adults are far from isolated from their adult children (Bengtson & Cutler, 1976). Most older adults have close relatives, or at least one child within visiting distance with whom they maintain frequent contact (Brown, 1960; Palmore, 1977; Troll, 1971). This is especially true for working-class populations. Middle-class children tend to live further away yet maintain strong family ties. Their moves are not to escape from parents but to follow career opportunities (Troll, 1971). The overall family life-cycle pattern involves maximum distance between middle-aged parents and their young adult children who are first establishing homes. Distances shrink between parent and at least one child by the time the parent is old (Baltes & Schaie, 1973; Hartup & Lempers, 1973; Troll, 1971).

Unlike their reports of mutual aid, elderly adults and middle-aged children perceive their visiting patterns accurately (Bengtson & Cutler, 1976). While older adults may lessen the extent of other social activities, they do not lessen the extent to which they interact with their families (Rosow, 1974). Even if children live far away, they telephone, write, and make long visits (Troll, 1971). Bonds of attachment cannot be erased by distance or by time (Troll & Smith, 1976).

The quality of the relationship takes precedence over the physical distance that separates parent and child. Research has shown that older adults not living with their child are no more likely than those who are to report feelings of neglect. Infrequent visits similarly do not always dampen the parent's morale (Brown, 1960). Feelings of neglect instead are more strongly related to a parent's expectations of a close relationship, particularly when the relationship fails to materialize (Brown, 1960; Lowenthal & Robinson, 1976). For example, a nine-year longitudinal study found no increase in feelings of neglect, although the elderly who were interviewed saw their families less and less over time (Britton & Britton, 1972). This is not to suggest, however, that frequent contact with one's child cannot boost morale (Rosow, 1967).

Overall, simply knowing how often the older adult sees his child tells us very little about the relationship they share. If, in turn, the relationship is one that is solidly grounded, the frequency of contact becomes that much less important. On the other hand, if the parent-child relationship is tense, the absence of a visit can be a powerful communication, with repercussions on both sides as they barter for power, dignity, and affection.

Family and Friends

Relationships with family and relationships with friends constitute two separate systems of social interaction (Rosow, 1967; Troll & Smith, 1976). Relationships between family members are intense but also compulsory. Relationships between friends are based more upon mutual consent (Troll, 1971). Often parent-child relationships are fraught with ambivalent feelings. There is more control over friendship relations that, in turn, can improve the quality of life (Lowenthal & Robinson, 1976). These two separate systems of relations each have implications for the other.

A study by Hampe and Blevins (1975) focused on the family and friendship relations among residents of a Western retirement hotel. The majority of residents were female, widowed or divorced, and of similar social background, satisfying the low-income requirement for residence in the housing unit. The researchers found that interaction with family members was strongly related to friendship patterns within the hotel setting. Those residents who visited more frequently with their adult children were less dependent upon hotel interactions than those who visited with other relatives. On the other hand, the number of friends the individual had, had no effect upon the frequency with which they visited relatives. Other research, too, has shown that frequency of neighboring cannot lessen the emotional ties with members of one's family (Rosow, 1967).

The study also found that those who received more visits from their adult children in actuality had more friends within the hotel as well. The researchers concluded that parent-child interactions carry over into interaction with friends. If the child fulfills emotional needs of the aging parent, there is energy left to expend upon friendships. A person who maintains a high morale and firm sense of the self finds it easier to initiate other meaningful relationships.

However, the researchers also found that high frequencies of interaction with either family or with friends did not eliminate a feeling of uselessness common to many older adults. They attributed this finding to three factors: many of the female adults acutely felt a loss of their cherished lifetime roles of mother and of wife; many visits with their children were much too superficial, since the children's visits may have been in response to society's unspoken law that children visit parents at least once in a while; and the elderly were no longer the initiators of many social encounters: they simply had no power over the timing of their visits.

For better or for worse, relationships with family have repercussions in one's friendship circles. Rosow's (1967) work illustrates a variety of patterns of neighboring as they become associated with relationships with adult children. Overall, he found that older people living in the community visited with their children more often than with neighbors; yet, if visiting with children was an infrequent event, the older adult did not necessarily make up for this lack by searching out friends.

If children lived nearby, and visits were rare and superficial, the older adult was more likely to depend upon his neighbors. In cases such as these, the self-confirmation desired in interaction is absent from the ritual visits of child and aging parent. The parent, therefore, improves his chances for confirmation through making friends. If children lived far away, however, the parents' reactions were not the same, since there were no high expectations of contact to begin with. The parent, in these cases, has an image of the self that he believes to be secure within the parent-child relationship. It cannot be denied if parent and child are apart. However, members of this latter group who were extremely dependent did attempt to compensate for the absence of children by means of neighboring.

Family and friendship groups become interconnected during old age. The nature of this connection is based upon factors such as place of residence, the family members that are seen, personality traits of the older adult, and the quality of the relationships. Relationships of high quality are sought in later life. To the extent that children cannot provide them from nearby or far away, the satisfactions of mutuality will be sought in other ways.

Reorganizing the Relationship

The quality of the parent-child relationship is dependent upon how power relations are handled by its members. A common pattern of parent-child interactions over the family life cycle involves a shift in the distribution of power and responsibility. When the child is young, the parent is in command. When the child grows up, the parent comes to rely upon the child. This transformation can take place at an imperceptible level if the relationship between parent and child is fulfilling and harmonious. On the other hand, some parents and children embark upon a power struggle, never quite able to renegotiate their relationship in a mutually satisfying way (Brim, 1968). Whether harmonious or hostile, both child and parent feel uneasy and anxious in dealing with these transformations within the relationship (Kalish & Knudtson, 1976; Pfeiffer, 1977).

In terms of basic principles of communication (as described in chapter two), if the relationship is ill defined, the message becomes distorted. This, in turn, contributes to further confusion and ambivalent feelings. The superficiality of many parent-child relationships is one means of coping with this ambiguity. Superficial behaviors allow the participants to conveniently avoid their deepest feelings about one another. Superficial interactions between parent and child can be described as a pseudocommunication. Misunderstanding and incorrect presuppositions are mutual. They go unprotested. On the other hand, if only the child, and not the parent, reacts in a ritual and routine way, the parent finds a mutual relationship impossible to achieve. Communication is stifling, not fulfilling.

On a practical level, dependency is fostered by the ill health of the parent who is primarily cared for by members of the family (Shanas & Maddox, 1976). The increased expenditure of energy and time in caring for an ailing parent often results in an implicit or explicit sense of resentment harbored by the child. The elderly parent, in turn, perceives those nonverbal cues of the child's feelings, leading to greater estrangement within their relationship (Lowenthal & Robinson, 1976).

On a less dramatic level, interviews with young adults revealed the belief that grown children should not have to accept or even listen to advice given by the parent, unless, of course, they themselves had actually sought the advice. The elderly adults who were interviewed, in contrast, felt that it was the parent's right and duty to advise their grown children (Britton & Britton, 1972). This conflict of presuppositions about the form of the relationship provides the perfect conditions for a stormy interchange, unless it is subdued by means of superficially blunting one's feelings.

The concept of role reversal in old age, however, need not prevail. The gerontologist Margaret Blenkner substitutes the concept of filial maturity (Troll, 1971). Filial maturity is achieved by the middle-aged adult who with maturity views his parent from a wider perspective. The parent is seen not only as he is during the present, but also as someone with a personal history contributing to his lifetime development.   As a result, the middle-aged adult can identify with the aging parent in a deeper and richer way. The parent too must contribute to the filial maturity of the child by providing an enviable view of development and adaptation to aging. If the tone of their relationship is one of respect and mutual affection, responsibilities may shift hands, but feelings remain secure at the least and enriched at the most throughout the process. Since at all stages of the life cycle, parent-child relations range from pathological to a healthy ideal, both the rewards of filial maturity and the conflicts of role reversals occur in varying degrees within and across the parent-child relationships during later life.

Emotional Investment

A related point of tension within the parent-child relationship involves the emotional energy each invests in the other. While both middle-aged children and elderly parents perceive solidarity in their relationship, the elderly parent perceives it even more strongly than the child (Bengtson & Cutler, 1976). Additionally, the middle-aged adult directs attention in action and thought to all members of the family, yet more attention is directed toward one's own child than one's aged parent (Troll, 1971). Hence, not only is power asymmetric, but so is the emotional investment within the joint relationship of child and aging parent.

Due to the busy and often overloaded schedule of the middle-aged child, and due to the anxieties that come with coping with an elderly parent, the attachment relation may suffer (Kalish & Knudtson, 1976).

The affection that the parent offers may not be returned in kind. Instead the child fulfills his obligations by providing services to the parent (Sussman, 1976). This constitutes another reason as to why there are misperceptions (mentioned earlier in this chapter) by both parent and child concerning the flow of mutual aid. If the child views his interaction with the parent as one based upon services rendered, he is likely to think that he gives far more to the parent than he receives, especially if all the parent has to offer is affection.

Since the elderly parent is more emotionally invested within the relationship, this provides optimal conditions for the principle of least interest (see chapter two). Based upon this principle, the parent, who appears to need the relationship more intensely, will be the more accommodating member of the pair: he has more to lose if the relationship dissolves. However, this is not to suggest that the middle-aged child fails to invest a great deal of emotion into the relationship. For example, most children support their parents through illness, disability, and stress, hesitant to let go even when professional help becomes essential (Troll & Smith, 1976).

Types of Troubles

A major source for identifying various areas of conflict between parent and child is derived from clinical evidence. Although clients who seek clinical help often have problems that approach pathological severity, elements of these problems are likely to occur at less intense levels in the context of more normal relationships. Simos (1970, 1973) describes several problems that middle-class adult children experienced with their aged parents while seeking advice from a family agency.

Nearly all the elderly parents of this group had psychological problems, yet in many cases physical problems were so severe that they prevented the child from dealing with the more psychological aspects of the relationship. Distortion of messages about the relationship between the parent and child were difficult to rectify, since they were overshadowed by physical concerns.

Additionally, it appeared that psychological problems that had occurred when parent and child were younger had intensified over the years. Adult children would easily accept a parent's psychological problem if they could attribute it to the process of aging. However, if it was simply another version of earlier parent-child conflicts, anger about the problem and towards the parent would result. Several relationships did improve when feelings were sorted out. But those relationships left unresolved were ones in which the adult child perceived his early childhood as deprived of parental affection. As a result, when the parent aged, he was cared for responsibly, but viewed as a burden. Within communication, resentments are perceived, whether explicit or implicit, verbal or nonverbal, exacerbating already highly tenuous relationships. For example, several of the adults experienced little pleasure interacting with their parents, yet felt obligated to the parent because of the blood relationship and because they felt it necessary to repay the parent for childhood care. Yet parents are often painfully aware, consciously or unconsciously, of these interpersonal feelings within their interactions.

Many problems surfaced directly as a function of the aging process and the losses of old age. Often the parent would turn to the child to take the place of those who had died, such as a husband or a wife. In these cases, the adult child would be unable and unwilling to play the role of the missing person. Communicatively, this represents an interactional impasse, since the role relationship is defined quite differently by each member of the pair, distorting any message content embedded within their exchanges.

In addition, the adult child was often unable to interpret the parent's feelings or social problems accurately. For example, many parental symptoms and psychological defenses against loss were interpreted as crankiness or emotional coolness when they were really due to depression. Similarly, adult children would react to their parents' social problems in ways they'd react to their own. Some would push their parents into activities no longer desirable to the older adult although attractive to the children themselves. These problems indicate that different presuppositions of both parent and child are underlying the messages they convey. Both the social context and personal needs of the other are misinterpreted. They perceive the content of each message from differing points of view, unable to achieve any semblance of mutuality or role taking in their exchange.

Finally, the child views the parent as a model for coping with old age, just as during childhood the parent had modeled adulthood behaviors. The adult child during middle age either accepts or rejects the parental example. When acceptance occurs, it is a prime example of filial maturity. If the model is rejected, it usually is done under circumstances where the child finds parental behaviors discomforting and threatening. This in turn contributes to the tension of the relationship and (in the extreme) discomfirmation of the parent as a source for self-definition. The self-concept and esteem of the aging parent are seriously challenged as a result.

A Rewarding Role

We tend to view the role of grandparent as one held by the elderly, yet it should be noted that many grandparents are actually middle aged (Troll, 1971). Neugarten and Weinstein (1964) identify several different styles of grandparenting that correspond largely to the age of the grandparent.

With regard to the dynamics of family relationships, Robertson (1975) has shown that it is the middle generation that shapes the grandparent-grandchild relationship. However, should the grandparent and grandchild have the opportunity to develop their relationship on their own, expectations transmitted by the middle generation will not be as compelling. In general, stronger ties with grandparents exist when parent and child live nearby. Regardless of distance, the role of grandparent is one that must be worked at. The grandparent must be dedicated and active in order to play the role well (Troll, 1971).

Because there are many styles of grandparenting and varying degrees of closeness in the relationship between generations, it is not surprising that the adult children's feelings toward grandparents are similarly varied (Troll, 1971). However, the majority of grandparents are satisfied and pleased with the role, for it gives them more of a sense of identity and place within society (Neugarten & Weinstein, 1964).

In recent times the four-generation family is increasingly common, because of the expanding length of life of elderly adults (Townsend, 1968; Troll, 1971). The presence of four generations influences the perception of grandparent-grandchild relationships. Bekker and Taylor (1966) have found that not only do college students tend to view their own grandparents more favorably than they do the aged in general, but members of four-generation families feel even more favorably than members of three-generation families. The researchers concluded that four-generation grandchildren are able to acquire more experience and understanding of the elderly, and that they view their grandparents as particularly youthful when compared with their older great-grandparents. The resultant picture is one of an active, responsible older adult. If others react to the grandparent in a positive, affirming way, the grandparent tends to view the self in a similarly favorable light.

The role of grandparent, overall, can be gratifying during old age. It reinforces a sense of self and purpose in relation to others, yet not all elderly adults desire this role; to others it is not available. Success in fulfilling the role of grandparent is conditioned by many factors, such as traveling distance, family structure, involvement, personality, and age.

Most older adults in modern society are embedded within a social network of family relations. Members of this kinship network, particularly the child, aid the parent in his dealings with the wider social world and the preservation of continuity and a positive sense of self. Communications within the family implicitly support the older adult's view of the world and self-image if the relationship is secure, yet the relationship between parent and child is asymmetric. Mutual aid and visiting patterns are often a means for displaying who has power within the relationship, and if mutuality is lacking or expectations of children unfulfilled, the older adult may be prone to seek self-confirmation in friendship relations.

The shift in power and control from parent to child during old age provokes anxiety and a sense of uncertainty among all parties concerned: their images of the relationship must undergo transformation, and their expectations of one another become inconsistent with their past. Some parents and children deal admirably with this role transition;

others endure a prolonged state of tension in an unresolved relationship. The feelings involved are expressed within their communications, be it by means of blunting external feelings to avoid a stormy exchange, or by subtle cues of resentment or a struggle for control. Whether positive or negative, conscious or unconscious, social cues are transmitted. In the process, they improve or reduce the quality of life in old age.

NEIGHBORS

The older adult's social activities are largely determined by where he lives. Accessibility of family, friends and social facilities depend upon neighborhood location. The dwellings of aged persons range from low-income subsidized housing to expensive retirement communities, and from areas heavily populated with other aged persons to neighborhoods that contain a wider mixture of age groups. It should be noted, however, that only a small proportion of the elderly live in either age-segregated public housing oir retirement communities (Neugarten & Hagestad, 1976). Each of these residential patterns has a differing effect upon the quality of the elderly adult's life style, social activities, and adaptation to aging.

Making a Move

The elderly move far less often than do young adults (Lawton, 1977). Most older adults report that they are satisfied with their current housing, yet when there are few alternatives to one's current residence – from lack of funds and the stress of a move – it is only reasonable to expect that the older adult will convince himself and others that he really wants to stay put (Lawton & Nahemow, 1973). Those elderly adults who do move more often tend to display rather specific characteristics, including marital separation, low income, less education, good health, a history of mobility, and a tendency to rent (Lawton, 1977).

On the other hand, many aged persons resist making a move because of the network of friendships they have built within the neighborhood. This network provides a valuable resource. When older adults actually do decide to move, it is often because they are unhappy with their neighborhood and home (Lawton & Nahemow, 1973).

Select Settings

The housing arrangement the older adult selects has major implications for his social life and sense of well-being. Personality is, however, an intervening factor: different types of people select different types of housing arrangements. One study, for example, found that those elderly who applied for residence in a high-rise public housing project for the aged saw themselves as middle aged (although they were 72 years and above), were low income but felt a strong personal need to live an independent life, and were dissatisfied with their social lives in their previous neighborhoods (Carp, 1968). Consequently, most older adults selecting to live in age-segregated public housing are satisfied with their choice after they make the move (Lawton & Nahemow, 1973). Most elderly adults, overall, prefer not to live in this type of housing and therefore would be unhappy, unlike the self-selected group (Teaff et al., 1978).

There is also a tendency by the management of age-segregated housing projects to choose as tenants individuals who are healthy, competent, and capable of independent living (Carp, 1976). These characteristics, from the beginning, of this select population, nearly guarantee a pleasant way of life. Because they are self-selected and the adults are competent and self-assured, adaptation to the new housing and facility in making friends are common.

Contented Communities

Many studies have been conducted on residents of age-segregated housing and neighborhoods that are densely populated by the elderly, as these are easy targets for the researcher who wants access to many older adults. Results have shown many positive effects of these types of communities upon the quality of life in old age and upon social interaction. Residents of these communities, whether in subsidized housing or neighborhood settings, often maintain a higher morale than aged adults in other areas. In these communities the older adults develop their own norms for behavior and give one another social roles to play in community affairs (Bennett & Eckman, 1973; Teaff et al., 1978). In essence, the elderly develop a speech community of their own. The meanings of the language they use are best comprehended by members of the community. Membership fosters a sense of security and identity. It gives the aged adult a place and purpose in relation to others. Mutual understanding is more readily achieved.

Additionally, residents are protected from ridicule and feelings of inadequacy when they are compared with younger adults (Carp, 1976; Streib, 1976). Older adults in all types of housing fear contact with the very young precisely for this reason. Teaff et al. (1978), in a study of varying living arrangements in which older adults reside, found that within the more age-mixed settings, activities sponsored by housing projects as open to those of all ages in fact tended to develop norms of behavior that favored the younger people. In these groups the old were subjected to unpleasant stereotypes of old age expressed by younger residents.

Comparisons of those who are accepted and those rejected among applicants to public housing projects for the aged show similarly positive effects of housing for the aged. A major study comparing these two groups was undertaken by Frances Carp (1968). She found that the residents who were accepted continued to perceive themselves as middle aged and maintained higher opinions of themselves. These characteristics were supported by appropriate age norms and expectations, and increased contact with other elderly who confirmed these favorable images.

Rosow (1967), in a study of community-dwelling elderly, found that greater density of an older-adult population within an immediate area (i.e., 50 percent or more residents are elderly) corresponded to a greater number of friends that the aged person tended to have. He also reported that the loss of roles, such as spouse, worker, and provider strengthened this relationship between density and neighboring. Other research on this topic has supported these results (Streib, 1976).

In the same vein, the study by Hampe and Blevins (1975) (discussed in the preceding section) found that the elderly adults of the retirement hotel misperceived themselves as receiving more visits than they paid to their neighbors and friends. This is interpreted as a direct result of one's self-perception as a desirable friend within the housing setting. The adults in this study did not show this pattern of misperception where they previously lived. Thus, not only are more friendships available, but they also are more personally satisfying in the new housing setting.

In conjunction with an increased number of friendships in housing environments that are heavily populated with older adults, there can be a relative decrease in contact with family yet increased satisfaction with both friendship and family relationships (Carp, 1968; Havighurst, 1973a). The increased independence and more fulfilling social life reduces the dependency of aged persons upon their families. In turn, an asymmetric, ambivalent, and frustrating parent-child relationship is avoided or repaired because of neighborhood satisfaction.

Overall, studies of age-density and age-segregated environments indicate increased opportunities for social interaction, high morale (regardless of level of activity), greater satisfaction with the housing arrangement, and increased neighborhood mobility (Bennett & Eckman, 1973; Carp, 1968, 1976; Lawton, 1977; Teaff et al., 1968). Compared to nonresident applicants, Carp (1968) reported improved physical and mental health and decreased requests for medical care, while the opposite trend appeared for nonresidents, who remained unhappy in their current environments. Research has continued to show that the positive effects of this type of housing are not short lived but continue over the period of residence (Carp, 1976). Although only a minority select age-segregated environments, a larger number of older adults live within a neighborhood community. The extent to which these communities house many older adults or not, strongly affects the aging adult's pattern of living, social life, and sense of well-being.

Status, Space and Transportation

Age density in the neighborhood is a critical factor for satisfaction and healthy adjustment for many elderly adults. However, factors other than density are involved in the maintenance of high morale. Material resources, for example, are an intervening factor. Participation and morale are higher in retirement communities than in hotels for the elderly precisely because of the privileged status of adults in retirement communities (Bennett & Eckman, 1973; Carp, 1976). The spatial composition of the housing environment has an additional impact upon social behaviors (Lawton, 1977). How often the residents see one another depends upon factors such as the position of apartments and open areas for social encounters. It is also quite possible that moves to new housing increase morale and well-being, simply because the opportunity for interaction with just about anyone has improved (Carp, 1976).

A final characteristic of residential environments that influences social activity and the quality of life is the convenience of transportation and the ease of mobility. Social isolation is often a result of poor transportation facilities (Lawton & Nahemow, 1973; Muth, 1976). Lawton and Nahemow (1973), in a review of research concerning this problem, find that inadequate transportation to social activities not only lessens one's social opportunities but sadly increases dependence on others. In a study of a community in New York City, elderly residents were totally dependent upon public transportation. Family members provided transportation services for family gatherings only. Hence, most activities were local. The elderly would do lots of walking, running their daily errands, or merely getting a breath of fresh air (Lawton & Nahemow, 1973).

In communities such as these, the neighbor relationship is crucial. One's neighbors provide an available social network for support and interaction, especially in light of the limited opportunities for branching one's contacts out into wider geographic areas. The availability of other aged adults improves the prospects for developing this network, a network that establishes age-appropriate modes of behavior and norms for communication. When this occurs, the older adult need look no farther for social support.

The place of residence of the older adult can enhance or discourage a sense of well-being and social opportunities. Whether one moves to a housing project designed for older adults or continues to live in a neighborhood where many others are old, the chances for the maintenance of high morale and social support are vastly improved beyond those settings where the elderly are isolated from others. The elderly set up speech communities with their surrounding neighbors, providing norms and social roles appropriate to their age group. Mutuality of expectations and understanding is enhanced, and as a result a positive image of self can be maintained. Other factors contribute or detract from a sense of well-being, such as economic status, spatial location, and ease in getting around. Throughout, however, neighbors provide a valuable network of social support.

FRIENDS

Throughout the life cycle, friends are a crucial element of one's social world. However, the nature and salience of these relations change over time. Many older adults have fewer friends in later life (Britton & Britton, 1972; Rosow, 1967). The number of friendships that one maintains is often a function of who is available. During old age friends and neighbors are often one and the same (Hampe & Blevins, 1975; Lawton & Nahemow, 1973; Rosow, 1967), and after retirement males often shift from the workplace to neighbors in pursuit of friends (Lawton, 1977).

Social-class differences in patterns of friendship relations should also be noted. Working-class aged turn more toward their neighbors for developing friendship ties. Middle-class adults tend to have more friends who are spread out over a wider area (Rosow, 1967, 1968).

What is a Friend?

The perception of friendship relations changes throughout the life cycle (Lowenthal & Robinson, 1976). Loeb (1973), for example, conducted a study of how the meanings attributed to the concept of friendship change across the life span. She found that pre-adults (aged 19 and under) felt friendship encompassed many qualities: acceptance, mutual liking, trust, enjoyment, respect, loyalty, mutual aid, and shared recreation, talk, and ideas. Mature adults (aged 50 to 59) attributed fewer qualities to the concept of friendship: respect, mutual liking, enjoyment, trust, and mutual aid. Elderly adults (aged 70 plus) characterized friendship as including only acceptance and trust. Loeb interpreted these results as indicative of value crystallization with age. However, on a practical level, the data may also indicate the older adult's openness to a wider range of people for potential friendships because of a greater need for friends, greater acceptance of others, plus a measure of cohort differences in attitudes toward friendship. Since the older adults of this study did not require much of friendship, these findings correspond to Rosow's (1967) observation that with old age many friendship ties may become more shallow. In truth, however, the patterns of friendship among the aged vary from shallow and superficial to intimate and confidential, an issue that is explored in the remainder of this section.

Mixed Feelings

Friendship relations during old age can be dampened by the person's feelings about his own old age. As a result, ambivalent emotions surround many friendships among aged adults (de Beauvoir, 1973). Elderly adults often enjoy the company of one another. They share common memories, perceptions, and interpretations about the world.

These shared perspectives foster a smooth and unruffled communication. Role taking is done with relative ease, for they are thinking on similar wavelengths, but viewing another aged adult can be a painful reminder of one's own old age, information that is unattractive to the individual.

This mixture of good and bad feelings is more common among middle-class adults, who are more defensive concerning old age. At times they actually prefer not to associate with others their own age rather than acknowledge that they are old (Rosow, 1967). This behavior is in line with Goffman's concept of 'saving face' (see chapter two). The face the older adult presents is one of a youthful person. Encounters with other aged adults who respond to this person as if he were old threaten the youthful social face so important to the person.

On the other hand, elderly adults who are old-old (aged 75 and over) are especially prone to seek many friends in neighborhoods with large populations of elderly (Rosow, 1967). By this stage in life, they cannot continue to deny personal aging simply by avoiding older adults. Instead they pursue a search for friends who themselves will support a youthful outlook. Research shows, for example, that after age 70 participation in friendship cliques results in reduced self-perception as old when compared with those outside these groups (Bell, 1967). Group members arrive at a consensual understanding of their social reality. This in turn provides the context for their communication with one another. The reality of these older adults is that they are youthful, not old. Their interactions are used to confirm each member's self-image in this manner, thereby supporting high morale, self-confidence, and desire to be consistent.

Selection and Status

A basic social tendency is to choose one's friends from one's status group. The most obvious status group is comprised of others of one's own age. This group best exemplifies a mutually shared background and values (Riley, 1976). Hence, even if fearful of having the self associated with old age, the older adult selects most of his friends from among those within his age range (Rosow, 1967). In fact, during the later stages of life, age may become a more important criterion for the choosing of friends, because other roles — such as those in the work world — are no longer available as bases upon which to build friendship circles (Neugarten & Hagestad, 1976). Other status similarities, however, also influence the selection of friends. These include sex, social class, ethnic group, marital status, beliefs, and life style (Riley, 1976; Rosow, 1967, 1968).

Older adults have more friends when their neighborhoods have high concentrations of elderly, further supporting the basic idea that peers are selected of similar age (Neugarten & Hagestad, 1976). In these areas, there is a preference for other aged persons as friends, and a decreased search for alternatives such as finding younger friends

(Rosow, 1967). As noted before, our society tends to be age graded. People of the same age-range are afforded the same opportunities and requirements by virtue of their age. This mutuality of experience makes friendships among age peers all the more comfortable. They share a basic starting point upon which to develop a rich relationship. Neugarten and Hagestad (1976) add that in our society we take it for granted that friends are people of the same age. In fact, when a close relationship exists between people of widely differing ages, it is sometimes not even called a friendship, or it is labeled with qualifiers by those involved. For example, a young adult might say, "I've become friendly with an old woman."

Approaches to Affiliation

The sociologist Irving Rosow (1967) conducted an in-depth analysis of friendship patterns of aged persons living in different apartment buildings in the Cleveland area. His results revealed that extensive friendship activities are not always desirable or necessary for the well-being of older adults. Instead, there are various patterns of interaction among elderly friends, with a variety of end results.

Rosow found that his elderly subjects fell into five friendship patterns: a) the cosmopolitan, who had least contact with neighbors and no desire for more friends. This group was predominantly middle class, with interests that did not include the immediate residential area; b) the phlegmatic (constituting only four percent of the sample), who had little contact with neighbors and no desire for more friends. This group was predominantly working class, significantly older, passive, withdrawn, and satisfied to have no social contact except for regular visits with children; c) the isolated, who had little contact with neighbors or friends, yet maintained a desire for more friends. This group was predominantly middle class with limited social opportunities, yet lacked the necessary social skills for initiating friendship relations; d) the sociable, who had frequent contact with friends and neighbors and no desire for more friends. This group was primarily working class, female, and widowed; e) the insatiable, who had frequent contact with friends and neighbors yet desired more. This group was similar to the sociable group in class, sex, and marital status, but also tended to be childless and lonely, regardless of number of contacts. They were so intensely in need of friends that their interactions had little purpose except to amass a large number of friends. Relations under these circumstances are highly unsatisfactory. They are initiated under false pretenses. Mutuality is avoided, and this in turn feeds the person's insatiable need for more friends.

Each of these groups clearly maintains a unique approach to social life. The cosmopolitan, phlegmatic, and sociable are not problematic older adults. They receive what they need from their social relations, be they extensive or confined. The isolated, on the other hand, fare poorly wherever they live. When confronted with sets of potential friends, they continue to live in isolation, never quite able to develop skills of social interaction. The insatiable live in a similar world of isolation. They pseudocommunicate with those they call friends, but never truly share. A frantic search for many friends precludes the investment of time and energy necessary to establish meaningful exchanges in a mutually constructed dialogue.

Rosow concluded that there is an inverse relationship between personal morale and the desire for more friends, regardless of the environment. The isolated remain unhappy because they want to make friends but can't. The insatiable remain unhappy because they make too many friends but lack the substance of social exchange. Because the elderly population is comprised of many and diverse personalities, it is important to qualify any conclusions about the impact of the setting upon interaction. For some older adults, increased opportunities for friendships are beneficial. For others there is no need to pursue any friendships beyond those that exist. For the problem group of adults, the sad conclusion is reached that all the potential friends in the world cannot allay their discontent.

Quality Friends

An enlightening research study that clarifies how the elderly experience their friendship relations was conducted by Lowenthal and Haven (1968). They focused upon the type of friend who is called a confidant — a friend with whom one shares one's deepest thoughts and concerns. Of all one's friends, the confidant provides the closest relationship.

Lowenthal and Haven (1968) found that if the aged adult had at least one person in whom he could confide, he could curtail many other social activities with little or no risk of depression. On the other hand, one could be quite depressed in the midst of an active social life if there is a conspicuous lack of a confidant relationship. Worst of all is the situation where a confidant and a social life are simultaneously absent from the life of the older adult.

The confidant relationship corresponds to a friendship pattern that includes extensive self-disclosure. Self-disclosure occurs only gradually between those who pursue a relationship. Once the pattern is established, a closeness begins to develop. The confidant relationship is the closest approximation in the social world of the older adult to a state of intersubjectivity (see chapter two). Confidants understand one another at their deepest feeling level. Taking the role of the other is accomplished well within this context. Underlying the process is a tacit understanding and acceptance of the self and of the other. Together they form a unified group, a 'we', when compared with all others. When these feelings are mutual, intersubjectivity is complete. It must be noted, however, that some relationships, valuable as they may be, only go one way. In these cases an interlacing of perspectives nevertheless occurs, as one shares with the other basic assumptions about the self and one's place in the world.

Lowenthal and Haven concluded that the confidant relationship serves as a buffer against the social losses that accompany the aging process. This basic idea serves well as a framework for viewing previous findings about the aged. For example, as the adult loses his social roles, he turns even more strongly towards the neighborhood to seek out friends. Certainly this is done in an effort to develop a buffering relationship. The loss of a confidant relationship nearly always results in depression.

However, Lowenthal and Haven also found that not all older adults have the benefit of a confidant. Those who do not have a confidant often have low morale, but do not present themselves as persons who are burdened with severe psychological problems. This was attributed to the fact that several of these loners had been isolates nearly all their lives; old age was no different. Others had maintained an intimate relationship in their past, thereby sustaining their current means of coping in old age. Morale, however, takes a plunge when a confidant is gone. For example, those who were widowed within seven years and who had confidants also, had higher morale than those who were married yet lacked confidants. Similarly, those retired and with confidants ranked the same on measures of morale as those who were still working but were lacking confidants.

Lowenthal and Haven also reported sex, status, and social class differences in the proclivity towards and selection of other persons as confidants. Females are more likely to participate in confidant relationships. This is no surprise in light of the sex differences in general friendship patterns. Females tend to have more friends and are more involved in neighborhood networks of social relations (Bengtson et al., 1977; Rosow, 1967). In light of these rich opportunities, they are bound to develop some intimate friendships. Females are the more sensitive sex when it comes to social settings. Lowenthal and Haven add that women are capable of establishing these close relations with a wider range of persons than are men.

For all the adults in the study, however, spouse, child, and friend were equally likely to serve as confidants. Siblings and other relatives less often played this role. Additionally, married persons were most likely to have confidants, single persons least, with widowed then divorced lying somewhere between. Correspondingly, Rosow (1967) has shown that married elderly are less likely than the widowed or the single to seek more friends in neighborhoods with many older adults. If satisfied with their relationship, they need not look any further. Similarly, the greater likelihood of confidant relationships among married adults may serve as a partial explanation for the lower incidence of psychopathology among elderly persons who are married (Pfeiffer, 1977).

Lowenthal and Haven surprisingly found that the wife frequently serves the confidant role for the husband, yet she mentions her husband less frequently as serving this role for herself. Females are more versatile in their choice of confidants. This serves later on as an aid to adjustment when the woman is widowed. Males, in contrast, often remarry soon after the wife has died. For a wife, in many cases, provides the only confidant relationship the husband knows and feels he needs.

In terms of social class, those above the median economic level are more likely to have a confidant than those who are below. This corresponds to Rosow's (1967, 1968) finding that middle-class aged adults have more friends than do the working class, and are also less reliant upon neighbors for social activities. Middle-class aged often forego superficial relations with many neighbors for the rewards of substantial and intimate ties.

No matter what class, the confidant can improve the quality of life, whether other social ties are extensive or nonexistent. Simply counting one's number of friends is like counting the number of visits. They tell us of the frequencies, but not of the basic substance. In studying the impact of friendship relations of elderly adults, we need to know how close or superficial the interactions are, be they with a family member, a distant friend, or the neighbor next door. If intersubjectivity and the mutuality it embodies is a part of the social encounters of the older adult, morale is enhanced, identity sustained, and the sharing of taking the role of the other enriches the quality of life.

Friendships remain an important part of life throughout old age, whether or not the older adult has many friends or just a few. Most of the friends of older adults are people of the same age. The mutuality of their past and present experience overrides the fear that one's age peer is a poignant reflection of one's own old age. In fact, during the latest stages of aging, friends can forestall self-perception as old.

There are many and varied patterns of interaction with friends among the aged, some of which are fulfilling and some in which mutuality is painfully lacking. The key to morale, however, is the knowledge that one has a confidant, someone with whom to disclose one's reflections about self, the other, and the context they share.

THE MASS MEDIA

A one-way communication in which most older adults participate is the reception of the messages of television, radio, and the newspaper. The mass media is a major component of the older adult's leisure activity. On the average, the older adult allocates approximately three to six hours per day to mass media consumption (Atkin, 1974).

Television viewing is the dominant form of media consumption during old age. Atkin (1976), in a review of the research on use of mass media by the elderly, finds that television viewing increases steadily from ages 40 through 80. However, the number of hours devoted to this activity varies with social class and geographic setting. Television provides the least obstacles to understanding by the older adult. It is both visual and auditory, providing sufficient redundancy for the older adult to understand, particularly if he is experiencing sensory deterioration. Most older adults, as a result, express satisfaction with television viewing (Atkin, 1976).

The aged are especially dedicated to news and information content, whether from television, radio, or the paper. By the age of 55, the adult reads newspapers more than the national average and increases this activity until 65 to 70 years of age. Informational television viewing increases more rapidly than entertainment viewing, so that exposure to news becomes greater for the elderly population than for younger age groups (Atkin, 1976). Atkin suggests that the preference for news and information in T.V. viewing is a direct attempt to compensate for the stable and unexciting world of the older adult. In this way it provides stimulation and subsequent adaptation. However, it may also stimulate the older adult in a very personal way, for news and information touch upon the concerns of the older adult as he reviews the events of his life and their place in historical time. By directly viewing current events, he is able to compare and contrast his own past time to the present from a widening perspective.

The mass media performs a number of other functions for the older adult. The most apparent function is its entertainment value. More significantly, the mass media can be used to compensate for decreasing social contacts and organization participation. Television becomes a new companion for the older adult, as he becomes familiar with the friendly and accepting faces that appear on the T.V. screen (Atkin, 1976; Graney & Graney, 1974; Hess, 1974). It is important to note, however, the research of Lowenthal and Boler (1965), which showed that those aged adults who voluntarily disengaged from their social activities actually decreased their use of the mass media, whereas those who had involuntarily disengaged had increased their media participation. For this latter group, therefore, the mass media may have served a substitute companionship function. The one-way direction of this form of exchange can certainly not sufficiently replace the two-way relations that have been lost. On the other hand, for those elderly adults who lead active social lives, television programs may serve as conversation pieces for subsequent interaction, providing a mutual context to initiate social exchange (Atkin, 1976).

Finally, it is important to note the potential detrimental effects of the media, and in particular television, upon older individuals. Most research indicates a predominance of negative stereotypes of the aged and the glorification of youthful images in television programs and their commercials (Aronoff, 1974; Atkin, 1976). If older adults are isolated with few opportunities for social contact, these images can be damaging to the aged adult's self-concept (Hess, 1974). As a result, he is never quite sure if the content of the media is accurate and real, or if his age peers can provide more attractive models of adaptation during old age.

The elderly are heavy consumers of the mass media, and in particular television programs. They are especially drawn towards the news and information content. The media serves several functions for the aged population, including entertainment, social relations, stimulation, and self-assessment. It is important, however, for the older adult to discuss media content with others like himself, in order to appraise the degree to which it is representative of the elderly person's competencies and the social environment most beneficial to adaptation in later life.

The stimulation of the media alone is insufficient in later life. The stress and strain of growing old requires more extensive support. The potential networks of social support for the older adult are provided by family, neighbors, and friends, who at times are one and the same. Each of these networks can make a unique contribution to the quality of the life of the older adult.

Relations with the family help to maintain a continuous sense of self. Emotional attachments with family members prevail over time and distance. The mutual aid and support of the family serve a practical purpose and also provide an indirect way for conveying social relations. The structure of family relationships develop and change throughout life, and with old age the adult child often must take on the responsibility of looking out for the aging parent. While some parents and children communicate with ease, others struggle for power and influence as they define and redefine an unsettled social relationship. When relationships within the family are harmonious and secure, the communication between members enables the aging adult to perceive the self in a positive manner. In contrast, if the family relations are ambiguous and tense, the older adult may feel compelled to seek self-confirmation from alternative sources.

A viable source of self-confirmation during later life is participation in a cohesive network of neighbors within the community. When neighbors are of a similar age and social status, they often form a system of norms for behavior and role relations among themselves. Playing a part within such networks bolsters one's sense of security and purpose. Communication is facilitated by a common social context and interpretation of events.

While family provides the emotional backbone and neighbors provide the social context, friends provide the aged adult with the opportunity to confide. The presence of a confidant during later life serves to boost morale. The communication between confidants is mutual and gratifying to the parties concerned. Implicit within their exchange is an acceptance of self, of other, and of the intimate group that they form and replenish each time they interact.

Communication with family, neighbors, and friends can be highly supportive. They can help the older adult to maintain a self-image of competence and worth. This image, in turn, enables the adult to effectively confront the wider environment, an encounter that is discussed in depth in chapter eight.

8 Communicative Interaction and the Aged

Communication with others is a vital human activity. The need to interact remains important to the individual through all stages of life. The elderly are no exception. This is not to say that the older adult must continuously interact with others. Quality, not quantity of communication is the crucial factor. Successful communication experiences contribute to the psychological, social, and biological well-being of the older adult. Opportunities for communication are essential for successful coping.

Communication with the older adult, however, is different in form and function from communication with others at different stages of life. The older adult has accumulated a lifetime of experience. He thinks about the world differently from those younger than himself. The older adult also confronts a different social world than the young, a world where roles have been taken away and where the number of social guidelines have been significantly reduced. Finally, the older adult is a different biological being. His senses are no longer quite as acute as they were earlier in life, and the way he deals with perceptual problems are different than the young. Hence, the needs of the older adult and the demands of the environment are qualitatively different from those at other stages of life. Communication with the older adult must account for these features of later life in order to ensure a successful, mutually satisfying exchange. This chapter applies the information discussed in previous chapters towards an examination of communication with the aged adult.

REMINISCING: A LOOK AT THE PAST

Prior to an examination of how older adults communicate within their social environment, it is important to understand just what is on the mind of the elderly adult. A personality development common to the transition from middle adulthood to old age is an increasing inner

135

orientation. The older adult has embarked upon a personal life review and assessment. The older adult thinks about the present and future, but reminiscing dominates many of his thoughts (Butler, 1968). Thus, within communication there is frequent reference to the past, sometimes quite explicitly, at other times implicit.

The older adult surveys his previous experiences throughout life and places them within a coherent, thematic framework for recall. Butler (1968) attributes the process of the life review in later life to the recognition that death is near, the increase in free and unstructured time, and the inability to use one's work to forestall deeper thoughts about the self. In the context of communication, increased reminiscence may involve an effort to defend one's self-esteem and to gain support for the validity of one's beliefs about the world — two factors which are seriously threatened with the onset of old age (Chown, 1977; Meacham, 1977). Yet reminiscence in solitude occurs quite frequently if others with whom to share the past are conspicuously absent (Beattie, 1976).

Reminiscing contributes to self-awareness, self-acceptance, and a sense of personal continuity. For these reasons, it is a highly adaptive process (Butler, 1968; Lowenthal & Chiriboga, 1973; Meacham, 1977). Negative consequences, however, are also possible during old age. These include depression, guilt, and a state of inner panic. Butler (1968) attributes these negative effects to the practice of life review in solitude. The older adult runs the risk of depression if isolated from those with whom he is emotionally attached, and if he lacks a system of social supports within his social environment. Additionally, the life review is to no avail if the personality of the older adult has never been well adjusted, and if the adult has many regrets about the way he has lived his life.

Research has shown that the elderly recall many people from their distant past when requested to list (within a ten-minute period) the people they have met during their lives. In contrast, young and middle-aged adults recall more people whom they've recently known (Riegel, 1972). The younger adult is much more involved with the present than is the older adult, who recalls more readily the people and events of his early history. This is not to suggest that the older adult's recall of the past is precise and accurate (Craik, 1977), for this is not the purpose that reminiscing serves. The older adult remembers what he needs and wants to recall, so that he may interpret his life in a more satisfying way (Meacham, 1977).

The way the elderly view the world and the part they have played within it differs in form and function from those younger than themselves. Both young and old must account for these differences if they attempt to interact, for if each does not take the role of the other, misunderstanding is inevitable. How this is managed by both is discussed later within this chapter.

THE SENSES AND COMMUNICATION

During the process of normal aging, the auditory and vocal biological systems no longer function at optimal levels (Botwinick, 1973; Corso, 1977; Hutchinson & Beasley, 1976; Jarvik & Cohen, 1973; Ryan & Capadano, 1978). Hearing difficulties of aged adults are exacerbated when speakers speak at rapid rates and when there is interference or stress. Simply speaking more loudly does not make speech more intelligible. In addition, the high degree of cautiousness of the elderly adult may prevent him from responding to the spoken word if he is not completely sure about the content he is hearing (Jarvik & Cohen, 1973).

These biological factors can impede the success of communication. At the extreme, Eisdorfer has reported that elderly adults with impaired hearing display poor communication skills and less than optimal adaptation to environmental demands (cited in Oyer & Oyer, 1976). The uncertainty about what is said is disturbing to the adult. It instills a sense of confusion that reduces adaptation in a cyclic manner. Britton and Britton (1972) also have found that over a nine-year period the majority of their elderly interviewees had decreased in their ability to see and hear. As a result their interaction skills had been reduced.

Hearing impairment often leads to difficulties if the older adult refuses to accept it as a problem and instead blames his poor understanding on the language of the speaker. This is certainly frustrating, as well as insulting to the individual speaking, and decreases the desirability of making further contact. The onset of presbycusis, the hearing impairment of old age, is usually insidious (Willeford, 1971). This unpleasant sequence therefore becomes a real possibility during old age.

Impaired vision further complicates communication. Joint visual reference, typically taken for granted, is more difficult to achieve. Participants appear to be looking in the same direction, yet they may be seeing and saying very different things. Topics have to be redefined and the conversation reorganized once these misunderstandings come to light. Additionally, the impaired sensory capacities of older adults often cause them to move closer to one another (Lawton & Nahemow, 1973). The younger adult, as a result, feels uncomfortable in this setting, for culturally he is more accustomed to greater physical distance during communication.

Paradoxically, as sensory and perceptual capacities decline, the elderly individual becomes increasingly more dependent upon communication (Corso, 1977). For only through communication can one keep in touch with one's surroundings. However, communication with the hearing or visually impaired adult constitutes an extremely stressful situation for the participants involved. The young adult becomes fatigued by the disrupted communication (Oyer, 1976). The older adult becomes frustrated by his inability to perceive the speech clearly and in turn to respond appropriately.

THOUGHT PROCESSES AND COMMUNICATION

Research on cognition during later life has shown that older adults take longer to react and that with age they become more susceptible to fatigue. Within communication settings these behaviors are deceiving. They give the appearance of a passive adult, or one who is disinterested, when in truth he is suffering from the slowness of old age (Oyer, 1976). If the adult's behavior is interpreted as lack of interest, the other party is likely to lose interest as well. Communication with such an adult is unrewarding: conversation that is not mutual is like no conversation at all.

Problem-solving research results indicate that the elderly have difficulties in asking appropriate, strategic questions and in synthesizing complex bits of information. These characteristics have implications for conversational interaction. On a practical level, the older adult may need help in learning to ask appropriate questions when there is a task at hand (Haack, 1976). On a social level, the elderly adult may find it difficult to maintain a smooth flow of conversation during interaction. The given-new strategy of conversation (see chapter two) proposes that with each utterance in dialogue the listener must determine what information is already given and what information is new for the proper interpretation of the content of the utterance. If the older adult finds it difficult to concentrate simultaneously on several different features of a cognitive task, he may also find it difficult to synthesize the differing features of each utterance in dialogue. In order to determine what is given and what is new, one must keep in mind what was previously said, the social context of the dialogue, and the information shared by participants as they interact.

However, one should not be too hasty to generalize from cognitive research: many older adults can hold a conversation quite competently. The key to successful communication is often its intrinsic interest. It is easier to keep in mind meaningful information, than the abstract concepts that are typically used in cognitive studies. Hence, those psychological studies where meaningful materials are used indicate little decrement in the older adult's performance. As noted in chapter five, meaningful cognitive tasks can even reduce the physiological differences between young and old adults. Thus, conversation with older adults can often be enhanced, by a mutual focus upon a topic that has meaning for both participants.

ARE THE ELDERLY EGOCENTRIC?

The social and cognitive changes which accompany old age have a major impact upon communication. The concept of egocentrism has been used to explain this impact. Before this concept can be accepted as an overall explanation, it is important to critically assess its merits in relation to old age, as the concept of egocentrism was originally conceived in order to describe the immature behavior of the little child.

Egocentrism is the inability to take the role of the other. The very young child is presumed to be egocentric in action and thought. Egocentrism has not been extensively studied in adult populations, however, because it has simply been assumed that adult speech is sensitive to listener needs (Looft, 1972).

Cross-sectional research by Neugarten (1964) has shown, however, that the verbalizations of elderly men and women tend to be more dogmatic, do not often clarify past-present and cause-effect relationships, express idiosyncratic and eccentric methods of communication, and display reduced sensitivity to the reactions of others, all of which characterize an egocentric strategy of communication. Similarly, Looft (1972) suggests a link between rigidity and egocentrism during later life. However, one must be cautious in interpreting these results. Often cross-sectional studies and the testing situation itself exaggerate a decrement model of the aging process. For example, longitudinal studies do not support the notion of increased rigidity in old age. Personality research similarly has shown that the elderly are not necessarily rigid when taking personal action, even if general, rigid opinions have already been expressed.

There is a shift in middle age toward an inner orientation and toward the development of strategies of interaction that deal with limited focal issues instead of the many smaller details that exist in the world. These changes, in turn, reduce both the cognitive and emotional overload of the middle-aged adult. Looft (1972) has suggested that these changes, beginning in middle age, result in egocentrism by the time the adult is old. He also suggests that the older adult's social disengagement and intensive personal life-review contribute to a rise in egocentrism in old age. He fails to note, however, that voluntary disengagement may often be accompanied by commitment to a less extensive but more intimate set of social relations. Similarly, the increased inner focus during later adulthood also involves an increasing concern by the individual about the social contributions he has, or will make to the outside world.

To the extent that one's social world does become constricted and the environment less diverse and stimulating, there is, however, a decreased need for the exercise of verbal skills (Gumperz, 1972). Recall from chapter three how during the child's early years increased social interaction and communication conflict facilitate the development of mature role-taking skills. Correspondingly, if the older adult communicates little with others because of reduced opportunities for social interaction, there is little opportunity to reflect upon the differing thoughts and concerns of the other and the self. An egocentric view of the world is the inevitable result. Because this form of egocentrism results from a poor social environment, it can be speculated that these results are reversible in old age. Egocentrism during late adulthood is the product of different processes than the egocentrism the child displays in the early, formative years (Looft, 1972).

Research has shown that on cognitive egocentrism measures (such as those of Kraus and Glucksberg as described in chapter three), older adults perform significantly less well than do young adults. However, these tasks are often actually removed from a natural social context and are characterized by greater emphasis upon abstract cognition rather than social skills. A study by Looft and Charles (1971) has shown that while college students achieve higher scores on a cognitive egocentrism task, there are no significant differences between the young and old on a measure of social interaction. This absence of any correlation between cognitive egocentrism and social interaction shows that the aged and children display a different form of egocentrism. Research on children indicates that cognitive egocentrism and social interaction are positively related. In contrast, older adults display no relationship at all.

Therefore, the discussion of egocentrism during old age, if evidenced at all, actually involves a different concept than that which is used to describe the child. When two concepts are structurally different, they should not be directly compared. It is also important to remember that, as for most cognitive and social measures among elderly adults, there is a wide range of variation in egocentrism among the aged.

WHEN GENERATIONS MEET

Older and younger generations are very different in nature. The old reflect upon their past, the young upon their future. The old attempt to compensate for failing physical stamina; the young, in contrast, have reached the heights of physical endurance. While the old shift their focus from an outer to inner world, the young adult begins to branch out in multiple directions. Eventually the young and old come into contact with one another, either voluntarily or as a product of haphazard circumstance. How they react to one another depends upon their mutual perception, which varies with the social setting in which they make their acquaintance.

Prior to describing how the generations perceive one another in interaction, it is important to define precisely what is meant by the concept of 'generation'. A generation is neither a concrete group that is formed for a specific purpose, nor does it always work collectively to give rise to social change. Membership within a generation or cohort simply implies a specific location in historical time. At that time, the members experience 'fresh contact' with the social world. Early impressions exert a continuing influence upon the members of each generation as they come and go in succession over time (Mannheim, 1952).

Members of different generations at any one point in time also represent differences of social position, economic situation, and life stage, as well as personal history, all of which contribute to the various ranges of experience and the characteristic view of the world expressed by each generation. It is these personal, social, and historical factors that contribute to the development of its members' individual identities (Back, 1976; Elder, 1977; Mannheim, 1952). Research has shown, for example, that while present-day college men and women perceive themselves as aggressive and managerial, elderly males and females perceive themselves as cooperative and nurturant (Fitzgerald, 1978). While young adults are concerned with creative enterprises, older adults are interested in the validation of their values (Bengtson & Black, 1973).

Nevertheless, the common experience of social and historical events (such as media coverage of the Vietnam War, economic recessions, and an energy crisis) by members of different cohorts provides substantial overlap between the perceptions of generations (Bengtson et al., 1977). This, in turn can provide the common basis of understanding that is a prerequisite to the successful initiation of communication. This is further facilitated by the fact that the way in which the parent generation interprets social events often influences the expectations and strategies of coping by the next generation (Elder, 1977).

To the extent that there is interchange between generations, however, there are likely to be discrepancies in the way they perceive their relationship. These differences, although stressful, need not result in out-and-out conflict (Bengtson & Black, 1973). The success of encounters between representatives of different generations depends upon how well these differences are accepted and understood, how these social perceptions and evaluations are negotiated, and how mutual is the willingness of the generations to learn from one another.

Recall from chapter two how subjective the process of perception is. The way two adults perceive one another is more crucial to the interaction than their true similarities or differences. The least misperception between generations occurs when their social relationship is close and emotionally sound. Thus, there exists a smaller generation gap within the family group than within the wider society; and attitudes toward grandparents are considerably less negative than those towards the elderly in general (Andersson, 1976; Bekker & Taylor, 1966; Bengtson & Cutler, 1976; Nardi, 1973).

In contrast, the age grading of our society segregates the members of different generations. Most social communication takes place between people of similar age and status (Rosow, 1967; Woelfel, 1976). This reduction of interaction between members of different age groups contributes to the development of unchallenged negative stereotypes, and the opportunity for mutual exchange is further impeded.

MISPERCEPTION BETWEEN GENERATIONS

Adults form the least misperceived group within society, and they represent the group that most misperceives other age cohorts (Ahammer & Baltes, 1972). The adult generation perceives itself as separate from the generation before it, and young adults are especially prone to misperceive the aged (Bengtson & Cutler, 1976). Simply being seen as old sets the elderly adult apart from people in general (Nardi, 1973). Consequently, young adults express more social interest when they hear someone referred to as a 'person' rather than as an 'old person'. They state an attitude of indifference when asked how they would react to an elderly individual seated near them on a bus (Bennett & Eckman, 1973; Kogan & Shelton, 1962).

Research over the past several decades has demonstrated significant differences between the descriptions of the elderly by young adults and by the elderly themselves. In general, there are misperceptions of the elderly by the young along the personal dimensions of valuation of autonomy and nurturance, hostility, skepticism, rejection, affiliation and related personal needs (Ahammer & Baltes, 1972; Bennett & Eckman, 1973; Fitzgerald, 1978; Kogan & Shelton, 1962). To a lesser extent, research has also shown some degree of agreement between young and old perceptions of the elderly (Britton & Britton, 1972; Kogan & Shelton, 1962). Were this not the case, communication on any level of intensity or satisfaction would be impossible to achieve.

Nevertheless, the prevalence of interpersonal misperceptions makes communication between members of different generations subject to both information distortion and social discomfort. Presuppositions concerning what is referred to in an informational sense, and the nature of the relationship in an interpersonal sense are made ambiguous under these conditions. As noted in chapter two, the relationship component of communication classifies the nature of the information exchanged. Thus, an ill-defined relationship inevitably distorts the participants' recognition and understanding of the meaning of their utterances as they attempt to construct a social dialogue.

DISTORTION OF COMMUNICATION

Young adults display ambivalent feelings about aging and aged persons. When the young adult is confronted with an elderly person, he may tend to cope with these feelings by behaving artificially rather than attempting to establish a social relationship (McTavish, 1971). If neither party recognizes the true nature of the exchange, it constitutes a prime example of pseudocommunication. Pseudocommunication occurs when neither party recognizes the faulty assumptions he has made about the interaction. A mutual sharing of meaning is absent. The interaction is inconsequential. However, if either of the speakers become aware of how contrived their exchange actually is, it is likely to be highly unpleasant, especially to the older adult, who suddenly recognizes that mutual understanding is clearly being avoided.

Surveys of attitudes towards the aged reveal additional information about the misunderstandings that occur when young and old interact. For example, Fitzgerald (1978) has found that the elderly view themselves as inclined towards affiliation and less concerned with any display of power and control. In contrast, young adults perceive the old as more hostile and anxious to achieve greater power and control. The incongruence between these perceptions of the social relationship provides the perfect conditions for a strained and stressful interaction.

Affiliative offers by the older adult are interpreted as attempts to control. This incorrect assumption by the young adult is transmitted to the older adult in direct or indirect ways. The older adult, in turn, becomes discouraged from interacting. The only possible solution is for him to withdraw: mutual commitment to the relationship is lacking. Within this social context, information cannot be exchanged, for the tension of the relationship will mask the message content. The older adult finds his identity difficult to maintain, for the image that he holds of himself is not the image that others perceive.

Another form of misperception leading to similar social strain involves the finding that young adults believe that the elderly compare the young unfavorably with their own generation. This results in defensiveness on the part of the young. It also leads to resentment on the part of the misunderstood old adult (Kogan & Shelton, 1962). In a similar vein, Rosow (1974) has noted that aged persons tend to be viewed as irrational and stubborn, when they are merely attempting to counteract the dependent social position in which they have been placed. The older adult would prefer a more dignified self-image, than to accept the minimal expectations of society.

Many middle-class aged adults prefer to deny their personal aging (Rosow, 1967, 1968, 1974). Consistent perception and treatment by others as if they are old often cause withdrawal from these disconfirming encounters. In the terms of Erving Goffman (see chapter two), the individual's 'social face' is discredited either overtly or subtly by the other when he is treated in a manner inconsistent with his self-image. The maintenance of one's face is a basic condition of interaction, and the encounter is, by necessity, distorted and eventually ended unless the older adult adopts a new face. Additionally, the older adult's implicit reference to the self as if he were middle aged is confusing and difficult to integrate within the existing set of presuppositions about the elderly that the younger adult believes to be true. Incongruence of presuppositions concerning the older adult's identity eliminates the sense of shared social context essential for communicating.

A similar situation characterized by 'loss of face' has been described by Miller (1968). Assuming the best of intentions of both young and old participants, specific characteristics of the aged may cause embarrassment within the shared relationship. These include: the inability of the older adult to return a favor because of the general decline in health and income during old age, the inability to perform a task that all had assumed he could do, and the outdated nature of the knowledge that the older adult has to offer. In these cases both the young and old become socially embarrassed. The presuppositions they held about the older adult have proved false, the older adult has lost face, and the younger adult is unable to 'save' the face of the other. Miller finds that this usually results not only in the hesitance of the older adult to participate in further interaction, but also in the exclusion of the elderly from participation. He suggests that such occurrences can be avoided by providing the aged participant with a social role that he is capable of fulfilling well. A new and realistic social face may then be adopted and mutually recognized. Loss of face no longer can threaten either the old or young participant.

A CONFLICT OF INTEREST

These examples of unsuccessful communicative encounters describe the distorting effects of ill-defined relationships and false presuppositions. Another form of unsatisfying social interaction results from the inherent conflict of interests of the young and old. The ways in which they approach their social world are different in form and function. While there is a predominant 'here-and-now' and future outlook by the young, older adults are more concerned with the past and their own history. One study, for example, examined the relationship between young and old adults who found themselves attending an academic college course over a semester. The researchers found that the young adults complained about the elderly students. They resented the older adults' continued reference to their past experiences. The young students felt that this behavior was irrelevant to the classroom setting (Auerbach & Levenson, 1977).

Young adults, rightly or wrongly, perceive a tone of defensiveness when older adults attempt to make reference to their past. They also resent the way attention is diverted from the present (Kastenbaum, 1966). However, this attitude of resentment is also the result of some degree of misperception on the part of the younger adult; Lowenthal (1977) notes that the very old try to convey through reminiscence a picture of their history that corresponds to the present stage of life of the younger listener. This is done in an attempt to achieve mutuality of reference and interest and is certainly not intended to alienate the listener. Nevertheless, a knowledge of the past is not shared by young adults. It therefore provides a shaky basis for mutual interaction, especially if the relationship is not on solid ground.

Many elderly adults are aware that they are misperceived by the young (Kogan & Shelton, 1962; Lowenthal & Boler, 1965). As described in chapter two, nonverbal communication alone, although vague, nonspecific, and often unconscious, is actively perceived. It serves to define the social relationship between the speaker and hearer. For example, Lowenthal and Boler (1965) found that most older adults do recognize the fact that the young do not understand their problems and underestimate their skills. However, it is difficult to dispel these misperceptions given the limited contact between generations. Additionally, an awareness of the negative attitudes held by younger adults discourages the initiation of any communication by the old. For example, in the classroom study discussed above, the elderly students tended to seat themselves only near their age peers within the college classroom. They stated that they feared the young would otherwise view them as intrusive. Unfortunately, this gave the appearance of indifference to the younger students, who in turn would fortify their poor opinions of the old (Auerbach & Levenson, 1977).

BACK TO BABY TALK

The attitudes that are held about the elderly influence the nature of social encounters between young and old adults, yet very little is known about the actual form and content of the spoken messages each conveys to the other within the interaction. A revealing study that does address this communication issue has been reported by researchers Rubin and Brown (1975). Their results suggest a qualitative difference in the way in which the young adult communicates to the old.

The researchers used a subject sample of college students. They requested each student to explain a set of game rules to a hypothetical person who was represented by an ink drawing on a card. Each student spoke to a picture representative of a single age group, ranging from preschool age children to elderly adults. The researchers found that when the young adults spoke to the drawings of the young child and the older adult, they would simplify the language they used. Middle-aged adults received the most complex explanation of rules. Young children and the elderly received the least complex explanations. Additionally, the degree of language complexity of the speaker was related to measures which evaluated the students' estimations of the intellectual skills of the various age groups. In general, the elderly were perceived as less competent than other adults and were considered less capable than others of caring for themselves. These attributions had clearly surfaced in the language the students had used. Those who are perceived as least competent are spoken to in the simplest language. However, ink drawings are not real persons. Real-life language in a mutual dialogue is likely to be quite different, but if the young adult immediately assumes that the old adult is incompetent, the language that he initially uses will be very much like the language used by the students in this study.

The results strongly suggest a shift in style of speech, also called a speech register (see chapter three), when communicating with the older adult. The register used with the older adult is the same type of register that is used with young children, commonly known as the baby-talk socialization function. It communicates to the older adult the social assessment of his capacities and his responsibilities within the interaction. In accord with common attitudes that are held about the elderly, both the capacities and responsibilities of the older adult are minimized. Unlike language to children, the simplified speech to the older adult is typically nonnurturant, yet it signifies a childlike status (Ferguson, 1977). Kalish and Knudtson (1976) note that no matter how dependent the older adult is within a social relationship, he does not evoke the tenderness displayed towards infants and small children. Should the older adult be experiencing hearing impairment or intellectual decline, simplified speech may be necessary and adaptive for the adult. However, should a competent and healthy elderly adult be addressed in simplified speech with its implicit connotation of intellectual deficiency, it is likely to result in a demeaning social encounter, either angrily protested or hastily ended by the older adult.

THE CONTEXT OF THE ENCOUNTER

A basic principle of social psychology is that increased social contact helps to dissolve the stereotypes and negative attitudes held between different groups. If conditions for contact are unfavorable, however, social prejudice tends to worsen. Contact between generations is no exception to this rule. The study cited previously by Auerbach and Levenson (1977) examining the participation of young and old students in a classroom setting provides a clear example of unfavorable contact conditions. Over the course of the college semester, the young adult students expressed increasingly more negative attitudes towards the older adults. They especially complained about the older students' excessive attention to the instructor both in and out of class and about the unfair competition within the classroom setting. They resented the fact that the elderly students were able to dedicate all their energy to the single college course that they were taking. In contrast, the younger students were burdened with other course-work demands. They could not compete at an equal level and felt frustrated as a result.

The researchers described these conditions of contact as competitive and involuntary. They suggested a more favorable outcome would result under intimate and casual conditions. Close family relationships, for example, provide this more intimate context. Attitudes held about family members are often complementary as a result.

Similarly, Birren (1978) found that joint participation of young and old adults in a university course on autobiography resulted in increased mutuality, understanding, and admiration between the young and old students. The classroom situation was composed of small, closely knit groups, who would meet weekly within the class to discuss features of their personal history. The willingness of the students to participate in these encounters, the mutual acknowledgment of their personal identities, and the constructive emphasis upon evaluating one's personal history resulted in a highly satisfying communication experience for all. It appears that intersubjective relationships had developed within these discussion groups. The mutual sharing of personal history, social identity and respect was achieved by means of the willingness of each to take the role of the other. The other was no longer alien, but was understood and well accepted. Birren noted, in fact, that several students of widely differing ages had continued to maintain contact after the course had ended.

WHEN THE SYSTEM BREAKS DOWN

The experience described by Birren represents a fairly unique occurrence within the research literature on contact between the young and old. Most studies instead suggest the tendency of the elderly adult to withdraw, due to rejection, ambiguous messages, overt embarrassment, and the desire to avoid highly arousing interpersonal events (Bettinghaus & Bettinghaus, 1976; Feffer, 1970; Miller, 1968). A theory of 'social breakdown', most explicitly described by Kuypers and Bengtson (1973), has been used to characterize a vicious cycle of disconfirming interactions and the threat they present to the self-perception of the older adult.

The individual's self-perception and sense of personal competence are largely reliant upon the social labels and values communicated by others. The elderly adult becomes especially susceptible to the effects of social labeling because of the ambiguous social position in which the aged are placed. These include the loss of roles, vagueness of norms, and inadequate models of optimal aging. Kuypers and Bengtson describe these conditions as a 'feedback vacuum', creating vulnerability to and dependence upon the social environment for self-definition. As described throughout this book, societal evaluations of the elderly are largely unfavorable. Hence, the older adult develops a poor sense of competence and self-worth, further increasing dependence upon the external world in a cyclic manner.

With age, the display of competent action no longer receives the reinforcement awarded to younger adults (Labouvie-Vief & Zaks, in press). Instead, the elderly individual's needs are supplied noncontingently. The older adult is not expected to display self-sufficient behavior (Cath, 1975). Responsibilities diminish, and the older adult can not depend upon others to notice those skills he has maintained and developed during old age. The result is a decreased sense of personal effectiveness. Interactions of this noncontingent nature correspond to Watzlawick et al.s' (1967) description of 'disconfirmation' within communication (see chapter two). The identity of the older adult is not simply rejected, but the reality of the individual as a source of self-definition is discredited. Watzlawick et al. characterize this form of interchange as the most destructive to personal identity. In essence, personal identity is negated, self-esteem denied. Accordingly, clinical observations suggest that depression in old age is generally based upon the loss of positive reinforcements rather than upon guilt, which is the more common cause of depression among younger individuals (Gottesman et al., 1973).

From this perspective one should take note of the revealing research finding that fluid intelligence (which is biologically based) of elderly adults is improved under conditions of social praise (Labouvie-Vief & Zaks, in press). This research result substantiates the idea that social confirmation is a crucial component of the older adult's sense of competence and successful behavior during later life. The general self-perception of low self-competence by the aged is used to explain the corresponding tendencies of elderly adults towards social conformity, hesitation to express opinions, and decreased intellectual performance (Birren & Renner, 1977; Labouvie-Vief & Zaks, in press; Maddox, 1964).

REDEFINING THE CONTEXT: DISTRIBUTING POWER

The transition to old age is accompanied by a new set of socializers, including peers, offspring, and former subordinates, who encourage the aging individual to accept his new social status (Inkeles, 1969). To ensure that this transition will not involve a loss of esteem, competence, or identity, the older adult should not view these others as socializers, teachers, or individuals upon whom he is dependent. Instead, they must be redefined as resources for the older adult, people who are available if necessary, and who can aid the elderly adult in adjusting to old age when specifically requested (Haack, 1976).

This process of redefinition is essential to successful aging. A major problem of the aged is one of decreasing power (Rosow, 1974; Sussman, 1976), and to remain continually in a subordinate position is demoralizing to the adult. For example, the older adult is frustrated by a subordinate position when he finds it difficult to initiate interaction with others. Much prerogative for interaction depends upon the younger adult. The elderly adult is often unable to alter his interaction patterns although he may desperately desire new relationships or a redefinition of old ones (Britton & Britton, 1972; Chown, 1977; Fitzgerald, 1978). As described in chapter six, even frequent visits with children do not eliminate discontent if the older adult does not feel he has any control over who initiates visits (Hampe & Blevins, 1975).

The asymmetry of power distribution in communication between generations provides the basic conditions for the principle of least interest (see chapter two). The individual most dependent upon maintaining the social relationship defers to the other more often for fear that the other will break off relations (Bengtson & Cutler, 1976). Hence, for example, research has shown that many older adults are easily persuaded, especially if they are isolated with few opportunities for interaction (Bennett & Eckman, 1973).

When relations between the old and young are asymmetric in power, it is nearly always the older adult who is in the dependent position (Oyer & Oyer, 1976). Part of the problem is that young adults view themselves as more mature when they make fewer demands upon the older adult (Gottesman et al., 1973). From this perspective, the elderly individual's behavior is of little consequence unless he makes extensive demands under the guise of dependency (Kalish & Knudtson, 1976; Rosow, 1976b). Yet this serves only to reinforce a subordinate position and eliminates the opportunity to present a self-image of competence. Resentment is inevitable and relationships are strained. Effective and mutually satisfying communication is stifled.

For the young and old to avoid these stressful interactions, they need to jointly redefine the social context of their exchange. The older adult must be recognized as a competent participant who is capable of contributing to the social world. In this way power within the relationship becomes more equitably distributed, and both participants are equally capable of constructing a social dialogue. The transmission of meaningful messages in social interaction requires that speaker and listener establish a mutually satisfying relationship, which in turn provides the basic context of communication.

A REMINDER

It is important to remember throughout how different the elderly are from each other. Their relationships with young and old vary from those which are mutually fulfilling to those which are sadly deficient and stressful. There are many competent, well-functioning, healthy, secure adults who are old. There are also many who require extensive assistance in coping with old age. The elderly are the most hetero-geneous age group of them all. Less heterogeneous, however, are the attitudes toward the aged and the consequent misperceptions that are communicated to the old. It is these forces which impinge upon the inner resources of the older adult, causing the adult to call into question his sense of personal competence. The secure and resourceful adult works to fortify his self-esteem and continuity with the past. A supportive environment and the availability of valued roles aids the less secure adult in maintaining his personal identity and sense of effective-ness. In this way he becomes more capable of negotiating power in interaction. Once the social relationship becomes equitably defined, the flow of information and opportunity for mutual development and enrichment continues through life.

At all stages of life, the individual needs to communicate with others. The quality not quantity of communication is the key to personal well-being. The older adult confronts a unique social world and a series of personal changes, thereby changing the nature of his communication with others. The older adult begins to focus intensely upon his past, a point of reference different from that which is used by the young. The older adult also experiences a series of sensory and cognitive changes to which he must adapt in order to communicate effectively. An insufficient social environment can cause a rise in egocentrism during later life, but this change is not irreversible. Egocentrism during old age is not the same as the egocentrism that is displayed by the very young child.

Given these basic changes that accompany old age, communication between the young and old is sometimes problematic, as each genera-tion in society represents a characteristic view of the world – a product of their place in historical time and current stage of life. As a result, there are misperceptions between young and old generations concerning the relationship that they share and their presuppositions about the world. These misperceptions can result in distorted or aborted com-munication, accompanied by loss of face and embarrassment by one or both. Attitudes are not necessarily conveyed by means of direct reference, but may be implicit within the form of speech that is used when addressing the other. For example, the use of excessively simpli-fied speech conveys to the older adult the fact that he is viewed as incompetent by virtue of his age. The conditions of contact between generations can enhance or discourage the development of a mutually satisfying exchange. This depends upon whether the participants are at odds or are willing to take the role of the other.

The ambiguous social environment that confronts the adult in old age renders the individual susceptible to a cycle of social breakdown. Increased isolation and loss of roles and norms to guide behavior leaves the aging individual more reliant upon the social environment for personal identity, yet negative messages from the environment only serve to increase vulnerability. Too often the older adult is not reinforced for competent behavior. Instead the needs of the aged are supplied in a noncontingent manner. A personal sense of effectiveness diminishes as a result, and the identity of the older adult is disconfirmed in the process.

The general loss of power and increased dependence during old age often serve to distort the social relationships of the aged. Continued subordination is difficult to withstand. Instead, the social position of the older adult must be redefined. The competencies he displays must be acknowledged and reinforced. In this way more mutually satisfying relationships can develop, and within this context both young and old can benefit from the give-and-take of a jointly constructed social dialogue.

9 A Final Note: Communication Throughout the Life Cycle

Many diverse ideas have been discussed in the chapters of this book. There are, however, common issues and themes that provide the conceptual links between the topics that have been covered. It is these issues and themes that are reviewed in this final note.

Throughout the life cycle, the developing individual undergoes qualitative change. Both the inner world and the outer world of the individual transform over time. Communication with others is central to the process. Both the environment and the individual interact in a dialectical manner to promote development and change in a cumulative way. There is no stepping backwards, no return to the past. The pattern is irreversible. This development occurs within a social context, where the individual is informed as to whether he is on time or off time, whether his behavior is acceptable or unacceptable, age-appropriate or non-age-appropriate. Communicating with others conveys these messages to the individual throughout development, and informs him of his place in the social structure.

Each successive cohort experiences the social structure and the process of development in a manner different from its predecessor. Each individual establishes fresh contact with the social environment at a time in history different from those before or after. World views differ not only with age and the cumulation of a developmental history, but with placement in historical time, and possessors of differing views of the world must work that much harder to establish mutual understanding in order to communicate with one another.

Different developmental progressions and cumulative experience lead to basic differences between the cohorts of society. Theorists and researchers of development who recognize this basic concept are alerted to the danger of comparing the young and old directly. The young and old see the world differently, manage crises differently, and are treated by others differently within their social world. However, throughout the life course there is a common need: communication.

151

Communication with others enables the individual to discover regularities in the social environment and to interpret new input in terms of how he understands the world. But the preference for consistency by the individual must be balanced by an openness to change and adaptability. This is achieved through role taking, the ability to put oneself in the other's shoes. This ability to take the perspective of the other enables participants within a social interaction to jointly construct a social reality, whether by means of mutual confirmation, or by active testing and negotiation. Throughout, however, participants must maintain some semblance of surface agreement in order to avoid loss of face and to confirm the dignity and self-esteem of both. Inability or lack of opportunity to participate in such exchanges denies the individual a necessary source of self-confirmation within the social structure.

Within the communication encounter, information is exchanged and the social relationship is defined, verbally and nonverbally, digitally and analogically. If the relationship is ambivalent, tenuous, or ill defined, little information can be conveyed, while participants are jockeying for power, attention, influence, change. On the opposite end is the establishment of intersubjectivity, the ideal of the communication episode, characterized by mutual recognition, acceptance, interlacing of perspectives, and social cohesion between speakers who interact. Most communications fall somewhere in between, although nearly all of us require some dose of intersubjective relationships in order to maintain self-esteem.

Early in life the communication process is established, primarily by means of the parent-child bond. Joint actions between mother and child are comprised of a mutual focus on some object, action, or topic, and mutual recognition of the other. Just as maternal sensitivity is a key variable in the development of the infant and young child, throughout the life cycle sensitivity to the needs of others remains a key variable in the success of communication exchanges. Just as sharing of mutually perceived topics in dialogue becomes increasingly sophisticated with the development of the child, it remains a crucial requisite to effective communication throughout adulthood and later life. A major achievement of childhood is the mastery of role-taking skills, which frees the individual from the narrowness of egocentrism. This is facilitated by conflict in communication and the ability to reevaluate oneself in accord with the views of others. Again, this process is vital throughout the human life cycle. Just as the child's social status is communicated to him by means of nurturant, simplified, 'baby talk' language, social status is conveyed to the adult throughout the life course both through language and behavior within the communication encounter.

The adolescent and young adult, through the course of development, proceed to absorb the messages and confront the multiple demands presented by the external world. The adult commits himself to values and goals and works towards their achievement. Middle-aged adults, as members of the most powerful age cohort within society, set the standards for societal functioning, yet they are not impervious to change. Middle adulthood often involves an increased turning inwards;

external sources of self-evaluation are compared with internal assessments of self-worth and social accomplishment. New, enlightened commitments are accompanied by an acceptance of contradiction, as compared with the absolutism of youth.

Middle adulthood and aging is accompanied by change on many levels. Biological, cognitive, personal, and social functions gradually transform. The dividing line between middle and late adulthood or old age, however, is unclear. Society informs the adult as to his changing status. Stereotyped expectations are conveyed through interactions, or the avoidance of interactions, with elderly adults. Roles are lost and left uncompensated. Norms become ambiguous and offer little guidance. Significant others, such as spouse and dear friends, pass away.

The loss of these sources of social confirmation induce a greater reliance upon the self for a sense of continuity and personal identity. Those who maintain their self-concept adapt best in later life. Informal roles, which are those self-defining personal characteristics, be it that of the intellectual, the nurturer, or the gossip, become crucial to identity. The family becomes an important means for conveying to the older adult a sense of personal continuity by sharing a common past and accepting the current identity of its older members within their communications. Confidant relationships similarly provide an emotional resource, helping the individual to cope with the insults of old age and allowing for the rewards of intersubjectivity between communicators. Communities that develop norms and roles that structure the social interactions of members boost morale and self-acceptance by the aging adult.

Nevertheless, the aged adult, in light of the diminishing external sources of self-confirmation, turns inwards for personal resources. There is a more intensive focus upon one's past history and personal reassessment as death approaches and there is more time to think. This manifests in communication in the form of reminiscence, which imparts information difficult for younger generations to identify with or understand. The present and the future are on the minds of younger adults. The young and old may converse, but fail to interlace perspectives or acknowledge each other's thoughts and cherished personal identities. Sharing and mutual confirmation occur when there is a common goal, such as the examination of common life themes by speaker and listener, be they young or old.

Such experiences are crucial to the functioning of the older adult, who must otherwise contend with rejecting or ambiguous communications.   Whether the individual avoids these unpleasant encounters or faces them head on, he loses. In the former case, his social world shrinks; in the latter case, he is demoralized. A sense of effectiveness can develop only out of interactions where the individual is understood and accepted by the other. This occurs within a context of intersubjective relationships. No matter how constricted the social environment of the aging adult, the mutual affirmation and maintenance of self-concept implicit within intersubjective communications continually provide the opportunity for personal development as well as the security of a predictable social world. This process is especially crucial to the aged adult, who is confronting a highly ambiguous set of norms and role relationships within the wider social world.

The success of a social encounter depends upon the presence of a mutually satisfying social relationship, agreement upon the social context, and sharing of basic reference between speakers who communicate. The success of communication throughout the human life cycle simultaneously enables the individual to express and affirm his view of the world, yet at the same time to undergo sufficient internal reassessment so that he may adapt successfully to an ever-changing social world.

Bibliography

Abelson, R.P. 1976. Script processing in attitude formation and decision making. In J.S. Caroll and J.W. Payne, eds., Cognition and social behavior. Hillsdale, N.J.: Lawrence Erlbaum Associates.

Ahammer, I.M. 1973. Social learning theory as a framework for the study of adult personality development. In P.B. Baltes & K.W. Schaie, eds., Life-span developmental psychology: Personality and socialization. N.Y.: Academic Press.

Ahammer, I.M., & Baltes, P.B. 1972. Objective vs. perceived age differences in personality: How do adolescents, adults, and older people view themselves and each other? Journal of Gerontology 27: 46-51.

Ahammer, I.M. & Bennett, K.C. 1976. On the biological decline model: The search for an alternative. Proceedings of the Australian Association of Gerontology.

Ainsworth, M.D.S., Bell, S.M., & Stayton, D.J. 1974. Infant-mother attachment and social development: 'Socialization' as a product of reciprocal responsiveness to signals. In M.P.M. Richards, ed. The integration of a child into a social world. N.Y.: Cambridge University Press.

Albrecht, G.L., & Gift, H.C. 1975. Adult socialization and adult life crises. In N. Datan & L.H. Ginsberg, eds., Life span developmental psychology: Normative life crises. N.Y.: Academic Press.

Aldrich, C.K., & Mendkoff, E. 1963. Relocation of the aged and disabled: A mortality study. Journal of the American Geriatrics Society 11: 185-194. Also in B.L. Neugarten, ed., 1968. Middle age and aging. Chicago: University of Chicago Press.

Anderson, J.E. 1958. A developmental model for aging. Vita Humana 1: 5-18.

Andersson, B. 1976. The generation gap: Imagination or reality? In K.F. Riegel & J.A. Meacham, eds., The developing individual in a changing world, vol. 2. The Hague: Mouton & Co.

155

Arenberg, D. 1973. Cognition and aging: Verbal learning, memory, problem solving, and aging. In C. Eisdorfer & M.P. Lawton, eds., The psychology of adult development and aging. Washington, D.C.: A.P.A.

Arenberg, D. & Robertson-Tchabo, E.A. 1977. Learning and aging. In J.E. Birren & K.W. Schaie, eds., Handbook of the psychology of aging. N.Y.: Van Nostrand Reinhold.

Argyle, M., Salter, V., Nicholson, H., Williams, M., & Burgess, P. 1972. The communication of inferior and superior attitudes by verbal and nonverbal signals. In S. Moscovici, ed., The psychology of language. Chicago: Markham.

Aronoff, C. 1974. Old age in prime time. Journal of Communication 24: 86-87.

Atchley, R.C. 1974. The meaning of retirement. Journal of Communication 24: 97-100.

Atchley, R.C. 1975. The life-course, age grading, and age-linked demands for decision making. In N. Datan & L.H. Ginsberg, eds., Life span developmental psychology: Normative life crises. N.Y.: Academic Press.

Atkin, C.K. 1976. Mass media and the aging. In H.J. Oyer and E.J. Oyer, eds., Aging and communication. Baltimore: University Park Press.

Auerbach, D.N., & Levenson, R.L. 1977. Second impressions: Attitude change in college students toward the elderly. The Gerontologist 17, no. 4: 362-66.

Austin, J.L. 1962. How to do things with words. Cambridge: Harvard University Press.

Back, K.W. 1976. Personal characteristics and social behavior: Theory and method. In R.H. Binstock & E. Shanas, eds., Handbook of aging and the social sciences. N.Y.: Van Nostrand Reinhold.

Baltes, P.B. 1968. Longitudinal and cross-sectional sequences in the study of age and generation effects. Human Development 11: 145-71.

Baltes, P.B. & Nesselroade, J.R. 1970. Multivariate longitudinal and cross-sectional sequences for analyzing ontogenetic and generational change: A methodological note. Developmental Psychology 2: 163-68.

Baltes, P.B., & Schaie, K.W. 1973. On life-span developmental research paradigms: Retrospects and prospects. In P.B. Baltes & K.W. Schaie, eds., Life-span developmental psychology: Personality and socialization. N.Y.: Academic Press.

Baltes, P.B., & Willis, S.L. 1977. Toward psychological theories of aging and development. In J.E. Birren & K.W. Schaie, eds., Handbook of the psychology of aging. N.Y.: Van Nostrand Reinhold.

Barker, R.G., & Barker, L.S. 1961. The psychological ecology of old people in Midwest, Kansas, and Yoredale, Yorkshire. Journal of Gerontology 16: 144-149. Also in: B.L. Neugarten, ed., 1968. Middle age and aging. Chicago: University of Chicago Press.

Barnlund, D.C. 1970. A transactional model of communication. In K.K. Sereno & C.D. Mortenson, eds., Foundations of communication theory. N.Y.: Harper and Row.

Basso, K.H. 1972. 'To give up on words': Silence in Western Apache culture. In P.P. Giglioli, ed., Language and social context. London: Cox Wyman Ltd.

Bates, E. 1975. Peer relations and the acquisition of language. In M. Lewis & L. Rosenblum, eds., Friendship and peer relations. N.Y.: Wiley.

Bates, E., Camaoni, L., & Volterra, V. 1975. The acquisition of performatives prior to speech. Merrill-Palmer Quarterly 21: 205-226.

Bates, J.E. 1976. Effects of children's non-verbal behavior on adults. Child Development 47: 1079-88.

Bateson, G. 1972. Steps to an ecology of mind. N.Y.: Ballantine Books.

Bateson, M.C. 1975. Mother-infant exchanges: the epigenesis of conversational interaction. Annals of the New York Academy of Sciences, Developmental Psycholinguistics, and Communication Disorders 263: 101-113.

Bayley, N. 1963. The life span as a frame of reference in psychological research. Vita Humana 6: 125-39.

Beattie, W.M. 1976. The relevance of communication for professionals involved with the elderly. In H.J. Oyer & E.J. Oyer, eds., Aging and communication. Baltimore: University Park Press.

Bekker, L.D., & Taylor, C. 1966. Attitudes toward the aged in a multi-generational sample. Journal of Gerontology 21: 115-18.

Bell, R.Q. 1971. Stimulus control of parent or caretaker behavior by offspring. Developmental Psychology 4: 63-72.

Bell, R.Q. 1974. Contributions of human infants to caregiving and social interaction. In M. Lewis & L. Rosenblum, eds., The effect of the infant on the caregiver. N.Y.: Wiley.

Bell, T. 1967. The relationship between social involvement and feeling old among residents in house for the aged. Journal of Gerontology 22: 17-22.

Bengtson, V.L. & Black, K.D. 1973. Inter-generational relations and continuities in socialization. In P.B. Baltes & K.W. Schaie, eds., Life span developmental psychology: Personality and socialization. N.Y.: Academic Press.

Bengtson, V.L., & Cutler, N.E. 1976. Generations and intergenerational relations. In R.H. Binstock & E. Shanas, eds., Handbook of aging and the social sciences. N.Y.: Van Nostrand Reinhold.

Bengtson, V.L., Dowd, J.J., Smith, D.H., & Inkeles, A. 1975. Modernization, modernity, and perceptions of aging: A cross-cultural study. Journal of Gerontology 30, no. 2: 668-95.

Bengtson, V.L., Kasschau, P.L., & Ragan, P.K. 1977. The impact of social structure on aging individuals. In J.E. Birren & K.W. Schaie, eds., Handbook of the psychology of aging. N.Y.: Van Nostrand Reinhold.

Bennett, K.C., & Ahammer, I.M. 1977. Toward a social deficit model of aging: A critique of the biological decline model. Australian Journal of Social Issues.

Bennett, R., & Eckman, J. 1973. Attitudes toward aging: A critical examination of recent literature and implications for future research. In C. Eisdorfer & M.P. Lawton, eds., The psychology of adult development and aging. Washington, D.C.: A.P.A.

Bernstein, B. 1970. Social class, language and socialization. In B. Bernstein, Class codes and control, vol. 1: Theoretical studies towards a sociology of language. London: Routeledge and Kegan Paul.

Bettinghaus, C.O., & Bettinghaus, E.P. 1976. Communication considerations in the health care of the aging. In H.J. Oyer & E.J. Oyer, eds., Aging and communication. Baltimore: University Park Press.

Birren, J.E. 1970. Toward an experimental psychology of aging. American Psychologist 25: 124-35.

Birren, J.E. 1978. Psychological development and autobiography. Colloquium Lecture. University of Michigan. Jan. 25.

Birren, J.E., & Renner, V.J. 1977. Research on the psychology of aging: Principles and experimentation. In J.E. Birren & K.W. Schaie, eds., Handbook of the psychology of aging. N.Y.: Van Nostrand Reinhold.

Birren, J.E., & Woodruff, O.S. 1973. Human development over the life span through education. In P.B. Baltes & K.W. Schaie, eds., Life span developmental psychology: Personality and socialization. N.Y.: Academic Press.

Blenkner, M. 1967. Environmental change and the aging individual. The Gerontologist 7: 102-105.

Bloom, L. 1976. An integrative perspective on language development. Papers and Reports on Child Language Development 12: 1-22.

Bloom, L., Rocissano, L., & Hood, L. 1976. Adult-child discourse: Developmental interaction between information processing and linguistic knowledge. Cognitive Psychology 8: 521-52.

Blount, B.G. 1972. Parental speech and language acquisition: Some Luo and Samoan examples. Anthropological Linguistics 14: 119-30.

Bochner, A. 1976. Conceptual frontiers in the study of communication in families: An introduction to the literature. Human Communication Research 2, no. 4: 381-97.

Botwinick, J. 1969. Disinclination to venture response vs. cautiousness in responding: Age differences. Journal of Genetic Psychology 115: 55-62.

Botwinick, J. 1973. Aging and behavior. N.Y.: Springer.

Botwinick, J. 1977. Intellectual abilities. In J.E. Birren & K.W. Schaie, eds., Handbook of the psychology of aging. N.Y.: Van Nostrand Reinhold.

Brazelton, T.B., Koslowski, B., & Main, M. 1974. The origins of reciprocity: The early mother-infant interaction. In M. Lewis & L. Rosenblum, eds., The effect of the infant on the caregiver. N.Y.: Wiley.

Brim, O.G. 1966. Socialization through the life cycle. In O.G. Brim & S. Wheeler, Socialization after childhood. N.Y.: Wiley.

Brim, O.G. 1968. Adult socialization. In J.A. Clausen, ed., Socialization and society. Boston: Little, Brown & Co.

Brim, O.G. 1974. Selected theories of the mid-life crisis: A comparative analysis. Paper presented at the 82nd Annual Convention of A.P.A., New Orleans, Sept., 1974.

Britton, J.H. & Britton, J.O. 1972. Personality changes in aging. N.Y.: Springer.

Broen, P.A. 1972. The verbal environment of the language-learning child. American Speech and Hearing Association Monograph 17.

Bronson, W.C. 1975. Developments in behavior with age mates during the second year of life. In M. Lewis & L. Rosenblum, eds., Friendship and peer relations. N.Y.: Wiley.

Brown, R.G. 1960. Family structure and social isolation of older persons. Journal of Gerontology 15: 170-74.

Brown, R., & Gilman, A. 1960. The pronouns of power and solidarity. In T.A. Seboek (Ed.), Style in language. Cambridge, Mass.: M.I.T. Press.

Bruner, J.S. 1974/75. From communication to language – a psychological perspective. Cognition 3, no. 3: 255-87.

Bruner, J.S. 1975. The ontogenesis of speech acts. Journal of Child Language 2: 1-19.

Butler, R.N. 1968. The life review: An interpretation of reminiscence in the aged. In B.L. Neugarten, ed., Middle age and aging. Chicago: University of Chicago Press.

Carp, F.M. 1968. Some components of disengagement. Journal of Gerontology 23: 382-86.

Carp, F.M. 1976. Housing and living environments of older people. In R.H. Binstock & E. Shanas, eds., Handbook of aging and the social sciences. N.Y.: Van Nostrand Reinhold.

Carp, F.M., & Nydegger, C. 1975. Recent gerontological developments in psychology and social sciences. The Gerontologist 15, no. 4: 270-368.

Cath, S.H. 1975. The orchestration of disengagement. International Journal of Aging and Human Development 6, no. 3: 199-213.

Cavan, R. 1962. Self and role adjustment during old age. In Rose, ed., Human behavior and social processes: An interactionist approach. Boston: Houghton-Mifflin.

Chandler, M.J. 1975. Relativism and the problem of epistemological loneliness. Human Development 18: 171-80.

Chown, S.M. 1961. Age and the rigidities. Journal of Gerontology 16: 353-62.

Chown, S.M. 1977. Morale, careers, and personal potentials. In J.E. Birren & K.W. Schaie, eds., Handbook of the psychology of aging. N.Y.: Van Nostrand Reinhold.

Cicourel, A.V. 1972. Basic and normative rules in the negotiation of status and role. In D. Sudnow, ed., Studies in social interaction. N.Y.: The Free Press.

Clark, H., & Haviland, S. 1974. Psychological processes as linguistic explanation. In D. Cohen, ed., Explaining linguistic phenomena. N.Y.: John Wiley & Sons.

Clark, R.A., & Delia, J.G. 1976. The development of functional persuasive skills in childhood and early adolescence. Child Development 47: 1008-1014.

Clayton, V. 1975. Erikson's theory of human development as it applies to the aged: Wisdom as contradictive cognition. Human Development 18: 119-28.

Corso, J.F. 1977. Auditory perception and communication. In J.E. Birren & K.W. Schaie, eds., Handbook of the psychology of aging. N.Y.: Van Nostrand Reinhold.

Craik, F.I.M. 1977. Age differences in human memory. In J.E. Birren & K.W. Schaie, eds., Handbook of the psychology of aging. N.Y.: Van Nostrand Reinhold.

Cross, T.G. 1975. Some relations between mothers and linguistic level in accelerated children. Papers and Reports on Child Language Development 10: 117-35.

Cross, T.G. 1977. Mother's speech adjustments: The contribution of selected listener variables. In C. Snow & C. Ferguson, eds., Talking to children. N.Y.: Cambridge University Press.

Cumming, E. 1975. Engagement with an old theory. International Journal of Aging and Human Development 6, no. 3: 187-91.

Cumming, E., & Henry, W.E. 1961. Growing old. N.Y.: Basic Books.

Dance, F.E.X. 1970. A helical model of communication. In K.K. Sereno & C.D. Mortenson, eds., Foundations of communication theory. N.Y.: Harper & Row.

De Beauvoir, S. 1970. The coming of age. N.Y.: Warner.

De Long, A.J. 1974. Environments for the elderly. Journal of Communication 24: 101-12.

Deutsch, F. 1974. Observational and sociometric measures of peer popularity and their relationship to egocentric communication in female preschoolers. Developmental Psychology 10: 745-47.

Deutscher, I. 1968. The quality of post-parental life. In B.L. Neugarten, ed., Middle age and aging. Chicago: University of Chicago Press.

Dore, J. 1975. Holophrases, speech acts and language universals. Journal of Child Language 2, no. 1: 21-40.

Dore, J. 1976. Conditions for the acquisition of speech acts. In I. Markova, ed., The social context of language. N.Y.: Wiley.

Duncan, S. 1972. Some signals and rules for taking speaking turns in conversation. Journal of Personality and Social Psychology 23, no. 2: 283-292.

Eisdorfer, C., & Altrocchi, J. 1961. A comparison of attitudes toward old age and mental illness. Journal of Gerontology 16: 340-43.

Eisdorfer, C., & Wilkie, F. 1977. Stress, disease, and aging. In J.E. Birren & K.W. Schaie, eds., Handbook of the psychology of aging. N.Y.: Van Nostrand Reinhold.

Elardo, R., Bradley, R., & Caldwell, B.M. 1977. A longitudinal study of the relation of infants' home environment to language development at age three. Child Development 48: 595-603.

Elder, G.H. 1977. Family history and the life course. Journal of Family History.

Elias, M.F., & Elias, P.K. 1977. Motivation and activity. In J.E. Birren & K.W. Schaie, eds., Handbook of the psychology of aging. N.Y.: Van Nostrand Reinhold.

Elias, M.F., Elias, P.K., & Elias, J.W. 1977. Basic processes in adult developmental psychology. St. Lewis: C.V. Mosby Co.

Emmerich, W. Socialization and sex-role development. 1973. In P.B. Baltes & K.W. Schaie, eds., Life span developmental psychology: Personality and socialization. N.Y.: Academic Press.

Erickson, F., & Schultz, J. 1977. When is a context? Some issues and methods in the analysis of social competence. Quarterly Newsletter of the Institute for Comparative Human Development 1: 5-10.

Erikson, E.H., 1950. Childhood and Society. N.Y.: Norton.

Erikson, E.H. 1977. Adulthood and world views. Paper prepared for the conference on Love and Work in Adulthood. American Academy of Arts and Sciences, Palo Alto, California, May 6-7, 1977.

Ervin-Tripp, S. 1968. An analysis of the interaction of language, topic, and listener. In T.A. Fishman, ed., Readings in the sociology of language. The Hague: Mouton.

Ervin-Tripp, S. 1972. On sociolinguistic rules: Alternation and cooccurrence. In J.J. Gumperz & D. Hymes, eds., Directions in sociolinguistics: The ethnography of communication. N.Y.: Holt, Rinehart & Winston.

Escalona, S.K. 1973. Basic modes of social interaction. The emergence and patterning during the first two years of life. Merrill-Palmer Quarterly 19, no. 3: 205-232.

Farwell, C.B. 1975. The language spoken to children. Human Development 18, no. 4: 288-309.

Fearing, F. 1953. Toward a psychological theory of human communication. Journal of Personality 22: 71-87.

Feffer, M. 1970. A developmental analysis of interpersonal behavior. Psychological Review 77: 197-214.

Feffer, M., & Suchotliff, L. 1966. Decentering implications of social interactions. Journal of Personality and Social Psychology 4: 415-22.

Ferguson, C. 1977. Baby talk as a simplified register. In C. Snow & C. Ferguson, eds., Talking to children. N.Y.: Cambridge University Press.

Fillmore, C.J. 1972. A grammarian looks to sociolinguistics. In R. Shuy, ed., 23rd Annual Round Table, Georgetown Monograph Series on Language and Linguistics. Washington, D.C.: Georgetown University Press.

Fishman, J.A. 1972. Domains and the relationship between micro and macro sociolinguistics. In J.J. Gumperz & D. Hymes, eds., Directions in sociolinguistics: The ethnography of communication. N.Y.: Holt, Rinehart & Winston.

Fishman, J.A. 1972. The sociology of language. In P.P. Giglioli, ed., Language and social context. London: Cox & Wyman, Ltd.

Fiske, M. 1977. Changing hierarchies of commitment in adulthood. Paper prepared for the conference on Love and Work in Adulthood. American Academy of Arts and Sciences, Palo Alto, California, May 6-7, 1977.

Fitzgerald, J.M. 1978. Actual and perceived sex and generational differences in interpersonal style: Structural and quantitative issues. Journal of Gerontology 33, no. 3: 394-401.

Flavell, J.H. 1970. Cognitive changes in adulthood. In L.R. Goulet and P.B. Baltes, eds., Life-span developmental psychology: Theory and research. N.Y.: Academic Press.

Flavell, J.H., Botkin, P.T., Fry, C.O., Wright, J.W., & Jarvis, P.E. 1968. The development of role-taking and communication skills in children. N.Y.: Wiley.

Fozard, J.L., Wolf, E., Bell, B., McFarland, R.A., & Podolsky, S. 1977. Visual perception and communication. In J.E. Birren & K.W. Schaie, eds., Handbook of the psychology of aging. N.Y.: Van Nostrand Reinhold.

Freedle, R. 1975. Dialogue and inquiring systems: The development of a social logic. Human Development 18: 97-118.

Freedle, R., & Lewis, M. 1977. Prelinguistic conversations. In M. Lewis & L. Rosenblum, eds., Interaction, conversation and the development of language. N.Y.: Wiley.

Frenkel-Brunswik, E. 1963. Adjustments and reorientation in the course of the life span. In R.G. Kuhlen & G.G. Thompson, eds., Psychological studies of human development. N.Y.: Appleton-Century-Crofts. Also in B.L. Neugarten, ed., Middle age and aging. Chicago: University of Chicago Press.

Frolkis, V.V. 1977. Aging of the autonomic nervous system. In J.E. Birren & K.W. Schaie, eds., Handbook of the psychology of aging. N.Y.: Van Nostrand Reinhold.

Garvey, K. 1974. Some properties of social play. Merrill-Palmer Quarterly 20: 163-180.

Garvey, K., & Hogan, R. 1973. Social speech and social interaction: Egocentrism revisited. Child Development 44: 562-68.

Gellert, E. 1961. Stability and fluctuation in the power relationships of young children. Journal of Abnormal and Social Psychology 62: 8-15.

Gelman, R., & Shatz, M. 1977. Appropriate speech adjustments: The operation of conversational constraints on talk to 2-year-olds. In M. Lewis & L. Rosenblum, eds., Interaction, conversation, and the development of language. N.Y.: Wiley.

Giele, J.Z. 1977. Adulthood as transcendence of age and sex. Paper prepared for the conference on Love and Work in Adulthood. American Academy of Arts and Sciences, Palo Alto, California, May 6-7, 1977.

Goffman, E. 1955. On face-work: An analysis of ritual elements in social interaction. Psychiatry 18: 213-31.

Goffman, E. 1959. The presentation of self in everyday life. N.Y.: Doubleday.

Goffman, E. 1962. On cooling the mark out: Some aspects of adaptation to failure. In A.M. Rose, ed., Human behavior and social processes. Boston: Houghton-Mifflin.

Goffman, E. 1964. The neglected situation. American Anthropologist 66, no. 6: 133-36.

Goode, W. 1960. A theory of role strain. American Sociological Review 25: 483-496.

Gordon, C., Gaitz, C.M., & Scott, J. 1976. Leisure and lives: Personal expressivity across the life span. In R.H. Binstock & E. Shanas, eds., Handbook of aging and the social sciences. N.Y.: Van Nostrand Reinhold.

Gordon, J.B. 1975. A disengaged look at disengagement theory. International Journal of Aging and Human Development 6, no. 3: 215-27.

Gottesman, L.E., Quarterman, C.E., & Cohen, G.M. 1973. Psychosocial treatment of the aged. In C. Eisdorfer & M.P. Lawton, eds., The psychology of adult development and aging. Washington, D.C.: A.P.A.

Gottman, J.M. 1977. Toward a definition of social isolation in children. Child Development 48: 513-17.

Gottman, J.M., Gonso, J., & Rasmussen, B. 1975. Social competence, social interaction, and friendship in children. Child Development 46: 709-718.

Gove, W., Grimm, J.W., Motz, S.C., & Thompson, J.D. 1973. The family life cycle: Internal dynamics and social consequences. Sociology and Social Research 57: 182-95.

Graney, M.J., & Graney, E.E. 1974. Communications activity substitutions in aging. Journal of Communication 24: 88-96.

Greene, D. 1976. Social perception as problem solving. In J.S. Carroll and J.W. Payne, eds., Cognition and social behavior. Hillsdale, N.J.: Lawrence Erlbaum Associates.

Gumperz, J. 1972. The speech community. In P.P. Giglioli, ed., Language and social context. London: Cox & Wyman, Ltd.

Gutmann, D. 1975. Parenthood: A key to the comparative study of the life cycle. In N. Datan & L.H. Ginsberg, eds., Life span developmental psychology: Normative life crises. N.Y.: Academic Press.

Gutmann, D. 1976. A cross-cultural view of adult life in the extended family. In K.F. Riegel & J.A. Meacham, eds., The developing individual in a changing world, vol. 1. The Hague: Mouton & Co.

Gutmann, D. 1977. The cross-cultural perspective: Notes toward a comparative psychology of aging. In J.E. Birren & K.W. Schaie, eds., Handbook of the psychology of aging. N.Y.: Van Nostrand Reinhold.

Haack, L.A. 1976. A retiree's perspective on communication. In H.J. Oyer & E.J. Oyer, eds., Aging and communication. Baltimore: University Park Press.

Habermas, J. 1970. Introductory remarks to a theory of communicative competence. Reprinted in Dreitzel, ed., Recent Sociology No. 2. London: Macmillan.

Halliday, M.A.K. 1973a. Talking one's way in: A sociolinguistic perspective on language and learning. In B. Dockrell, ed., Papers of the S.S.R.C. Research Seminar on Language and Learning. Edinburgh, Jan., 1973.

Halliday, M.A.K. 1973b. Early language learning: A sociolinguistic approach. Paper presented for the Ninth International Congress of Anthropological and Ethnological Sciences, Chicago, Aug.-Sept., 1973.

Hamilton, D.L. 1976. Cognitive biases in the perception of social groups. In J.S. Carroll & J.W. Payne, eds., Cognition and social behavior. Hillsdale, N.J.: Lawrence Erlbaum Associates.

Hampe, G.D., & Blevins, Jr., A.L. 1975. Primary group interaction of residents in a retirement hotel. International Journal of Aging and Human Development 6, no. 4: 309-20.

Harris, A.E. 1975. Social dialectics and language: Mother and child construct the discourse. Human Development 18: 80-96.

Hartup, W.W. 1975. The origins of friendship. In M. Lewis & L. Rosenblum, eds., Friendship and peer relations. N.Y.: Wiley.

Hartup, W.W. Peer relations and the growth of social competence. To appear in M.W. Kent & J.E. Rolf, eds., The primary prevention of psychopathology, vol. 3: Promoting competence and coping in children. Hanover, N.H.: University Press of New England.

Hartup, W.W., & Lempers, J. 1973. A problem in life span development: The interactional analysis of family attachment. In P.B. Baltes & K.W. Schaie, eds., Life span developmental psychology: Personality and socialization. N.Y.: Academic Press.

Havighurst, R.J. 1973a. Social roles, work, and education. In C. Eisdorfer & M.P. Lawton, eds., The psychology of adult development and aging. Washington, D.C.: A.P.A.

Havighurst, R.J. 1973b. History of developmental psychology: Socialization and personality development through the life span. In P.B. Baltes & K.W. Schaie, eds., Life span developmental psychology: Personality and socialization. N.Y.: Academic Press.

Havighurst, R.J., Neugarten, B., & Tobin, S.H. 1964. Disengagement and patterns of aging. Gerontologist 4: 217-28. Also in B.L. Neugarten, ed., 1968. Middle age and aging. Chicago: University of Chicago Press.

Heider, F. 1958. Psychology of interpersonal relationships. N.Y.: Wiley.

Hess, B. 1974. Stereotypes of the aged. Journal of Communication 24: 76-85.

Hickey, T., Bragg, S.M., Rakowski, W., & Hultsch, D.F. 1978. Attitudes toward aging and the aged: An analytical study. International Journal of Aging & Human Development, in press.

Hickey, T., Hickey, L.A., & Kalish, R. 1968. Children's perceptions of the elderly. Journal of Genetic Psychology 112: 227-35.

Hickey, T., & Kalish, R. 1968. Young people's perceptions of adults. Journal of Gerontology 23: 215-19.

Hickey, T., Rakowski, W., Hultsch, D.F., & Fatula, B.J. 1976. Attitudes toward aging as a function if in-service training and practitioner age. Journal of Gerontology 31, no. 6: 681-86.

Hulett, J.E. 1966a. A symbolic interactionist model of human communi-
    cation: Part 1. Audio-visual Communication Review 14: 5-33.
Hulett, J.E. 1966b. A symbolic interactionist model of human communi-
    cation: Part 2. Audio-visual Communication Review 14: 203-20.
Hultsch, D.F., & Hickey, T. 1978. External validity in the study of
    human development. Human Development 21: 76-91.
Hutchinson, J.M., & Beasley, D.S. 1976. Speech and language func-
    tioning among the aging. In H.J. Oyer & E.J. Oyer, eds., Aging and
    communication. Baltimore: University Park Press.
Hymes, D. 1971. Competence and performance in linguistic theory. In
    R. Huxley & E. Ingram, eds., Language acquisition: Models and
    methods. N.Y.: Academic Press.
Hymes, D. 1972a. Toward ethnographies of communication: The analysis
    of communicative events. In P.P. Giglioli, ed., Language and social
    context. London: Cox & Wyman, Ltd.
Hymes, D. 1972b. Models of interaction of language and social life. In
    J.J. Gumperz & D. Hymes, eds., Directions in sociolinguistics: The
    ethnography of communication. N.Y.: Holt, Rinehart & Winston, Inc.
Hymes, D. 1974. Foundations in sociolinguistics. Philadelphia: Univer-
    sity of Pennsylvania Press.
Inkeles, A. 1966. Social structure and the socialization of competence.
    Harvard Educational Review 36: 265-83.
Inkeles, A. 1969. Social structure and socialization. In D.T. Goslin, ed.,
    Handbook of socialization theory and research. Chicago: Rand
    McNally and Co.
Jaffe, J., & Feldstein, S. 1970. Rhythms of dialogue. N.Y.: Academic
    Press.
Jarvik, L.F., & Cohen, D. 1973. A biobehavioral approach to intellectual
    change with aging. In C. Eisdorfer & M.P. Lawton, eds., The
    psychology of adult development and aging. Washington, D.C.:
    A.P.A.
Kagan, J., Kearsley, R.B., & Zelazo, P.R. 1975. The emergence of
    initial apprehension to unfamiliar peers. In M. Lewis & L. Rosen-
    blum, eds., Friendship and peer relations. N.Y.: Wiley.
Kalish, R.A., & Knudtson, F.W. 1976. Attachment vs. disengagement: A
    lifespan conceptualization. Human Development 19: 171-81.
Kastenbaum, R. 1966. On the meaning of time in later life. Journal of
    Genetic Psychology 109: 9-25.
Kaye, K. 1976. Toward the origin of dialogue. In H.R. Schaffer, ed.,
    Interaction in infancy – The Loch Lomond Symposium. London &
    N.Y.: Academic Press.
Kaye, K. 1977. Thickening thin data: The maternal role in developing
    communication and language. In M. Bullowa, ed., Before speech.
    N.Y.: Cambridge University Press.
Kelley, H.H. 1973. The processes of causal attribution. American
    Psychologist 28: 107-128.
Kilty, K.M., & Feld, A. 1976. Attitudes toward aging & toward the
    needs of older people. Journal of Gerontology 31, no. 5: 586-94.
Kimmel, D.C. 1974. Adulthood and aging. N.Y.: Wiley.

Klausner, S.Z. 1973. Life span environmental psychology: Methodological issues. In P.B. Baltes & K.W. Schaie, eds., Life span developmental psychology: Personality and socialization. N.Y.: Academic Press.

Knudtson, F.W. 1976. Life span attachment: Complexities, questions, considerations. Human Development 19: 182-96.

Kogan, N. 1961. Attitudes toward old people in an older sample. Journal of Abnormal and Social Psychology 62: 616-22.

Kogan, N., & Shelton, F. 1962. Beliefs about "old people": A comparative study of older and younger samples. Journal of Genetic Psychology 100: 93-111.

Kogan, N., & Wallach, M. 1961. Age changes in values and attitude. Journal of Gerontology 16: 272-80.

Kohlberg, L., Yaeger, J., & Hjertholm, E. 1968. The development of private speech: Four studies and a review of theories. Child Development 39: 691-736.

Konner, M. 1975. Relations among infants and juveniles in comparative perspective. In M. Lewis & L. Rosenblum, eds., Friendship and peer relations. N.Y.: Wiley.

Korner, A.F. 1974. The effect of the infant's state, level of arousal, sex, and ontogenetic stage on the caregiver. In M. Lewis & L. Rosenblum, eds., The effect of the infant on the caregiver. N.Y.: Wiley.

Kraus, R.M., & Glucksberg, S. 1970. Socialization of communication skills. In R.A. Hoppe, G.A. Milton, & E.C. Simmel, eds., Early experiences and the processes of socialization. N.Y.: Academic Press.

Kuhlen, R.G. 1964. Developmental changes in motivation during the adult years. In J.E. Birren, ed., Relations of development and aging. Illinois: Charles C. Thomas, 1964. Also in: B.L. Neugarten, ed. 1968. Middle age and aging. Chicago: University of Chicago Press.

Kuypers, J.A., & Bengtson, V.L. 1973. Social breakdown and competence. Human Development 16: 181-201.

Labouvie-Vief, G. 1977. Adult cognitive development: In search of alternative interpretations. Merrill-Palmer Quarterly 23, no. 4: 227-263.

Labouvie-Vief, G. & Zaks, P.M. Adult development and aging. To appear in A.E. Kazdin, A.S. Bellack, & M. Hersen, eds., New perspectives in abnormal psychology. Oxford University Press.

Labov, W. 1970. The study of language in social context. Studium Generale 23: 66-83.

Lakoff, R. 1972. Language in context. Language 48, no. 4: 907-27.

Lawton, M.P. The impact of the environment on aging and behavior. In J.E. Birren & K.W. Schaie, eds., Handbook of the psychology of aging. N.Y.: Van Nostrand Reinhold, 1977.

Lawton, M.P., & Nahemow, L. 1973. Ecology and the aging process. In C. Eisdorfer & M.P. Lawton, eds., The psychology of adult development and aging. Washington, D.C.: A.P.A.

Lee, L.C. 1975. Toward a cognitive theory of interpersonal development: Importance of peers. In M. Lewis & L. Rosenblum, eds.,
Friendship and peer relations. N.Y.: Wiley.

Lehr, V., & Rudinger, G. 1969. Consistency and change of social
participation in old age. Human Development 12: 255-67.

Levinson, D.J. 1977. The midlife transition: A period in adult psychosocial development. Psychiatry 40: 99-112.

Levinson, D.J. 1978. The seasons of a man's life. N.Y.: Alfred A. Knopf.

Lewis, M., & Cherry, L. 1977. Social behavior and language acquisition.
In M. Lewis & L. Rosenblum, eds., Interaction, conversation, and the
development of language. N.Y.: Wiley, 1977.

Lewis, M., & Freedle, R. 1973. Mother-infant dyad: The cradle of
meaning. In P. Pilner, L. Krames, & T. Alloway, eds., Communication and affect, language and thought. N.Y.: Academic Press.

Lewis, M., & Lee-Painter, S. 1974. An interactional approach to the
mother-infant dyad. In M. Lewis & L. Rosenblum, eds., The effect of
the infant on the caregiver. N.Y.: Wiley.

Lewis, M., Young, G., Brooks, J., & Michalson, L. 1975. The beginning
of friendship. In M. Lewis & L. Rosenblum, eds., Friendship and peer
relations. N.Y.: Wiley.

Lewis, M.M. 1936. Infant speech. London: Kegan Paul, Trench, Tribner
& Co., Ltd.

Lieberman, M.A. 1968. Psychological correlates of impending death. In
B.L. Neugarten, ed., Middle age and aging. Chicago: University of
Chicago Press.

Lieberman, M.A. 1969. Institutionalization of the aged: Effects on
behavior. Journal of Gerontology 24: 330-40.

Lieberman, M.A. 1975. Adaptive processes in late life. In N. Datan &
L.H. Ginsberg, eds., Life span developmental psychology: Normative
life crisis. N.Y.: Academic Press.

Ling, D., & Ling, A.H. 1974. Communication development during the
first three years of life. Journal of Speech and Hearing Research 17:
146-59.

Loeb, M.B. 1975. Adaptation and survival: New meanings in old age. In
N. Datan & L.H. Ginsberg, eds., Life span developmental psychology: Normative life crisis. N.Y.: Academic Press.

Loeb, R. 1973. Disengagement, activity, or maturity? Sociology and
Social Research 57: 367-82.

Longhurst, T.M., & Turnure, J.E. 1971. Perceptual inadequacy and
communicative ineffectiveness in interpersonal communication.
Child Development 42: 2084-88.

Looft, W.R. 1972. Egocentrism and social interaction across the life
span. Psychological Bulletin 78: 73-92.

Looft, W.R. 1973. Socialization and personality development throughout
the life span: An examination of contemporary psychological approaches. In P.B. Baltes & K.W. Schaie, eds., Life span developmental psychology: Personality and socialization. N.Y.: Academic
Press.

Looft, W.R., & Charles, D.C. 1971. Egocentrism and social interaction in young and old adults. International Journal of Aging and Human Development 2: 21-28.

Lopata, H.Z. 1975. Widowhood: Societal factors in life span disruptions and alternatives. In N. Datan & L.H. Ginsberg, eds., Life span developmental psychology: Normative life crisis. N.Y.: Academic Press.

Lord, C. 1975. Is talking to baby more than baby talk? Paper presented at the Biennial Meeting of the Society for Research in Child Development, Denver, April, 1975.

Lowenthal, M.F. 1968. Social isolation and mental illness in old age. In B.L. Neugarten, ed., Middle age and aging. Chicago: University of Chicago Press.

Lowenthal, M.F. 1977. Toward a sociological theory of change in adulthood and old age. In J.E. Birren & K.W. Schaie, eds., Handbook of the psychology of aging. N.Y.: Van Nostrand Reinhold.

Lowenthal, M.F., & Boler, D. 1965. Voluntary vs. involuntary social withdrawal. Journal of Gerontology 20: 363-75.

Lowenthal, M.F., & Chiriboga, D. 1973. Social stress and adaptation: Toward a life course perspective. In C. Eisdorfer & M.P. Lawton, eds., The psychology of adult development and aging. Washington, D.C.: A.P.A.

Lowenthal, M.F., & Haven, C. 1968. Interaction and adaptation: Intimacy as a critical variable. American Sociological Review, 1968, 33 no. 1: 20-30. Also in: B.L. Neugarten, ed., 1968 Middle age and aging. Chicago: University of Chicago Press.

Lowenthal, M.F. & Robinson, B. 1976. Social networks and isolation. In R.H. Binstock & E. Shanas, eds., Handbook of aging and the social sciences. N.Y.: Van Nostrand Reinhold.

Maddox, G.L. 1964. Disengagement theory: A critical evaluation. The Gerontologist 4: 80-82.

Maddox, G.L. 1965. Fact and artifact: Evidence bearing on disengagement theory. Human Development 8: 117-30.

Maddox, G.L. 1968a. Retirement as a social event in the United States: In B.L. Neugarten, ed., Middle age and aging. Chicago: University of Chicago Press.

Maddox, G.L. 1968b. Persistence of life style among the elderly: A longitudinal study of patterns of social activity in relation to life satisfaction. In B.L. Neugarten, ed., Middle age and aging. Chicago: University of Chicago Press.

Maddox, G.L., & Wiley, J. 1976. Scope, concepts, and methods in the study of aging. In R.H. Binstock & E. Shanas, eds., Handbook of aging and the social sciences. N.Y.: Van Nostrand Reinhold.

Mannheim, K. 1952. The problem of generations. In K. Mannheim, ed., Essays on the sociology of knowledge. London: Routeledge & Kegan Paul.

Maratsos, M.P. 1973. Nonegocentric communication abilities in preschool children. Child Development 44: 697-700.

Markson, E.W. 1975. Disengagement theory revisited. International Journal of Aging and Human Development 6, no. 3: 183-86.

Marsh, G.R., & Thompson, L.W. 1977. Psychophysiology of aging. In J.E. Birren & K.W. Schaie, eds., Handbook of the psychology of aging. N.Y.: Van Nostrand Reinhold.

Maudlin, C.R. 1976. Communication and the aging consumer. In H.J. Oyer & E.J. Oyer, eds., Aging and communication. Baltimore: University Park Press.

McCall, R.B. 1977. Challenges to a science of developmental psychology. Child Development 48, no. 2: 333-44.

McLeod, J.M. 1967. The contribution of psychology to human communication theory. In F.E.X. Dance, ed., Human communication theory. N.Y.: Holt, Rinehart, & Winston, Inc.

McTavish, T. 1971. Perceptions of old people: A review of research, methodologies, and findings. Gerontologist 11: 90-101.

Meacham, J.A. 1977. A transactional model of remembering. In N. Datan & H.W. Reese, eds., Life span developmental psychology: Dialectical perspectives on experimental research. N.Y.: Academic Press.

Mead, G.H. 1934. Mind, self, and society, C.W. Morris, ed. Chicago: University of Chicago Press.

Miller, S.J. 1968. The social dilemma of the aging leisure participant. In B.L. Neugarten, ed., Middle age and aging. Chicago: University of Chicago Press.

Mischel, W. 1969. Continuity and change in personality. American Psychologist 24: 1012-18.

Moerk, E. 1974. Changes in verbal child-mother interactions with increasing language skills of the child. Journal of Psycholinguistic Research 3, no. 2: 101-16.

Moerk, E.L. 1977. Processes and products of imitation: Additional evidence that imitation is progressive. Journal of Psycholinguistic Research 6, no. 3: 187-202.

Mueller, E. 1972. The maintenance of verbal exchanges between young children. Child Development 43: 930-38.

Mueller, E., Bleier, M., Krakow, J., Hegedus, K., & Cournoyer, P. 1977. The development of peer verbal interaction among 2-year-old boys. Child Development 48: 284-87.

Mueller, E., & Brenner, J. 1977. The origins of social skills and interaction among peer group toddlers. Child Development 48: 854-61.

Mueller, E., & Lucas, T. 1975. A developmental analysis of peer interaction among toddlers. In M. Lewis & L. Rosenblum, eds., Friendship and peer relations. N.Y.: Wiley.

Muth, T.A. 1976. Legal and public problems in communication arising with aging. In H.J. Oyer & E.H. Oyer,, eds., Aging and communication. Baltimore: University Park Press.

Nardi, A.H. 1973. Person perception research and the perception of life-span development. In P.B. Baltes & K.W. Schaie, eds., Life span developmental psychology: Personality and socialization. N.Y.: Academic Press.

Nelson, K. 1973. Structure and strategy in learning to talk. Monographs of the Society of Research in Child Development. Serial No. 149. 38, nos. 1-2.

Nesselroade, J.R. 1977. Issues in studying developmental change in adults from a multivariate perspective. In J.E. Birren & K.W. Schaie, eds., Handbook of the psychology of aging. N.Y.: Van Nostrand Reinhold.

Nesselroade, J.R., & Baltes, P.B. 1974. Adolescent personality development and historical change: 1970-1972. Monographs of the Society for Research in Child Development. Serial No. 154. 39, no. 1.

Neugarten, B.L. 1964. Summary and implications. In B.L. Neugarten & Associates, eds., Personality in middle and late life. N.Y.: Atherton Press.

Neugarten, B.L. 1966. Adult personality: A developmental view. Human Development 9: 61-73.

Neugarten, B.L. 1968a. Adult personality: Toward a psychology of the life cycle. In B.L. Neugarten, ed., Middle age and aging. Chicago: University of Chicago Press.

Neugarten, B.L. 1968b. The awareness of middle age. In B.L. Neugarten, ed., Middle age and aging. Chicago: University of Chicago Press.

Neugarten, B.L. 1969. Continuities and discontinuities of psychological issues into adult life. Human Development 12: 121-30.

Neugarten, B.L. 1970. Dynamics of transition of middle age to old age. Journal of Geriatric Psychiatry 4, no. 1: 71-87.

Neugarten, B.L. 1977. Personality and aging. In J.E. Birren & K.W. Schaie, eds., Handbook of the psychology of aging. N.Y.: Van Nostrand Reinhold.

Neugarten, B.L., & Datan, N. 1973. Sociological perspectives and the life cycle. In P.B. Baltes & K.W. Schaie, eds., Life span developmental psychology: Personality and socialization. N.Y.: Academic Press.

Neugarten, B.L., & Gutmann, D.L. 1968. Age-sex roles and personality in middle age: A thematic apperception study. In B.L. Neugarten, ed., Middle age and aging. Chicago: University of Chicago Press.

Neugarten, B.L., & Hagestad, G.O. 1976. Age and the life course. In R.H. Binstock & E. Shanas, eds., Handbook of aging and the social sciences. N.Y.: Van Nostrand Reinhold.

Neugarten, B.L., Havighurst, R.J., & Tobin, S.S. 1968. Personality and patterns of aging. In B.L. Neugarten, ed., Middle age and aging. Chicago: University of Chicago Press.

Neugarten, B.L., & Moore, J.W. 1968. The changing age-status system. In B.L. Neugarten, ed., Middle age and aging. Chicago: University of Chicago Press.

Neugarten, B.L., Moore, J.W., & Lowe, J.C. 1965. Age norms, age constraints, and adult socialization. American Journal of Sociology 70: 710-717. Also in: B.L. Neugarten, ed. 1968. Middle age and aging. Chicago: University of Chicago Press.

Neugarten, B.L., & Weinstein, K.K. 1964. The changing American grandparent. Journal of Marriage and the Family 26: 199-204. Also in: B.L. Neugarten, ed. 1968. Middle age and aging. Chicago: University of Chicago Press.

Newport, E., Gleitman, H., & Gleitman, L. 1977. Mother, I'd rather do it myself: Some effects and noneffects of maternal speech style. In C. Snow & C. Ferguson, eds., Talking to children. N.Y.: Cambridge University Press.

Osofsky, J.D. 1976. Neonatal characteristics and mother-infant interaction in two observational situations. Child Development 47: 1138-47.

Oyer, E.J. 1976. Exchanging information within the older family. In H.J. Oyer and E.J. Oyer, eds., Communication and aging. Baltimore: University Park Press.

Oyer, H.J., & Oyer, E.J. 1976. Communicating with older people: Basic considerations. In H.J. Oyer & E.J. Oyer, eds., Aging and communication. Baltimore: University Park Press.

Palmore, E. 1977. Facts on aging. The Gerontologist 17, no. 4: 315-20.

Pearce, W.B., & Sharp, S.M. 1973. Self disclosing communication. Journal of Communication 23: 409-25.

Pfeiffer, E. 1977. Psychopathology and social pathology. In J.E. Birren & K.W. Schaie, eds., Handbook of the psychology of aging. N.Y.: Van Nostrand Reinhold.

Phillips, B.S. 1957. A role theory approach to adjustment in old age. American Sociological Review 22: 212-17.

Piaget, J. 1955. The language and thought of the child. U.S.A.: World Publishing Co.

Piaget, J. 1977. Intellectual evolution from adolescence to adulthood. Human Development 15: 1-12.

Pineo, P.C. 1968. Disenchantment in the later years of marriage. In B.L. Neugarten, ed., Middle age and aging. Chicago: University of Chicago Press.

Rabbitt, P. 1977. Changes in problem solving ability in old age. In J.E. Birren & K.W. Schaie, eds., Handbook of the psychology of aging. N.Y.: Van Nostrand Reinhold.

Ratner, S.C., & Rice, E.F. 1963. The effect of the listener on the speaking interaction. Psychological Record 13: 265-68.

Reese, H.W., & Overton, W.F. 1970. Models of development and theories of development. In L.R. Goulet & P.B. Baltes, eds., Life span developmental psychology: Research and theory. N.Y.: Academic Press.

Reichard, S., Livson, F., & Peterson, P.G. 1962. Adjustment to retirement. In P.G. Peterson, ed., Aging and personality. N.Y.: John Wiley & Sons. Also in: B.L. Neugarten, ed. 1968. Middle age and aging. Chicago: University of Chicago Press.

Rheingold, H.L., Hay, D.F., & West, M.J. 1976. Sharing the second year of life. Child Development 47: 1148-58.

Richards, M.P.M. 1974a. The development of psychological communication in the first year of life. In K. Connolly & J. Bruner, eds., The early growth of competence. N.Y.: Academic Press.

Richards, M.P.M. 1974b. First steps in becoming social. In M.P.M. Richards, ed., The integration of a child into a social world. N.Y.: Cambridge University Press.

Riegel, K.F. 1966. Development of language: Suggestions for a verbal fallout model. Human Development 9: 97-120.

Riegel, K.F. 1972. Time and change in the development of the individual and society. In H.W. Reese, ed., Advances in child development and behavior, vol. 7. N.Y.: Academic Press.

Riegel, K.F. 1973. Dialectic operations: The final period of cognitive development. Human Development 16: 346-70.

Riegel, K.F. 1975a. Toward a dialectical theory of development. Department of Psychology, Report #62, Developmental Report Series. Univ. of Mich., Ann Arbor, Mich. 48109.

Riegel, K.F. 1975b. Adult life crisis: A dialectic interpretation of development. In N. Datan & L.H. Ginsberg, eds., Life span developmental psychology: Normative life crisis. N.Y.: Academic Press.

Riegel, K.F., & Brumer, S. 1975. History of psychological gerontology. Department of Psychology, Report #63, Developmental Report Series. University of Michigan, Ann Arbor, Michigan, 48109.

Riegel, K.F., & Riegel, R.M. 1960. A study of changes of attitudes and interests during later years of life. Vita Humana 3: 177-206.

Riegel, K.F., & Riegel, R.M. 1972. Development, drop, and death. Developmental Psychology 6: 306-19.

Riley, M.W. 1976. Age strata in social systems. In R.H. Binstock & E. Shanas, eds., Handbook of aging and the social sciences. N.Y.: Van Nostrand Reinhold.

Riley, M.W., Foner, A., Hess, B. & Toby, M.L. 1969. Socialization for the middle and later years. In D. Goslin, ed., Handbook of socialization: Theory and research. Chicago: Rand McNally & Co.

Robertson, J.F. 1975. Interaction in three-generation families, parents as mediators: Toward a theoretical perspective. International Journal of Aging and Human Development 6, no. 2: 103-10.

Rommetveit, R. 1972. Linguistic and nonlinguistic components of communication: Notes on the intersection of psycholinguistics and social psychological theory. In S. Moscovici, ed., The psychosociology of language. Chicago: Markham Publishing Co.

Rose, A.M. 1962a. A systematic summary of symbolic interaction theory. In A.M. Rose, ed., Human Behavior and Social Processes. Boston: Houghton-Mifflin.

Rose, A.M. 1962b. The subculture of aging: A topic for sociological research. The Gerontologist 2: 123-27. Also in: B.L. Neugarten, ed. 1968. Middle age and aging. Chicago: University of Chicago Press.

Rosow, I. 1967. Social integration of the aged. N.Y.: Free Press.

Rosow, I. 1968. Housing and local ties of the aged. In B.L. Neugarten, ed., Middle age and aging. Chicago: University of Chicago Press.

Rosow, I. 1974. Socialization to old age. Berkeley: University of California Press.

Rosow, I. 1976a. Affluence, reciprocity, and solidary bonds. In K.F. Riegel and J.A. Meacham, eds., The developing individual in a changing world, vol. II The Hague: Mouton & Co.

Rosow, I. 1976b. Status and role change through the life span. In R.H. Binstock & E. Shanas, eds., Handbook of aging and the social sciences. N.Y.: Van Nostrand Reinhold.

Ross, H.S., & Goldman, B.D. 1977. Infants' sociability toward strangers. Child Development 48: 638-42.

Rubin, K.H., & Brown, I.D.R. 1975. A life-span look at person-perception and its relationship to communicative interaction. Journal of Gerontology 30, no. 4: 461-68.

Rubin, K.H., Hultsch, D.F., & Peters, D.L. 1971. Non-social speech in four year-old children as a function of birth order and interpersonal situation. Merrill-Palmer Quarterly 17: 41-49.

Ryan, E.B., & Capadano, H.L. 1978. Age perceptions and evaluative reactions toward adult speakers. Journal of Gerontology 33, no. 1: 98-102.

Ryan, J. 1974. Early language development: Towards a communicational analysis. In M.P.M. Richards, ed., The integration of a child into a social world. N.Y.: Cambridge University Press.

Sachs, J., & Devin, J. 1976. Young children's use of age-appropriate speech styles. Journal of Child Language 3: 81-98.

Sacks, H., Schegloff, E., & Jefferson, G. 1974. A simplest systematics for the organization of turn-taking for conversation. Language 50, no. 4: 696-735.

Sameroff, A. 1975. Transactional models in early social relations. Human Development 18: 65-79.

Sarbin, T.R. 1954. Role theory. In G. Lindzey, ed., Handbook of social psychology, vol. 1. Cambridge: Addison Wesley.

Schachter, F.F., Kirshner, K., Klips, B., Fredricks, M., & Sanders, K. 1974. Everyday preschool interpersonal speech usage: Methodological, developmental, and sociolinguistic studies. Monographs of the Society for Research in Child Development. Serial no. 156. 38, no. 3.

Schaie, K.W. 1965. A general model for the study of developmental problems. Psychological Bulletin 64: 92-107.

Schaie, K.W. 1977. Quasi-experimental research designs in the psychology of aging. In J.E. Birren & K.W. Schaie, eds., Handbook of the psychology of aging. N.Y.: Van Nostrand Reinhold.

Schegloff, E.A. 1972a. Notes on conversational practice: Formulating place. In P.P. Giglioli, ed., Language and social context. London: Cox & Wyman, Ltd.

Schegloff, E.A. 1972b. Sequencing in conversational openings. In J. Gumperz and D. Hymes, eds., Directions in sociolinguistics. N.Y.: Holt, Rinehart & Winston.

Schegloff, E., & Sacks, H. 1973. Opening up closings. Semiotica 8: 289-327.

Schmitz-Scherzer, R., & Lehr, V. 1976. Interaction of personality, SES, and social participation in old age. In K.F. Riegel & J.A. Meacham, eds., The developing individual in a changing world vol. 2. The Hague: Mouton & Co.

Schulz, J.H. 1976. Income distribution and the aging. In R.H. Binstock & E. Shanas, eds., Handbook of aging and the social sciences. N.Y.: Van Nostrand Reinhold.

Searle, J. 1965. What is a speech act? In M. Black, ed., Philosophy in America. Ithaca, N.Y.: Cornell University Press.

Searle, J.R. 1969. Speech Acts. N.Y.: Cambridge University Press.
Searle, J. 1975. Indirect speech acts. In P. Cole & J. Morgan, eds., Speech Acts. N.Y.: Academic Press.
Seltzer, M., & Atchley, R.C. 1971. The concept of old: Changing attitudes and stereotypes. The Gerontologist 11: 226-30.
Shanan, J. 1976. Levels and patterns of social engagement and disengagement from adolescence to middle adulthood. In K.F. Riegel & J.A. Meacham, eds., The developing individual in a changing world vol. 2. The Hague: Mouton & Co.
Shanas, E., & Maddox, G.L. 1976. Aging, health, and the organization of health resources. In R.H. Binstock & E. Shanas, eds., Handbook of aging and the social sciences. N.Y.: Van Nostrand Reinhold.
Shatz, M. 1977. On the development of communicative understandings: An early strategy for interpreting and responding to messages. In J. Glick & A. Clark-Stewart, eds., Studies in social and cognitive development. N.Y.: Gardner Press.
Shatz, M. 1978. The relationship between cognitive processes and the development of communication skills. In B. Keasey, ed., Nebraska Symposium on Motivation, 1977. Lincoln: Univ. of Nebraska Press.
Shatz, M., & Gelman, R. 1973. The development of communication skills: Modifications in the speech of young children as a function of listener. Monographs of the Society for Research in Child Development. Serial no. 152. 38, no. 5.
Shatz, M., & Gelman, R. 1977. Beyond Syntax: The influence of conversational constraints on speech modifications. In C. Snow & C. Ferguson, eds., Talking to children. N.Y.: Cambridge University Press.
Shaver, K.G. 1975. An introduction to attribution processes. Cambridge: Winthrop Publishers, Inc.
Shock, N.W. 1977. Biological theories of aging. In J.E. Birren & K.W. Schaie, eds., Handbook of the psychology of aging. N.Y.: Van Nostrand Reinhold.
Sigel, I.E., & Cocking, R.R. 1977. Cognition and communication: A dialectic paradigm for development. In M. Lewis & L. Rosenblum, eds., Interaction, conversation, and the development of language. N.Y.: Wiley.
Siman, M.L. 1977. Application of a new model of peer group influence to naturally existing adolescent friendship groups. Child Development 48: 270-74.
Simos, B.G. 1970. Relations of adults with aging parents. The Gerontologist 10, no. 2: 135-39.
Simos, B.G. 1973. Adult children and their aging parents. Social Work 18: 78-85.
Snow, C.E. 1972. Mothers' speech to children learning language. Child Development 43: 549-65.
Snow, C.E. 1977. Mother's speech research: From input to interaction. In C. Snow & C. Ferguson, eds., Talking to children. N.Y.: Cambridge Univ. Press.

Soderbergh, R. 1974. The fruitful dialogue. Stockholms Universitet: Project Child Language Syntax.

Soskin, W.F., & John, V.P. 1963. The study of spontaneous talk. In R. Barker, ed., The stream of behavior. N.Y.: Appleton-Century-Crofts.

Speier, M. 1972. Some conversational problems for interactional analysis. In D. Sudnow, ed., Studies in social interaction. N.Y.: Free Press.

Spilton, D., & Lee, L.C. 1977. Some determinants of effective communication in four year olds. Child Development 48: 968-77.

Stern, D. 1971. A micro-analysis of mother-infant interaction. Journal of the American Academy of Child Psychiatry 10: 501-17.

Stern, D. 1974. Mother and infant at play: The dyadic interaction involving facial, vocal, and gaze behaviors. In M. Lewis & L. Rosenblum, eds., The effect of the infant on the caregiver. N.Y.: Wiley.

Stern, D., Jaffee, J., Beebe, B. & Bennett, S. 1975. Vocalizing in unison and in alternation: Two modes of communication within the mother-infant dyad. Annals of the New York Academy of Sciences, Developmental Psycholinguistics and Communication Disorders 263: 89-100.

Strayer, F.F., & Strayer, J. 1976. An ethological analysis of social agonism and dominance relations among preschool children. Child Development 47: 980-89.

Streib, G.F. 1965. Are the aged a minority? In A.W. Gouldner & S.M. Miller, eds., Applied sociology. N.Y.: Macmillan Co. Also in: B.L. Neugarten ed., Middle age and aging. Chicago: University of Chicago Press.

Streib, G.F. 1976. Social stratification and aging. In R.H. Binstock & E. Shanas, eds. Handbook of aging and the social sciences. N.Y.: Van Nostrand Reinhold.

Strumpel, B. 1973. The aged in an affluent economy. In C. Eisdorfer & M.P. Lawton, eds., The psychology of adult development and aging. Washington D.C.: A.P.A.

Sussman, M.B. 1960. Intergenerational family relationships and social role changes in middle age. Journal of Gerontology 15: 71-75.

Sussman, M.B. 1976. The family life of old people. In R.H. Binstock & E. Shanas, eds., Handbook of aging and the social sciences. N.Y.: Van Nostrand Reinhold.

Sussman, M.B., & Burchinal, L. 1962. Kin family network: Unheralded structure in current conceptualizations of family functioning. Marriage and Family Living 24, no. 3: 231-40. Also in: B.L. Neugarten, ed. 1968. Middle age and aging. Chicago: University of Chicago Press.

Tamir, L. 1979a. Interrogatives in dialogue: Case study of mother and child 16-19 months. To appear in Journal of Psycholinguistic Research, 1979.

Tamir, L. 1979b. Language development: New directions. To appear in Human Development, 1979.

Teaff, J.D., Lawton, M.P., Nahemow, L., & Carlson, D. 1978. Impact of age integration on the well being of elderly tenants in public housing. Journal of Gerontology 33, no. 1: 126-33.

Thomae, H. 1970. Theory of aging and cognitive theory of personality. Human Development 13: 1-16.

Thoman, E.B., Korner, A.F., & Beason-Williams, L. 1977. Modification of responsiveness to maternal vocalization in the neonate. Child Development 48: 563-69.

Thomas, A., Chess, S., & Birch, H.G. 1968. Temperment and behavior disorders in children. N.Y.: University Press.

Tobin, S., & Neugarten, B.L. 1971. Life satisfaction and social interaction in the aging. Journal of Gerontology 16: 344-46.

Toch, H., & MacLean, M.S., Jr. 1967. Perception and communication: A transactional view. Audio-visual Communication 10: 55-77. Also in K.K. Sereno & C.D. Mortenson, eds., Foundations of communication theory. N.Y.: Harper & Row, 1970.

Townsend, P. 1968. The emergence of the four-generation family in industrial society. In B.L. Neugarten, ed., Middle age and aging. Chicago: University of Chicago Press.

Trager, N.P. 1976. Available communication networks for the aged in the community. In H.J. Oyer & E.J. Oyer, eds., Aging and communication. Baltimore: University Park Press.

Troll, L.E. 1971. The family in later life: A decade review. Journal of Marriage and Family 263-90.

Troll, L.E., & Smith, J. 1976. Attachment through the life span: Some questions about dyadic bonds among adults. Human Development 19: 156-70.

Tuckman, F., & Lorge, I. 1953. Attitudes toward old people. Journal of Social Psychology 37: 249-60.

Turner, J.G. 1975. Patterns of intergenerational exchange: A developmental approach. International Journal of Aging and Human Development 6, no. 2: 111-15.

Turner, R. 1974. Words, utterances, and activities. In R. Turner, ed., Ethnomethodology. N.Y.: Penguin.

Van den Daele, L.D. 1969. Qualitative models in developmental analysis. Developmental Psychology 1: 303-10.

Van den Daele, L.D. 1975. Ego development in dialectical perspective. Human Development 18: 129-42.

Van Lieshout, C.F.M., Leckie, G., & Smits-Van Sonsbeck, B. 1976. Social perspective-taking training: Empathy and role-taking ability of preschool children. In K.F. Riegel and J.A. Meacham, eds., The developing individual in a changing world, vol. 2. The Hague: Mouton & Co.

Vygotsky, L.S. 1962. Thought and language. Cambridge: M.I.T. Press.

Wallach, M.A., & Green, L.R. 1961. On age and the subjective speed of time. Journal of Gerontology 16, no. 1: 71-74. Also in: B.L. Neugarten, ed. 1968. Middle age and aging. Chicago: University of Chicago Press.

Watson, J.S. 1972. Smiling, cooing, and "The Game." Merrill-Palmer Quarterly 18, no. 4: 323-39.

Watzlawick, B.J., Beavin, J.H., & Jackson, D.D. 1967. Pragmatics of human communication. N.Y.: W.W. Norton.

Werner, H., & Kaplan, B. 1963. Symbol formation. N.Y.: Wiley.

Wheeler, S. 1966. The structure of formally organized socialization settings. In O.G. Brim & S. Wheeler, Socialization after childhood. N.Y.: Wiley.

Wilensky, H.L. 1968. Orderly careers and social participation: The impact of work history on social integration in the middle mass. In B.L. Neugarten, ed., Middle age and aging. Chicago: University of Chicago Press.

Willeford, J.A. 1971. The geriatric patient. In D.E. Rose, ed., Audiological assessment. N.J.: Prentice Hall.

Williams, R.H., & Loeb, M.B. 1968. The adult's social life space and successful aging: Some suggestions for a conceptual framework. In B.L. Neugarten, ed., Middle age and aging. Chicago: University of Chicago Press.

Woelfel, J. 1976. Communication across age levels. In H.J. Oyer & E.J. Oyer, eds., Aging and communication. Baltimore: University Park Press.

Wohlwill, J.F. 1970. Methodology and research strategy in the study of developmental change. In L.R. Goulet & P.B. Baltes, eds., Life span developmental psychology: Research and theory. N.Y.: Academic Press.

Woodruff, D.S., & Birren, J.E. 1972. Age changes and cohort differences in personality. Developmental Psychology 6, no. 2: 252-59.

Wozniak, R.H. 1975. A dialectical paradigm for psychological research: Implications drawn from the history of psychology in the Soviet Union. Human Development 18: 18-34.

Name Index

Subject Index

About the Author

Lois Tamir is a research fellow at the Institute for Social Research and a doctoral candidate in the Department of Psychology at the University of Michigan. A member of Phi Beta Kappa, she received her B.A. in Sociology, Summa Cum Laude, 1974 from S.U.N.Y. at Stony Brook, and her M.A. in Psychology, 1976 from the University of Michigan. Her research is in the field of Developmental Psychology, and she has published work on the topics of language, life span development, and the family life cycle.

Pergamon General Psychology Series

Editors: Arnold P. Goldstein, Syracuse University
Leonard Krasner, SUNY, Stony Brook